HUMAN RIGHTS IN A DIVIDED WORLD

HUMAN RIGHTS
IN A DIVIDED WORLD

Catholicism as a Living Tradition

DAVID HOLLENBACH, SJ

FOREWORD BY TERRENCE L. JOHNSON

GEORGETOWN UNIVERSITY PRESS / WASHINGTON, DC

© 2024 Georgetown University Press. All rights reserved. No part of this book may be reproduced or utilized in any form or by any means, electronic or mechanical, including photocopying and recording, or by any information storage and retrieval system, without permission in writing from the publisher.

The publisher is not responsible for third-party websites or their content. URL links were active at time of publication.

Library of Congress Cataloging-in-Publication Data

Names: Hollenbach, David, 1942- author. | Johnson, Terrence L., writer of foreword.
Title: Human rights in a divided world : Catholicism as a living tradition / David Hollenbach, S.J. ; foreword by Terrence L. Johnson.
Description: Washington, DC : Georgetown University Press, 2024. | Includes bibliographical references and index.
Identifiers: LCCN 2023031186 (print) | LCCN 2023031187 (ebook) | ISBN 9781647124267 (hardcover) | ISBN 9781647124274 (paperback) | ISBN 9781647124281 (ebook)
Subjects: LCSH: Human rights—Religious aspects—Catholic Church. | Freedom of religion. | Refugees. | Christian sociology—Catholic Church.
Classification: LCC BX1795.H85 H65 2024 (print) | LCC BX1795.H85 (ebook) | DDC 261.7—dc23/eng/20231204
LC record available at https://lccn.loc.gov/2023031186
LC ebook record available at https://lccn.loc.gov/2023031187

♾ This paper meets the requirements of ANSI/NISO Z39.48-1992 (Permanence of Paper).

25 24   9 8 7 6 5 4 3 2   First printing

Printed in the United States of America

Cover design by Jeremy John Parker
Cover art by Jen Norton Illustration and Design
Interior design by BookComp, Inc.

This book is dedicated to my friends at Georgetown University's Berkley Center for Religion, Peace, and World Affairs, in gratitude for their intellectual and personal support.

CONTENTS

Foreword   ix

Acknowledgments   xiii

1 A Living Tradition   1

PART I. THE ROOTS OF RIGHTS   13

2 Human Dignity: Experience and New Understandings   15

3 Shared Humanity after Genocide in Rwanda   31

4 Dignity in Solidarity: Rights as Relational   46

PART II. THE RIGHT TO RELIGIOUS FREEDOM   63

5 Religious Freedom, Morality, and Law:
Vatican II and John Courtney Murray Today   65

6 Religion in Public: The Challenge of Freedom   85

7 Global Lessons for the United States   99

PART III. ECONOMIC RIGHTS AND EQUALITY   117

8 Equality, Inequality, and Justice   119

9 Challenges of Globalization: Many Agents of Justice   133

viii CONTENTS

PART IV. THE RIGHTS OF REFUGEES AND MIGRANTS 147

10 Borders and the Rights of the Displaced 149

11 Welcoming Refugees and Migrants:
The Need for Inclusion 166

PART V. THE RIGHTS OF WOMEN 181

12 Universality and Women's Rights 183

Notes 203

Index 237

About the Author 245

FOREWORD

Duty to take positive action . . . does not end at the national borders
of the countries where crisis is present. When people become aware of
crisis in a neighboring country or even in a country at a great distance,
this awareness leads to what might be called intellectual or psychological
proximity. It puts them in *moral* proximity to those who are suffering.
(D. Hollenbach, *Human Rights in a Divided World*, in this volume, p. 159)

David Hollenbach is a globe-trotter. His mission is to scavenge the borders
and regions of the world in search of the unnoticed, forgotten, and sometimes ignored human wreckage from war, international trade, famine, dis-
ease, and government tumult. He meticulously maps out the political and
theological consequences of civil conflicts and humanitarian crises with a
primary objective: to place his students, readers, and parishioners within a
heartbeat of calamity. Holding scripture in one hand and a pen in the other,
he prods the consciousness of anyone within reach through his probing
analysis of humanitarian crises and refugees, justice, and religion in public
life. He exposes to an audience often submerged in middle-class comforts
a world suffocating from human-driven crises. No one can say they didn't
know the depths of human rights violations both far and near. Hollenbach
won't accept any excuses. The awareness of injustice, Hollenbach suggests
to his readers, makes them witnesses to rampage and repression and subsequently morally responsible for their inaction or apathy.

For Hollenbach, moral culpability is not limited to the individual or
the close community. He holds institutions and governments accountable
for their inaction as well. As he says, expanding human rights "requires the
efforts of multiple agents. These many agents include states themselves plus
a wide range of nongovernmental organizations and international agencies.
The multiplicity of agents needed to secure social and economic rights is
particularly important in today's globalizing world." Hollenbach is undoubt-
edly extending and expanding scholarly debates about the common good
and about Catholic ethics in relationship to liberalism, theories of justice,
and theology, but a central goal of his scholarship is to stimulate just and
moral actions: from the Catholic Church, from all religious and political
leaders, from social activists, from laypeople, and from students in a world

increasingly divided by ethnicity, class, race, gender, and religion. Knowledge of Catholic social thought and theology is a moot and, dare I say, dangerous endeavor unless it is tied to sustained efforts to address human rights through a sustained engagement with global ethics.

Hollenbach is one of the nation's premier theological ethicists and is the most renowned living Catholic scholar of human rights and global ethics. Drawing upon Catholic social and theological teachings, Hollenbach investigates religious traditions as well as political and economic policies that impede global justice based on the human rights platform established by the United Nations Universal Human Rights Declaration of 1948.

Pluralism is central to his theological thinking. He often turns to sources outside Catholicism, including within Islam, Buddhism, and Protestant traditions, to help delimit global ethics and define rights in—and in tension with—political philosophy and liberalism. He focuses on conceptions held in common by multiple religious traditions, by atheists, and by humanist traditions to explain how humans can, as he says, "reach agreement that some forms of human behavior whose harmful effects they have all witnessed, such as genocide, should never be permitted to happen again. Shared experience could also show those from very different traditions that some goods, such as freedom of belief and thought, adequate nutrition, health care, and work, should be provided to all persons when such provision is possible." Hollenbach's hermeneutical shift extends Western theories of rights and human dignity to include resources that expand the interpretive lens retrieved through scholarly debate. The move is a shift away from liberal philosophies of individualism to an ethical theory animated by community and communal well-being, or what Hollenbach characterizes as a "relational understanding" of human rights and dignity. To be sure, Hollenbach appeals to figures such as Aristotle and Kant to unpack critical concepts like autonomy and freedom. But he does so with an acknowledgment of existing concerns raised by feminist and liberation theologians as well.

The writings of Confucians, Muslims, and those with no religious belief, for example, inform Hollenbach's understanding of the social goods that underscore fundamental preconditions of dignity (and rights) among many non-Christian traditions. He writes, "The human good is that of a bodily being and it has material preconditions. Human dignity can be realized only if the material conditions needed for bodily flourishing are present. Protecting human dignity, therefore, requires securing a person's capacities for knowledge, freedom, and relationship; and it requires guaranteeing access to food, shelter, medical care in sickness, and other needed material supports." Human rights and dignity must be contextualized and read in context of many religious and cultural traditions. Human dignity, he notes, should be theorized alongside the material concerns and existential fears facing any community or region of the world.

From Russia's war in Ukraine to political violence in South Sudan, from religious freedom and the rights of refugees to the controversial and contested treatment of migrants at the US southern border and elsewhere, Hollenbach grapples with the global consequences of actions by nation-states that deviate from established legal and moral norms. *Human Rights in a Divided World* is a reminder of Hollenbach's ongoing significance within scholarly and public debates on justice, human rights, and global ethics. Without losing sight of tradition, most notably Catholic tradition, Hollenbach explores the theological limits of relying on a single creed to understand, for instance, suffering, economic inequality, or women's rights. By engaging multiple religious traditions and political theories, Hollenbach can account for the "limits" of his own tradition without denying its ongoing veracity and viability for addressing human rights and global injustice.

Unlike some US-based political scientists and philosophers, Hollenbach is not afraid to investigate possible domestic cases of human rights violations. Hollenbach likens US Black poverty rates, for instance, to humanitarian crises emerging throughout the globe. "The severity of their poverty accounts for the fact that in the US regions of the Mississippi Delta and Appalachia, life expectancy is lower than in Bangladesh and Vietnam," according to Hollenbach. "Whether one is poor is clearly influenced by race, class, and gender. Racial inequality has a significant impact on the well-being of Black people, both within the United States and in comparison to some parts of the developing world." The data of US Black poverty rates have been available since Reconstruction. Some legal and political scholars characterize the disproportionate poverty rates and income and wealth gaps to systemic racism, racial capitalism, and embedded biases. Hollenbach sees something else at play. Human rights activists cannot develop strategies for economic justice alone. Religious traditions, specifically Christianity and Catholicism, are also responsible for the "well-being" of humans, which involves addressing the economic instability facing countless people throughout the globe.

When I proposed the publication of this volume of collected essays to Al Bertrand, director of Georgetown University Press, I assumed the project would look back into the archives of human rights atrocities to critique previous moral and political failures of both governments and moral actors. Of course, Hollenbach contextualizes human rights and global ethics historically and theologically. But he also analyzes human rights as a tool to address today's economic, social, and political well-being. This is done to motivate immediate and sustained interventions from the living witnesses of ongoing global injustices. Indeed, Hollenbach's ongoing interest in ameliorating human suffering and building an enduring hope for justice and freedom motivated my own interest. I stumbled upon his scholarship as a graduate student, and his early writings on the development of a "human rights ethic" within Catholicism served as an example of how I might retrieve my primary religious tradition to engage political ideals that may or may not mirror the commitments and norms of my personal theological commitments. The interchange between competing traditions and ideals guided me to questions that may not have been otherwise considered. Hollenbach's writings played a role in my then-developing interest in the role of African American political thought in shaping social ethics and moral inquiry among Black leftist thinkers who often were not Christian. I hope the inspiration I gained from his scholarship holds true for a new generation of students, activists, and religious leaders.

In this historical moment, when the category of human rights is contested and ambiguously detached from "real-world" problems, *Human Rights in a Divided World* seeks to invigorate human rights and global ethics by acknowledging both their limits and their possibilities for healing a broken world. From explorations of Rwanda, the Mississippi Delta, and Ukraine, Hollenbach builds a convincing argument for the ongoing necessity of human rights and global ethics, as they often tackle the underlying moral beliefs and religious doctrines at play in sustaining economic and political injustice. Engaging thinkers ranging from Kant and Hans Küng to Margaret Farley, Jomo Kenyatta, and Pope Francis's teachings on "a culture of encounter," Hollenbach yearns to awaken the consciousness of those sleeping or standing, immobilized and in silence, as the world implodes from human-driven turmoil, greed, and selfishness. Global ethics on human rights is more than a normative commitment: it is a reminder of the collective responsibility to join in efforts to ameliorate suffering and exploitation wherever it exists.

—Terrence L. Johnson

ACKNOWLEDGMENTS

The chapters of this book are slight revisions of chapters published earlier in journals and other books. Some were written for a specific purpose, but it is hoped that bringing them together with minor revisions will show that the Catholic community's work for human rights has solid intellectual backing and can be practically effective. The Catholic tradition on human rights is genuinely alive and it can continue to develop in ways that enable it to address new challenges in our divided world.

First publications are indicated here and are used with permission:

Chapter 1: *Irish Theological Quarterly* 84, no. 3 (May 21, 2019): 259–67.

Chapter 2: In *Understanding Human Dignity*, edited by Christopher McCrudden, 123–39. *Proceedings of the British Academy* 192. Oxford: Oxford University Press, 2013.

Chapter 3: In *Reinventing Theology in Post-Genocide Rwanda: Challenges and Hopes*, edited by Marcel Uwineza, Elisée Rutagambwa, and Michel Segatagara Kamanzi. Washington, DC: Georgetown University Press, 2023.

Chapter 4: Festschrift in honor of Michael J. Perry. *Emory Law Review* 71, no. 7 (May 2022): 1487–1507.

Chapter 5: *Journal of Moral Theology* 1, no. 1 (2012): 69–91.

Chapter 6: In *The Legacy of Vatican II*, edited by Massimo Faggioli and Andrea Vicini, 248–72. Mahwah, NJ: Paulist Press, 2015.

Chapter 7: *Theological Studies* 81, no. 3 (September 2020): 540–59.

Chapter 8: In *A World of Inequalities: Christian and Muslim Perspectives*, edited by Lucinda Mosher, 21–35. Washington, DC: Georgetown University Press, 2021.

Chapter 9: In *The Almighty and the Dollar: Reflections on Economic Justice for All*, edited by Mark J. Allman, 98–113. Winona, MN: Anselm Academic Press, 2012.

Chapter 10: *Journal on Migration and Human Security* 4, no. 3 (2016): 148–65. Republished in *Journal on Migration and Human Security*, March 2018, S20–S37.

Chapter 11: *Annals of the American Academy of Political and Social Science* 690 (July 2020): 153–67.

Chapter 12: In *A Just and True Love: Feminism at the Frontiers of Theological Ethics; Essays in Honor of Margaret A. Farley*, edited by Maura Ryan and Brian Linnane, 47–74. Notre Dame, IN: University of Notre Dame Press, 2007.

1

A LIVING TRADITION

The Catholic Church's stance toward human rights has developed in a dramatic fashion over the decades since the United Nations General Assembly proclaimed the Universal Declaration of Human Rights in 1948. This book will illustrate several of the shifts that have taken place and suggest some reasons why they occurred. Among these developments that stand out as particularly noteworthy is Pope John XXIII's strong support for a broad human rights agenda. His 1963 encyclical, *Pacem in Terris*, affirms an array of human rights that strongly resembles those presented in the UN's Universal Declaration of Human Rights. Then came the Second Vatican Council's unambiguous support for the right to religious freedom, a dramatic shift in the official Catholic stance on human rights. In addition to sketching these developments, I also present some of the Catholic community's more important practical contributions to human rights in recent decades, including the Church's commitment to rights in the economic sphere. The commitment to the economic rights of all people raises the question of the role of equality in any approach to human rights. In addition to treating the issue of equality, I will also sketch approaches to human rights on two other practical matters where continuing growth of the Catholic tradition is occurring today: the rights of refugees and the rights of women.

A distinguished historian of Christian doctrine, the late Jaroslav Pelikan, described tradition as "the living faith of the dead," in contrast to traditionalism, which he called "the dead faith of the living."[1] Following Pelikan, I argue here that the Catholic approach to human rights is shaped by a "living tradition." Catholic reflection on human rights is very much alive today: it draws on past Catholic thought in innovative ways, bringing the past into lively interchange with the realities of contemporary social and international life.

The vitality of the Church's commitment to human rights is especially important today. Some recent commentators maintain that belief in the importance of human rights is a "dead faith." For example, Stephen Hopgood argues that the recent failures to protect human rights in countries like Cambodia, Rwanda, and Syria show that we are in "the endtimes of human rights." Yascha Mounk sees the rise of nationalist populism and its often-accompanying authoritarian politics as severely threatening democratic commitment to individual rights. Samuel Moyn holds that the human rights movement's frequent focus on individual freedoms makes it incapable of addressing the inequality and injustice brought by the free market, the bedrock idea of economic neoliberalism.[2]

The approach taken here does not agree with the critics who forecast doom for the human rights movement. Indeed, this book supports Harvard professor Kathryn Sikkink in her insistence that both history and empirical data suggest that human rights have a lively future. Nonetheless, there is little doubt that human rights face serious challenges today. In the face of these challenges, I argue that the Catholic tradition on human rights is very much alive today. The vitality of a living tradition, Pelikan observed, gives it a capacity to develop in new ways while at the same time maintaining its identity and continuity.[3] My goal is to illustrate that Catholicism's living tradition on human rights can remain faithful to its roots and also develop in ways that enable it to make contributions that are urgently needed today.

CATHOLICISM'S DEVELOPING APPROACH TO HUMAN RIGHTS

The dynamism of the Catholic approach to human rights is evident from a look at its recent history. In the late nineteenth and early twentieth centuries, Catholic leaders rejected modern human rights standards—such as freedom of religion—that had emerged in the eighteenth and nineteenth centuries. They saw modern freedoms as tied to the secularism of the French Revolution, which relegated religious belief to the margins of society and saw rights as being held by isolated individuals, both of which undermined long-standing Catholic commitment to the common good. Thus, in his 1832 encyclical, *Mirari Vos*, Pope Gregory XVI declared that freedom of conscience was "crazed insanity" (in Latin, *dileramentum*).[4]

Less than a century and a half later, however, Vatican II's Dignitatis Humanae (Declaration on Religious Freedom) proclaimed that "the right to religious freedom has its foundation in the very dignity of the human person, as this dignity is known through the revealed word of God and by reason itself" (no. 2). In Gaudium et Spes (Pastoral Constitution on the Church in the Modern World) the council further declared that the Church, "by virtue of the Gospel committed to her, proclaims the rights of the human person; she acknowledges and greatly esteems the dynamic movements of today by which these rights are everywhere fostered" (no. 41.) Thus, the council linked the full gamut of human rights to the very core of Christian faith. Since 1963 the Church has become an important institutional activist for human rights.

Why did this extraordinary change occur? The same historical experiences that led to the drafting of the Universal Declaration also led the Church to discover resources within the Christian tradition that support human rights. The bloody wars of the twentieth century led both secular society and the Catholic community to see that peace depends on respect for human dignity and universal human rights. Disastrous conflicts like World War I and World War II follow almost inevitably when peoples are divided by attitudes of us-versus-them based on religion, nationality, or ethnicity. Such in-group/out-group division led to the barbarous Nazi genocide of the Jewish people that the Preamble of the Universal Declaration suggests "outraged the conscience" of humankind.[5] The drafters of the Declaration also feared that such divisions could leave oppressed peoples no alternative but to resort to violent revolt as the only way to throw off the domination oppressing them, including colonial domination. Chapter 2 will argue that the evolving social experience of the Catholic community led to recovery of aspects of the tradition that enabled it to address new problems in new ways.

To counteract bloody outcomes such as the world wars of the twentieth century, the universality of human rights means we must tear down the walls that divide people into those who count and those who do not count. The dignity of *all* members of the human family must be the basis for the social and political life of global society. No white rule over nonwhites; no Aryan over Jew; no European colonist over non-European colonized; no male superiority to female. The experience of the deeply harmful consequences of dividing the human community into "us" and "them" led to the Universal Declaration.

This same experience stimulated development in Church teaching on human rights. As chapter 3 shows, key voices in the Catholic tradition, such as those of Bartolomé de las Casas and Francisco de Vitoria, were raised against Western colonial domination of the Indigenous peoples of the Americas in the sixteenth century. These earlier voices need to be heard again as we confront the humanitarian crises and genocides of more recent times. Indeed, the experience of World War II led Pope Pius XII, in his Christmas messages of the 1950s, to begin the Church's initially hesitant support for human rights in their contemporary form. Pope John XXIII's *Pacem in Terris (Peace on Earth)* moved to unambiguous support for human rights based on the dignity of the person created in the image of God. *Pacem in Terris* supported both civil-political rights, such as free speech and self-governance, and social-economic rights, such as rights to food and health care. This recognition of social and economic rights as part of the full human rights agenda meant the Church no longer saw rights as having an individualistic basis. An exploration of this understanding of rights as rooted in human solidarity is in chapter 4.

The full range of rights, both civil/political and social/economic, are necessary preconditions for the world peace that John XXIII sought to promote in the midst of the Cold War. *Pacem in Terris* has become the Catholic charter of human rights, playing a role in the Church analogous to the role the Universal Declaration of Human Rights plays in the global political community. Further, Vatican II's Declaration on Religious Freedom explicitly stated that the council was carrying out a *development* of Church teaching in light of signs of the times. In the declaration's words, "The council intends to develop the doctrine of recent popes on the inviolable rights of the human person and the constitutional order of society" (no. 10). This development led to a rejection of distinctions in civic life between persons based on their membership or nonmembership in the Church. Current developments of Catholic approaches to religious freedom, some good and some not so good, are considered in chapters 5, 6, and 7.

The central importance of human dignity in the Christian vision of the person also led to a strong emphasis on the importance of social and economic rights in the developing Catholic tradition. Some important aspects of this commitment to rights in the economic sphere are examined in chapters 8 and 9. The tradition's stress on economic justice and economic rights emerged in distinctively modern form in the late nineteenth century, when Pope Leo XIII responded to Marxism by insisting on the Christian duty to secure justice for the working class and for the poor. He insisted on the rights of workers to organize and their right to a wage sufficient to lift them out of poverty. In doing so he launched what has become the modern Catholic commitment to social and economic rights. Economic institutions and those who control them are accountable for the effects of their decisions, especially what they do to the most vulnerable members of society. In Leo's words, "No man may with impunity outrage the dignity which God Himself treats with great reverence."[6] Indeed, employers have a responsibility to not treat workers as "mere instruments for money making," to recognize the rights to a living wage, and to organize labor unions. This emphasis has led to the development of what has come to be called "social Catholicism"—a tradition that appeals to human dignity as the basis for the full range of rights, including the rights to freedom of religion, speech, and self-governance, the rights to adequate nutrition, shelter, education, and health care, and the right to the social protection of all these rights.

Thus, the signs of the times have led the Catholic tradition to see that its deepest values support the full range of human rights against the abuses of nationalistic and authoritarian politics and against economic approaches that lead to grinding poverty and deep inequality.[7] Religious convictions must never be used to deny human dignity in the name of God. The Church should resist all tendencies to turn national or ethnic identity into in-group privileges that oppress outsiders. Catholics should work to secure basic economic necessities for all, especially for those who are poor or marginalized. These developments have put the Church in a position to challenge some of the major contemporary threats to human rights.

RECENT CHURCH ACTION FOR HUMAN RIGHTS

Because of these dynamic developments in the tradition of Catholic social thought, since Vatican II the Church has in fact become a global leader in the defense of human rights. The Catholic community has helped advance democracy in numerous countries and has contributed to the defense of the social and economic rights of poor and marginalized people. For example, in the early 1970s the Chilean Catholic Church's Vicaría de la Solidaridad was a clear voice in opposition to the torture and disappearances carried out under the dictatorship of Gen. Augusto Pinochet, who had aligned himself with the economically privileged in Chile. Similarly, in 1986 the Philippine bishops stood firmly against Ferdinand Marcos's effort to steal an election. The bishops issued a ringing declaration that Marcos's claim to have won the election was fraudulent and that his effort to remain in power lacked moral legitimacy. The bishops' defense of the right to self-government stimulated the "people power" movement that brought Corazon Aquino to the presidency. Similar forms of Church support for democracy have occurred in South Korea, Lithuania, Brazil, Peru, and elsewhere. Indeed, Pope John Paul II's advocacy of human rights in Poland made a significant contribution to the collapse of the Soviet Union.

In light of these activities, the late Samuel Huntington, a distinguished specialist on international politics, argued that since Vatican II, the Catholic Church has become highly effective in its contributions to the global advancement of democracy.[8] On the basis of further study of the role of religion in recent democratic transitions, Monica Duffy Toft, Daniel Philpott, and Timothy Shah conclude that between 1972 and 2009, the Catholic community played a role in advancing democracy in thirty-six of the seventy-eight countries that made substantial democratic advances and was a leader in the democratization of twenty-two of these countries.[9] It is clear, therefore, that the Catholic tradition on human rights is very much alive, both intellectually and in the Church's practical engagement in the modern struggle for human rights.

It is true, of course, that the Church's engagement in the struggle for human rights has not been uniform and consistent in all countries. In Argentina, during the so-called Dirty War of the late 1970s and early 1980s, Church leaders remained too closely linked with the repressive regime. In the horrific Rwanda genocide of 1994, this most Catholic country in Africa descended into the ultimate form of human rights violation, genocide. Some Rwandan clerics supported the genocidal murders, and some bishops failed to resist. Nonetheless, it is clear that despite these grave failures, Church leaders and members have helped create a major global force for the promotion of human rights. This invites us to reflect on how to build on the recent human rights achievements of Catholicism as we move into the future.

INTO THE FUTURE

The Catholic community can further contribute to the advancement of human rights today by continuing to stress that the universality of human rights remains of the utmost importance. Among the most important threats to human rights today are conflicts based on ethnic or religious identity, especially where religion or ethnicity intertwines with nationalism and/or economic privilege. Examples include the ethnic cleansing and crimes against humanity that took place in Bosnia, the ethnic and religious animosities in African countries like Nigeria, South Sudan, and Central African Republic, the strife among Hindus, Muslims, and Christians in India, and the Buddhist persecution of Muslim Rohingyas in Myanmar. The rising forms of populism in a number of European countries and the resistance to migration and asylum for refugees in many countries, regrettably including the United States in recent years, are also based in part on ethnic and religious antipathies. Drawing upon reliable empirical data, Brian Grim and Roger Finke conclude that in 86 percent of the 143 counties with populations of more than two million, at least some people have been abused or displaced because of their religion in recent years. Religious persecution is today so widespread in parts of the Middle East and South Asia that it has nearly become the norm in those regions. The injustice of such persecution is one of the principal causes of the conflict and bloodshed in many parts of the world.[10]

The conflicts of today have led to the denial of the rights to life, to political freedom, and to minimum economic necessities in many places around the globe. These in-group/out-group divisions have also led to the tragic fact that in 2022, over 100 million people had been forcibly driven from their homes, both as refugees and as persons internally displaced within their own countries. This is one of every seventy-eight people on earth, a dramatic and tragic record.[11] Protecting the rights of these forcibly displaced people should be near the top of the human rights agenda today. Displaced people face major threats to their basic human rights, starting with their right to live in their own homes and homelands. They are discriminated against because of their race, religion, ethnicity, or national origin. Their right to life is regularly threatened because of their identity. They often have no way to secure their rights to food, water, medical care, education, or a job, especially when they are confined to refugee camps or forced to live in very poor urban settings for protracted periods.

Pope Francis has modeled the relevance of the universalist call to respect rights across borders by making the rights of refugees one of the central emphases of his pontificate. When Francis visited the refugee camps of the Greek island of Lesbos, he stressed the theological conviction that "God created humankind to be one family."[12] Drawing on this vision of our common humanity, Francis called on developed countries to "build bridges" to welcome refugees rather than "putting up walls" to exclude them. He translated this teaching into action by taking twelve Syrian Muslim refugees back to the Vatican aboard the papal plane for resettlement. In the same vein, in *Pacem in Terris* Pope John XXIII stressed that "refugees are persons and all their rights as persons must be recognized. Refugees cannot lose these rights simply because they are deprived of citizenship of their own States" (no. 105). This implies that we must respect a person's right "to enter a country in which he hopes to be able to provide more fittingly for himself and his dependents. It is therefore the duty of State officials to accept such immigrants and—so far as the good of their own community, rightly understood, permits—to further the aims of those who may wish to become members of a new society" (no. 106).

An issue that has become central today, therefore, is whether protection of the well-being of the citizens of richer countries in the Northern Hemisphere is compatible with granting asylum to more refugees than are presently being admitted. Here some data will be useful. As we reflect on whether refugees have the right to asylum in the countries of the European Union (EU) or the United States, we should note that low- and middle-income countries host 83 percent of world's refugees and that the world's least-developed countries host 27 percent of global total.[13] For example, very poor Uganda is hosting 1.5 million refugees, mostly from South Sudan, and even poorer Bangladesh has recently welcomed close to 1 million, mostly from Myanmar. In Lebanon, a very small middle-income country, one out of every eight persons within the country's borders is a refugee from a conflict raging elsewhere. In addition, in judging the capacity to grant asylum to refugees, it is important to note that data show that in the United States, refugees on average contribute more to their host country than the social services they draw upon. For example, refugees resettled in the United States have higher employment rates and the same median incomes as do Indigenous citizens.[14] Thus, the countries of the European Union and the United States have the capacity to receive considerably more asylum seekers than they are in fact receiving. I consider the duties of the better off to protect the rights of the displaced in chapters 10 and 11.

It is true that some of those who oppose granting asylum to additional refugees do so because of fears rooted in their own deprivation or vulnerability. Princeton economist Anne Case and her husband, the Nobel Prize–winning economist Angus Deaton, have shown that over the past two decades in the United States, the death rate of middle-aged, non-Hispanic whites with a high school education or less has risen notably. Growing numbers of these people succumb to what Case and Deaton call "deaths of despair" due to drug overdose, alcohol abuse, or suicide. The rising death rate of these people is due not simply to inadequate income but to what Case and Deaton call "cumulative disadvantage"—in the labor market, in marriage and family outcomes, and in health—a disadvantage triggered by declining labor market opportunities for whites with low levels of education.[15] These disadvantages lead to loss of hope, which in turn leads to behavior that increases the death rate of the overall group.

These disadvantages among less-educated whites in the United States often generate resentment against refugees and other migrants. The same is true in Western Europe. The working poor come to see refugees as a threat to their jobs and the cause of rising taxes because of their need for social assistance. The data on the contributions of refugees to the United States just cited indicate that these beliefs are often erroneous. Nevertheless, the growing inequality in the US makes it easier for demagogic leaders to persuade working-class people that refugees and migrants should be excluded. The situation in the EU is somewhat different from the United States, but anti-refugee and anti-migrant attitudes have risen among disadvantaged people in Europe for similar reasons.

This suggests that increasing respect for the rights of refugees will require reducing inequality and providing better protection for the social and economic rights of working-class people in the richer countries. The linkage between the rights of refugees and the rights of working-class people in the Global North supports the thesis that diverse human rights are often interconnected. It also implies that the Church's efforts to protect the rights of refugees today should be seen as closely linked with its more traditional efforts to secure the rights of workers in the past. Working for the rights of refugees is thus an important new development in the Church's social ministry that should be pursued vigorously. It is also closely tied to the other dimensions of social ministry, such as support for working people.

It is clear, therefore, that Catholic social teaching on human rights is a historically developing body of thought—a living tradition. Nevertheless, official Church teachings rarely mention that the Church has not always affirmed many of the human rights they strongly proclaim today. In fact, the Church formerly opposed many of these rights and sometimes even violated them in practice.[16] That official Church teaching takes minimal notice of the fact that it is the latest phase of a developing tradition unfortunately leads some to conclude that recent Church teaching on these matters is the final word on them. As past developments clearly show, however, historicity and development need not be threats to the Catholic tradition. They can lead to growth in understanding, of both the requirements of the gospel and the demands of human reasonableness. In my view there are aspects of the Catholic understanding of human rights where ongoing development must continue.

Let me mention just one area where further change is surely needed: rights in the domain of gender, including the rights of women. The fact that a right is a human right implies that it is possessed by all persons, independent of their distinctive characteristics such as religion, ethnicity, race, or gender. Debates about the universality of the equal rights of women is the subject of lively debate, both in secular society and within the Catholic Church today. In the secular realm, the issue of what the dignity and well-being of women require in different cultural contexts is often vigorously debated. Chapter 12 explores what the universality of human rights can require in the face of cultural differences that lead to treating women in ways that can be seen as violations of their dignity. It also explores different ways the rights of women can be protected and that persuasion and education can sometimes be appropriate ways to ensure the equal dignity of women, for example, when their culture calls for female initiation practices that involve genital cutting. On the other hand, securing the rights of women can sometimes require coercive restraint of their abusers. Such coercion was needed in order to protect the human rights of Tutsi women from the violence of rape and murder that many of them experienced during the genocide in Rwanda.

Beyond the question of the requirements of universality, recent Catholic thought also faces other questions concerning women's rights that call for significant new developments in the tradition. The *Compendium of the Social Doctrine of the Church* affirms that "the glory of God shines on the face of every person," giving each person a dignity that is "the ultimate foundation of the radical equality" of all people, regardless of their race, nation, sex, origin, culture, or class.[17] The Church stresses this "radical equality" of persons when it opposes using religious, racial, or national differences as legitimate grounds for discrimination on the level of fundamental rights. It is not clear, however, that discrimination among persons based on sex or gender is always seen as unacceptable by Church leadership today.

Church discussion of the equality of men and women is often accompanied by support for the "complementarity" of the sexes.[18] Pope Francis has criticized what he calls an "ideology of gender that denies the difference and reciprocity in nature of a man and a woman."[19] The difference, reciprocity, and complementarity of male and female affirmed by Francis means that men and women can have different social roles. This can easily slide into the exclusion of women from some of these roles. Thus, support for gender complementarity can negate equality in practice. For example, male/female complementarity is used to justify the exclusion of women from important leadership roles in the Church itself. It is also invoked to oppose some of the international efforts underway at the United Nations to ensure gender equality and further invoked to argue that homosexual orientation is itself disordered. How the stress on the complementarity of male and female is compatible with equal human dignity and equal human rights is, therefore, not evident in current Church teaching and practice.

In dealing with this matter, it is salutary to remember that Catholic tradition once combined a commitment to the equal dignity of all persons before God with the practice of slavery. We should also recall that the Church once believed that the commitment to the truth of the Catholic faith could require forbidding people of other faiths from expressing their beliefs in public. Being equal before God did not necessarily mean being equal before one's fellow humans. The current stress on gender complementarity in Church teaching risks denying human equality in a similar way.

Much experience and rigorous theological discussion were required to develop the teachings on the equal human dignity of persons of different religions and cultures that is affirmed in recent Catholic thought and ministry. We would do well today to seek to bring about similar developments in

Catholic teachings and practice on gender roles and the equality of women. Catholic teaching is making important contributions to both the understanding of human dignity and to practical respect for human rights today. We need to appropriate this teaching with gratitude and respect. Current teaching is not the last word, however. Therefore, we should remain attentive to ways that the struggles of women and gay people are calling the tradition to further development today. Such a development would be a further illustration of the fact that the Catholic approach to human rights is rooted in a living, developing tradition.

This book explores a number of the developments that have taken place in recent generations as the Catholic community has deepened and expanded its understanding of and commitment to human rights. The chapters are slight revisions of arguments that were first presented in other venues. It is my hope that presenting these ideas in a single volume will contribute to a deepening of the Catholic commitment to human rights and to more effective protection of human rights by all.

PART I

THE ROOTS OF RIGHTS

The declaration of human rights that was proclaimed in 1948 at the initial session of the United Nations General Assembly, titled the Universal Declaration of Human Rights. It sets forth normative standards that should govern human interactions in all countries and all cultures. In recent years, however, the universality of the rights in the declaration has been challenged. Some claim that the diversity of the world's cultural and religious communities challenges the notion that communities can come to share common standards for social and political life. Others argue that individual states' pursuit of their national interests undermines the claim that human rights can be protected for all people and that all communities are obligated to respect these rights. These challenges to the universally binding force of human rights are sometimes directed at religious communities, which are seen as holding values that conflict with those the declaration sets forth as the rights of all.

This objection is sometimes aimed at Roman Catholicism in a particular way. Indeed, in the nineteenth and early twentieth centuries, official Catholic teaching rejected human rights as rooted in the secularizing thought of the French Revolution and as based on an excessively individualistic understanding of humanity. However, since the Second Vatican Council the Catholic community has become a major contributor to the promotion of human rights worldwide. This part explores how this significant change in Catholic teaching took place and shows that the experience of the Holocaust and of authoritarian repression in the Soviet Union under Stalin awakened Church leaders to the dangers of the denial of human rights. The more recent experience of the genocide of the Tutsi people in Rwanda has reinforced the Church's recognition of the importance of human rights and has stimulated remembrance of Catholic approaches to the human rights of Indigenous peoples in the face of sixteenth-century colonial threats. These Catholic appropriations of human rights standards have also been accompanied by a recognition that human rights need not be understood individualistically. Rights can be seen as relational, as guarantees of people's full participation in social life and in active relationships with others. Thus, the Catholic tradition has moved to vigorous support for the human rights agenda.

2

HUMAN DIGNITY

Experience and New Understandings

Human dignity has moved to the forefront of recent discourse about the normative standards that should govern human affairs. Since the promulgation of the Universal Declaration of Human Rights in 1948, the duty to respect the dignity of all human beings has come to be seen as the most fundamental duty men and women owe each other in their interpersonal and social interactions. The concept of human dignity as a standard of morality is surely not an invention of recent decades. Some argue that it has deep roots in Greek philosophy and biblical religion. Others trace it back to medieval theories of natural law, to the French and American Revolutions with their roots in Enlightenment reason, or to the antislavery movements of the nineteenth century. Nearer to today, the Nazi Holocaust of the Jewish people "shocked the conscience" of humankind and has become a standard point of reference in reflection on the role that respect for human dignity ought to play in human affairs, as has the revulsion at the consequences of the two world wars that made the twentieth century the bloodiest in European history. Postwar rejection of colonial domination and the struggle against Soviet tyranny further strengthened the emerging conviction that respect for the dignity of persons is a central social value.

Each of these explanations of why human dignity has become so central to normative approaches to social life has implications for what dignity means and how we interpret its requirements. This chapter will certainly not attempt to give a full treatment of the history of our understanding of human dignity or its contemporary importance, meaning, and practical implications. Rather, by appealing to historical experience of the violation and attainment of dignity, some partial suggestions will be offered about how we might come to a better understanding of what it means and what it requires.

OBJECTIONS TO DIGNITY

Despite the centrality of human dignity and the human rights it supports in contemporary social debate, some scholars have raised questions about whether the idea of human dignity is useful and whether it will bear the weight placed on it in today's normative and ethical discourse.[1] For example, Ruth Macklin, a philosopher specializing in bioethics, has written an essay titled "Dignity Is a Useless Concept."[2] She argues that "dignity" is too vague a standard to be useful in making judgments about difficult ethical matters. If dignity is to function effectively as a norm, we need to be able to determine with some precision when it is being violated. Macklin believes, however, that this is impossible due to the abstractness of the idea of dignity. Thus, she holds that respect for the liberal principle of autonomy is much more helpful than appeals to dignity, especially in domains as complex as contemporary biomedical ethics. In Macklin's view, therefore, appeals to an abstract concept of human dignity can be dispensed with in the field of bioethics without any notable loss.

Others have argued that appeals to human dignity should be avoided in secular or pluralistic societies because such appeals depend on metaphysical or religious convictions that are not broadly shared in such societies. For example, irritation at the references to religious grounds for dignity in the volume of essays *Human Dignity and Bioethics,* produced by the US President's Council on Bioethics, led evolutionary psychologist Steven Pinker to write a dismissive essay titled "The Stupidity of Dignity." Pinker sees the appeal to dignity in the council's volume as an effort to "impose a radical political agenda, fed by fervent religious impulses, onto American biomedicine."[3] Indeed, he sees some of the understandings of dignity in that volume as a sign that the council has been co-opted by a group seeking to impose a "Catholic agenda" on US pluralism.[4]

In a similar way, Michael Ignatieff maintains that arguments in support of human rights should avoid appealing to dignity because such appeals overlap with contestable religious claims about the sacredness of human persons. In secular and pluralistic contexts, appeals to metaphysical or even religious convictions about human sacredness as the basis of human rights are not helpful. Through the title of his book, *Human Rights as Politics and Idolatry,* Ignatieff suggests that calling on a religious or quasi-religious interpretation of dignity in defense of human rights verges on being a form of idolatry. Some people may be quite ready to affirm dignity as a way of speaking about the sacredness of the person on religious grounds. But those who do not believe in God will reject this and see it as raising the human to a level it does not deserve and thus as a kind of idolatry. To be sure, Ignatieff wants to support human rights. But he believes we should forgo efforts to ground them on claims about a dignity or nature allegedly shared by all human beings. Support for human rights will be more secure if we avoid metaphysical or religious claims about their foundations and rely simply on historical, prudential, or pragmatic evidence that support for rights is desirable.[5] So human rights will be better served if we forgo appeals about their grounding. Again, we can dispense with the idea of dignity.

Still others object to dignity because they see claims to having identified it as the basis for human rights that is shared among all human beings as falsely universalizing what are in fact Western cultural or religious standards. Dignity could thus be used to try to justify the imposition of Western religious or cultural beliefs on those outside the West who do not share these beliefs. This argument has been raised in an Asian, Confucian perspective in a particularly pointed way by Lee Kuan Yew and from an African standpoint by Mahmood Mamdani.[6] In their views, seeking to advance human well-being by proposing a universalist understanding of human dignity and human rights carries overtones of colonial or imperial domination. People in diverse cultures are different enough from each other that it is dangerous to claim that one has identified a set of universal norms like human rights that should govern how all people should be treated. Similarly, asserting a common human dignity supposedly shared by all people across cultural boundaries risks granting the interpretation of dignity in one cultural context a dominant and even repressive role in relation to other cultures.

The idea of human dignity, therefore, faces considerable challenges today. Some of the authors cited use harshly negative terms to characterize the role played by human dignity in contemporary discourse. Dignity is variously described as useless, stupid, idolatrous, and imperialistic. These critiques of the normative status of human dignity are analogous to the critiques of human rights sketched earlier. This is certainly not a promising situation. So should we abandon the effort to understand human dignity and human rights before spending any more time on such a debatable undertaking?

THE CONTEXT OF DIGNITY'S EMERGENCE AS A KEY SOCIAL NORM

By no means. I argue that the concept of human dignity is not abstract and useless, insensitive to religious pluralism, or a potential threat to cultural difference. Such an argument can begin by giving some attention to the experiential basis for the emergence of the contemporary focus on human dignity and human rights.

First, we should note that the preamble to the Universal Declaration of Human Rights states that the document is affirming human dignity and human rights because of some utterly concrete evidence for why the idea is needed. The declaration's starting point is what happens to human beings when dignity is *not* respected. Disregard for dignity, the preamble states, has "resulted in barbarous acts which have outraged the conscience of mankind."[7] The reference is to the slaughter of six million Jews in the Holocaust, an abomination that the drafters hold to be utterly offensive to all but the socially obtuse. The importance of this context is reinforced by the fact that the 1948 Convention on the Prevention and Punishment of the Crime of Genocide was adopted by the UN General Assembly just one day before the assembly proclaimed human dignity as the basis of human rights in the Universal Declaration.[8] The contrast between respect for dignity and descent into barbarisms like genocide indicates one of the most important functions of appeals to human dignity in recent discourse. Respecting human dignity means avoiding those violations of the human person that are so grave that nearly all persons see them as outrageous and shocking. The affirmation of human dignity as the basis of rights begins from the objection to such outrages and is proposed as an alternative to them. It points to the utterly concrete experience of those who suffered and died in the Holocaust camps, those who lost spouses, children, and parents to campaigns based on racist ideology, and those who were forced to flee their homes as refugees and asylum-seekers because of the effort of an authoritarian demagogue to shape the world according to his deluded image of what it should look like. The affirmation of dignity, therefore, is far from an abstract norm that provides only ambiguous guidance. Rather, it is a normative declaration that such outrages should never happen. Indeed, dignity is proposed as a way of understanding our relation to each other that explains why we see such actions as outrageous.

The preamble of the Universal Declaration invokes not only the Holocaust as the antithesis of its affirmation of dignity but also the human destruction of two twentieth-century world wars. As an alternative to such destruction, the declaration affirms that "recognition of the inherent dignity and of the equal and inalienable rights of all members of the human family is the foundation of freedom, justice and peace in the world." In addition, the preamble implicitly alludes to the rising anticolonial spirit of the times in which it was drafted. Anticolonial efforts were arising in India in the 1940s under Mahatma Gandhi's leadership and would soon spread across other parts of Asia and across Africa in the 1950s and 1960s. Respect for dignity, the preamble maintains, is required if people are "not to be compelled to have recourse, as a last resort, to rebellion against tyranny and oppression." If respect for dignity and rights is lacking, the resulting injustice will likely lead to the violence of war and to rebellion against colonial oppression.[9] Respect for human dignity is seen thus as the antithesis of the evils that flow from oppression and violence.

This kind of appeal to human dignity can be called the "Kantian moment" in discourse about human dignity. For Immanuel Kant, the fundamental standard of morality is that all human beings be treated with respect, as ends in themselves rather than only as means to be used for some other purpose. The value of a human being—the person's dignity—is beyond price. Things with prices can be exchanged for each other in the marketplace. But humans, having dignity, are valuable in themselves and thus cannot be simply traded one for another.[10] The response due to human dignity is respect for the inherent worth of the person, not the kind of fairness that is involved in setting a just price for a commodity being exchanged in the marketplace.

One aspect of Kant's understanding of dignity, therefore, is that it affirms *who counts* when we are distributing the benefits of our life together in political, social, and interpersonal interaction. It concerns the scope of the community that the standards of morality should govern. Who are included in the "we" that are to be governed by the standards of morality being proposed? The idea of dignity insists that the most fundamental moral "we" includes *all* human persons. *All* deserve to be treated in a way that takes account of their common humanity.

Dignity is used in a similar way by the Universal Declaration of Human Rights. The declaration affirms the reality of a global community to which *all* human beings belong.[11] This is evident in the way the terms "all," "everyone," and "no one" are used throughout the declaration to indicate the subjects of the enumerated human rights. All persons possess human rights without distinctions based on "race, color, sex, language, religion, political or other opinion, national or social origin."[12] The idea that *all* persons share human dignity, therefore, relativizes all in-group/out-group boundaries. It challenges understandings of religious, national, and cultural identities that suggest only those people who possess that identity have the kind of worth that is deserving of respect.

The use of the idea of human dignity in contemporary human rights discourse thus follows Kant's lead not only in affirming the existence of universal moral obligations but also in closely linking these obligations with the requirement of respect for humanity as such. In response to the experience of the Holocaust, the violence of world wars, the potential harms that can be caused by anticolonial struggles, and the oppression of supposedly revolutionary states such as those that formed the Soviet bloc, contemporary appeals to human dignity affirm both the universal reach of moral obligation beyond all in-group/out-group divides and the duty to treat every human being with the respect due to their irreplaceable worth.

AN INDUCTIVE UNDERSTANDING OF DIGNITY

It is true, of course, that Kant's moral philosophy is not without problems. But I believe there are alternative routes to the affirmation that all persons are due the respect that Kant calls for that do not depend on the whole of his systematic moral philosophy. Let me suggest the very general outlines of an approach to understanding human dignity that avoids Kant's effort to deduce an understanding of dignity from the preconditions of rational thought. It follows a more inductive approach that begins in human experience. Because of this, it can be called a more Aristotelian approach to an understanding of human dignity. Aristotle sought to identify the concrete dimensions of the good life in an inductive way by considering evidence from all the societies known to him.[13] In like manner we can seek to determine what sort of respect is due to human beings, and thus what their dignity requires, by paying attention to the diverse religious, cultural, and political communities of our world and observing how they believe persons should be treated. This will surely surface considerable pluralism regarding how people think they should be treated and how they should treat others. In the midst of this pluralism, however, through practical reflection on the agreements, disagreements, and relative strengths of these diverse conceptions of dignity, some common standards may emerge. Such an inductive, experience-based approach may lead to transcultural agreement on at least some of the most basic requirements of respect for human worth. In fact, this is just what happened when people from many diverse traditions reached consensus on the most basic requirements of dignity when they drafted the Universal Declaration in 1948.

Using a phrase borrowed from Margaret Farley, one can call the requirements of respect for dignity "obligating features of personhood."[14] One might also call them obligating features of human dignity. These are dimensions of personal dignity that indicate not only *that* we should show respect toward one another but *what* it will mean to show such respect. Farley identifies two such features: autonomy (the capacity to be self-determining and not have one's life simply shaped by other persons or external powers) and relationality (the fact that persons cannot survive, thrive, or even exist as persons without some fundamental relatedness to other persons).[15] Because autonomy can be interpreted in an excessively individualistic way, I would prefer to call the first of these features of personhood "freedom" rather than "autonomy." In addition, I want to add "basic needs"—such as the need for food or health care—as a third obligating feature of personhood that will help specify the meaning of human dignity and what respect for dignity requires.

The importance of these freedoms, relationships, and needs as crucial features of personhood emerges from reflection on the experience of what it is to be human. Long ago Aristotle drew from his experience the conclusion that human beings are different both from beasts and from gods, and should be treated differently both from beasts and from gods.[16] This conclusion surely remains intelligible and valid today, even in the midst of our experience of cultural diversity. It points to some key ways our human personhood generates both negative and positive obligations in our interaction with each other. Not being a beast is having a capacity for self-transcendence that is unique to beings with self-consciousness or spirit. It is a key index of the distinctive worth of human personhood and it points to a central aspect of how humans can reasonably expect to be treated by each other. We should support one another in undertaking activities of the spirit, such as growing in knowledge and exercising freedom. In addition, the capacity of human consciousness to move beyond itself is a kind of self-transcendence that is evident in the formation and sustaining of personal relationships in friendship and love. Respecting humanity requires, as a minimum, that we refrain from denying each other the most basic freedoms and relationships of these kinds, unless we have solid justification for doing so.

To respect a person's ability to know, make choices, and form bonds of relationship and love is to respect the claim of what she is and to acknowledge what she can become. Similarly, a second person is capable of experiencing that claim precisely because the second person also possesses the capacity for self-transcendence. This other person is not confined within the limits of self-consciousness but can genuinely encounter the other as a fellow human being. Thus, one human being *is* a kind of *ought* in the face of another. Each person's capacity for self-transcendence makes a claim on the other's capacity for self-transcendence. One person's ability to know and understand calls out for acknowledgment in the understanding shown by others. One person's freedom places requirements on the freedom of another. One person's capacity to form bonds of relationship with others calls for acknowledgment and support through the concern of others.[17] These affirmations lead to a vision of the human race as a genuine moral community possessing reciprocal obligations among all its members. This is a cosmopolitan vision of a universal human community. Along with its respect for cultural differences, it also holds that basic common standards of dignity can be identified across cultures.

Aristotle also held that human beings are not gods. The human good is that of a finite and limited being, a bodily being whose well-being has material conditions. Human dignity can be realized only if these material conditions are present, and it cannot be realized if they are lacking. Dignity requires not only that one's freedom and relatedness be secured and protected; it also requires the existence of food, shelter, bodily integrity, medical care in sickness, and a number of other material supports. Therefore, it can be reasonably affirmed that we have some responsibilities to enable one another to share in material goods and physical, bodily activities, activities that are among the conditions required for living with dignity. At minimum we have a duty not to deprive one another of these material basics.

Respect for all three of these features of personhood—freedoms, relationships, and basic needs—were evidently seen as requirements of human dignity by the drafters of the Universal Declaration of Human Rights. They saw dignity not as an abstract standard but as a way of referring to those inductively identified characteristics of personhood that make concrete demands for respect on other persons and on social institutions. Some, perhaps many, of these characteristics were identified through their absence. Thus, the experience of the effects of denial of freedoms because of religion, ethnicity, or race led to the affirmation that respect for freedom and dignity is due to all persons independent of their religious, ethnic, or racial identity. Further reflection on experience led to a more inclusive list of the features of personhood that must be respected if persons are to be treated as such. These include the freedoms that enable one to be a self-determining person of one's own: freedom from slavery or arbitrary arrest, freedom of movement, freedom of thought, conscience, religion, expression, and assembly. They include patterns of relationship that enable people to participate actively in the interpersonal and social interactions that are necessary for the well-being both of the individual persons and of the communities of which they are members. Finally, they imply that respect for persons and their dignity requires securing basic levels of subsistence, meeting other bodily needs such as the requirements of basic health, and protecting persons through respect for their bodily integrity.

These forms of freedom, relationship, and need-fulfillment are seen to be essential to human well-being through reflection on experience, especially on the experience of their absence. Indeed, reflection on experience leads to the conclusion that some truly basic freedoms, relations, and needs are required if persons are to live lives that can be judged to meet the minimum requirements of humanity. In other words, the most basic freedoms, relationships, and needs are essential to the attainment of human dignity. They specify in a concrete way what is required if human dignity is to be respected. They are obligating features of human dignity. Their full development leads to the articulation of human rights that specify the minimum standards for the protection of human dignity.

DEMANDS OF DIGNITY KNOWN THROUGH PRACTICAL REASON

This specification of the dimensions of human dignity in the Universal Declaration's catalog of human rights is an example of practical reason in action. Jacques Maritain, who participated in the drafting of the declaration, saw the process as a vivid illustration of how practical reason can lead people from diverse religious and cultural traditions to agreement on moral values even when their understandings of ultimate meanings are different. In a much-quoted comment, Maritain observed that the drafters could "agree about the rights but on condition that no one asks us why."[18] Representatives of diverse religious and cultural traditions might be unable to reach agreement about the requirements of human dignity if they sought to deduce them from their ultimate beliefs about the world and God. But this did not prevent the attainment of practical agreement about dignity and rights. Through practical reason it was possible to reach common practical ideas that led to "the affirmation of a single body of beliefs *for guidance in action*."[19] That the reasoning involved was practical rather than theoretical did not mean that the agreement reached was simply fortuitous, purely accidental, or even irrational. The agreement on dignity and rights was in fact a vivid example of human reason in action—practical reason reflecting on human experience. Thus, the understanding of human dignity attained by the drafters of the Universal Declaration was not simply an expression of their preferences, biases, or cultural dispositions. In light of the shared experiences and reflection that led to it, this understanding of dignity can be called reasonable.

In other words, there can be *good reasons* for conclusions about practical affairs even when their ultimate significance is interpreted differently in diverse religious and cultural traditions. We can give *reasons* for affirming that human beings should not be slaughtered because they are Jews or Armenians or Tutsi, that they should be allowed to express their religious beliefs and intellectual convictions in freedom, that they should not be excluded from participation in political community or denied access to work, that their need for food or health care should be met when their community has the capacity to do so, and so on. The reasons we provide will take the form of a statement like this: our experience has led us to the practical conclusion that treating a person as a human being requires this. We have learned from experience and it is reasonable for us to affirm that these freedoms, relationships, and needs are obligating features of human dignity. Thus, if we are to treat people as they deserve, we must respect this dignity in its multiple dimensions. We have a duty to respect the human rights that spell out these features of dignity in more detail when we have the capacity to do so.

INTERACTION OF PRACTICAL AND THEOLOGICAL INTERPRETATIONS

Thus, practical reason can lead to shared understanding of the dimensions of human dignity and rights across the boundaries of different religious traditions and cultures. This is one of the most important contributions of the human rights ethos in a world simultaneously aware of its diversity and its increasingly global interdependence. Because religious traditions articulate understandings of the ultimate meaning and purpose of human activity, however, they will surely affect people's motives for respecting dignity and, in the end, will influence how believers interpret the full meaning of dignity and rights. At the same time, because understandings of human dignity and rights arrived at through practical reasoning specify morally obligatory duties, they will have an impact on the ways religious traditions are themselves interpreted. In other words, there is a mutually illuminating movement between the conclusions reached by practical reason about dignity and rights and the more theoretical orientations provided by the doctrines and beliefs of religious traditions.

This mutual illumination is evident in the way Catholicism grounds its affirmation of human dignity, both on a theological understanding of the creation of human beings in God's image and on a more secular, philosophical understanding of human capacities. The theological approach begins from the biblical teaching in the book of Genesis that human beings are created in the image and likeness of God (Gen. 1:26). Persons possess a worth that deserves to be treated with the reverence shown to that which is holy. In the thirteenth century Thomas Aquinas expressed this biblical perspective in a way that has notable parallels to Kant's affirmation that persons are ends in themselves. Aquinas wrote that of all the creatures in the universe, only humans are "governed by divine providence for their own sakes."[20] If God governs people for their own sakes, humans surely have an obligation to treat one another in a similar way. In addition, Catholicism draws on the further theological conviction that human beings have been redeemed and recreated in Christ, which calls for an even greater level of respect for personal dignity.[21] These theological warrants lead to a strong commitment to defend human dignity and human rights, a commitment that the Second Vatican Council saw as flowing from the gospel that is at the heart of Christian faith.[22]

The Catholic tradition holds that human dignity can be recognized by all human beings and makes claims upon all, both Christian and non-Christian. This is very much in line with Catholicism's long-standing natural law–based conviction that ethical responsibilities can be grasped by human reason and philosophical reflection on what it is to be human. Thus, in addition to its explicitly theological grounding for human dignity the Catholic tradition offers secular warrants for its affirmation of human dignity. The Second Vatican Council not only invoked the theological theme of creation in the image of God as the basis of dignity, but also argued that this dignity can be seen in the transcendent power of the human mind. Through their intellects, human beings transcend the material universe, and the mind's capacity to share in divine wisdom gives humans a worth that reflects God's worth analogously. For the council, human dignity is also manifest in the capacity of the human conscience to search for moral truth and to adhere to it when it has been found. Obedience to the dictates of conscience—which is the deepest core and sanctuary of a person—"is the very dignity of the human person." The council further held that dignity is evident in the excellence of human liberty. Freedom is "an exceptional sign of the divine image within the human person." The dignity of freedom requires that persons act with free choice and that they seek to direct their freedom through knowledge of the true good.[23]

These three secular warrants for human dignity—the transcendence of the mind, the sacredness of conscience, and the excellence of liberty—are all aspects of the power of human reason and a prime manifestation of the likeness of humans to God. But because intellect, conscience, and liberty are rationally knowable through reflection on experience, they possess a certain autonomy from the doctrinal beliefs of the Church. This relative autonomy of the secular philosophical warrants for human dignity enabled thinkers such as Jacques Maritain and John Courtney Murray to draw on secular argument as a kind of fulcrum for the lever of their successful efforts to persuade the Church to abandon its nineteenth-century rejection of the rights to freedom of conscience and religion. In the nineteenth and early twentieth centuries several popes had seen modern arguments for freedom of religion and thought as the manifestation of relativism and thus as threats to the truth of Christian faith. Prior to and during the Second Vatican Council, however, Maritain and Murray successfully argued that, through the reflection of practical reason on the historical experience of modern democratic life, these freedoms could be seen to be true expressions of human dignity.[24] Thus, practical reflection on experience led to a dramatic development of the Catholic stance on religious freedom and related human rights. It brought the Second Vatican Council not only to reject the nineteenth-century papacy's suspicion of human rights but to the ringing positive statement that "the right to religious freedom has its foundation in the very dignity of the human person as this dignity is known through the revealed word of God and by reason itself."[25]

The reciprocal movement between practical and theoretical reason, or between secular reflection and faith, can therefore lead a religious tradition like Catholicism to reconsider and to revise its understanding of what human dignity requires. The movement can also go the other way. It can lead a religious tradition to critique the understanding of human dignity prevailing in a culture or society by drawing on its deep religious convictions to highlight aspects of human dignity being overlooked or denied. This critique of practical understanding in light of the convictions of faith has been evident in the way the Catholic tradition has stressed the communal and social dimensions of human dignity against the individualistic approaches commonly found in much of the modern West. The Catholic tradition, for both theological and secular reasons, insists that human dignity cannot be reduced to an individualistic understanding of freedom. Freedom can only be realized in relationship and interaction with other persons. The ongoing exercise of personal freedom depends on social interaction and on social institutions that support such freedom.

The theological stress on the social dimensions of human dignity has several sources. The biblical story narrates how God's covenant draws those with faith into community and makes them "a people." Both the Hebrew Bible and the New Testament teach that the commandment to love one's neighbor as oneself is a key norm in social life, thus making the call to solidarity central for both Jews and Christians. The Christian eschatological hope that human destiny is realized in a communion of saints reinforces these communal dimensions of human personhood. Further, Catholic tradition sees the image of God in persons as a reflection of a God that Christians believe is a trinitarian union of three Persons who are interrelated in mutual love. The God of Christian faith is not a monadic being isolated in sublime solitude but rather is radically relational. As images of this trinitarian God, human persons are also relational. Human beings achieve their dignity only in communal solidarity with each other. As the council put it, "God did not create the human being as a solitary. . . . For by his innermost nature the human being is a social being, and unless he relates himself to others he can neither live nor develop his potential."[26]

This theological understanding of human dignity as a relational reality also has secular warrants. For example, Vatican II cites Aquinas's appropriation of Aristotle's philosophical defense of the "social nature" of the human person, which implies that the development of the person and the advance of society "hinge on each other" and that each person "stands completely in need of social life."[27] Thus, on both theological and secular grounds, the dignity of the person can be achieved only when persons enter into fraternity and community with each other. Human dignity is not realized by persons acting autonomously on their own but rather only through collaboration and solidarity. An individualistic ethic is thus inadequate in light of Catholicism's relational understanding of human dignity. Protection of human dignity and realization of the common good go together. Neither personal flourishing nor communal well-being can be secured without the other. (This communal, relational understanding of human dignity and rights is further developed in chapter 4.)

This relational understanding of the image of God and of human dignity has important practical implications, particularly for the way human rights are understood. During the Cold War, the West was inclined to conceive human rights largely in individualistic terms and give priority to the civil and political rights to freedom of belief, speech, and association as well as due process of law. The negative rights not to be interfered with often took primacy in the West in its ideological struggle with the Soviet bloc. In contrast, Eastern bloc nations and some in the Southern Hemisphere adopted ideologies stressing social interdependence and the priority of community provision over individual initiative. This led to granting priority to social and economic rights, such as the right to adequate food, work, and housing.

The Catholic affirmation of the importance of freedom and the simultaneous claim that freedom is dependent on and realized in community leads to a rejection of the need to choose between the two types of rights. Neither individualistic understandings that see human rights primarily as rights to be left alone nor collectivist approaches that subordinate persons to the community in a totalitarian way are adequate. The Catholic tradition holds that opposition between individual freedoms, on the one hand, and mutual solidarity in society, on the other, is a false dichotomy. Persons can live in dignity only when they live in a community of freedom—a community in which both personal initiative and social solidarity are valued as essential aspects of human dignity.

Thus, the Catholic tradition will challenge any understanding of human rights that stresses solely the protection of individual freedom in an economy based entirely on the free market. The free market can be productive and lead to economic growth. But the communal understanding of human dignity means that the participation of all persons in the economic *and social* life of society must be protected. If persons are left out of such participation, the market may need to be regulated or limited in order to guarantee the basic requirements of their dignity. In the context of current economic problems that have pushed many into poverty and unemployment, Pope Benedict XVI stressed this social aspect when he stated that "the worldwide financial breakdown has . . . shown the error of the assumption that the market is capable of regulating itself, apart from public intervention and the support of internalized moral standards."[28] This does not, of course, mean that the Church endorses total state control of the economy. The communal understanding of dignity calls for a prudent blend of freedom and regulation in order to secure the agency of all, through their participation in the dynamics of social and economic life. It calls for an approach to dignity and rights in which persons have political space for action (civil and political rights) and also the material and institutional prerequisites of communal life that make such action possible (social and economic rights). Thus, both civil-political and social-economic rights are required if human dignity is to be respected in its multiple aspects. This has opened the way for the Church to become an active voice for human dignity in the face of the problems raised both by free markets and by centralized, authoritarian political systems as well.

Catholic understandings of human dignity and rights are thus shaped both by an inductive use of practical reason reflecting on experience and also on a more theoretical or imaginative vision of humanity shaped by Christian faith. Practical reason and faith play interacting roles in shaping the understanding of dignity. This interaction is itself a historical, experience-based process. It has led to notable revisions in the Catholic stance toward human rights, including religious freedom and democracy, on which the Church moved from strong opposition to full support in the century from 1865 to 1965. This also raises the question of whether further developments in the Catholic understanding of dignity and rights might be expected in the future. It suggests that the question of possible continuing development in how dignity is understood needs to be faced in other religious traditions and in secular traditions as well.

Let me conclude by suggesting that the inductive role played by practical reason in formulating the concrete demands of human dignity means that we should expect our understanding of human rights to continue to change and develop. The historical nature of practical reason's reflection on experience can help us understand how the Catholic understanding of human dignity has developed in such notable ways over the past few centuries. It also suggests that we can expect further developments in the Catholic understanding of human dignity and rights in the future. For example, recent Church teachings on the equality of men and women is often accompanied by an affirmation of a complementarity of male and female gender roles that leads to a rejection of some of the rights claimed by women and by persons involved in same-sex relationships. Similarly, recent Church teachings reject some innovative forms of medical and technological support for human reproduction as threats to human dignity.[29] Clearly, affirming the equality of men and women, the legitimacy of some forms of same-sex relationship, and the appropriateness of some types of technologically assisted reproduction as supportive of human dignity requires a notable shift in aspects of the Catholic moral tradition. Though this is not the place to assess these matters, developments in Catholic thought on such issues should not be ruled out a priori, for Catholic understandings of the requirements of human dignity have clearly changed in a number of other domains. These changes occurred when practical reason indicated they would serve the human good and promote human dignity. We need further reflection today on how human dignity might be affected by new practices in these areas.

In a reflection on the role of Islam in the world today, Pope Benedict stressed the role of reason in assessing whether particular religious visions of the moral life are to be judged to truly reflect God's intent for humanity. The pope noted that some Muslims' appeal to the Qur'an and to Islamic tradition to justify Muslim resort to holy war to advance the spread of Islam. But the pope sees such resort to violence as contrary to God's intent precisely because it rejects the use of reason, a key component of authentic faith. Quoting the fourteenth-century Byzantine emperor Manuel II Paleologus, the pope stated, "Not to act reasonably, not to act with *logos*, is contrary to the nature of God."[30] In appealing to what he calls the "rationality of faith," Pope Benedict was certainly not reducing faith to what can be known within the limits of reason alone. But he was clearly rejecting Muslim forms of holy war or jihad that fail to meet the kind of reasonable standards for the use of force that have become embodied in the tradition of just war, which combines practical human reasonableness with the Christian vision of the dignity of the person.

I would suggest that the Catholic tradition will be true to itself by being ready to apply similar standards of the "rationality of faith" to the assessment of how human dignity is supported or threatened by the impact of shifting gender roles on the rights of women and same-sex relations, by development of new forms of intervention in human reproduction, and by other new and perhaps controversial forms of human interaction. Inductive reflection on experience through practical reason on these issues may well lead us to conclude that change in traditional standards is the best way to secure human dignity and human rights. Human dignity raises ongoing challenges for all traditions of moral reflection. We can expect Catholicism to be an active participant in developing effort to respond to these challenges.

3

SHARED HUMANITY AFTER GENOCIDE IN RWANDA

The contemporary context makes remembrance of the genocide against the Tutsi people in Rwanda especially important for efforts to protect human rights today. Some of today's political currents threaten to undermine the commitment to "never again" tolerate genocide or other atrocities that massively violate human rights. The former UN high commissioner for human rights, Zeid Ra'ad Al Hussein, put the political challenge this way: "The number and scale of raging conflicts continue to cause immense suffering and force unprecedented numbers of people to flee their homes. . . . Yet rather than dealing with them, we seem to be turning away and looking inwards."[1] In numerous contexts people are turning inward to reaffirm their own identities and the interests of their own groups, even if doing so threatens the common humanity they share with others. This turning inward is evident in the populist nationalism that has led to Brexit in the United Kingdom and to Donald Trump's efforts to build a wall to insulate the United States from its neighbors to the south or to ban all Muslims from entering the United States. Antipathy toward those who are "different" is especially evident from the fact that at the end of 2022 over 108 million people were driven from their homes as forced migrants, an all-time high.[2] Despite the current generous reception of Ukrainian refugees in countries of the European Union, the walls some want to erect to separate themselves from people who are different threaten to undermine commitment to human rights.

The events of April to June 1994 in Rwanda show us how dangerous the division into "us-versus-them" can be. The lines of exclusion between Hutus and Tutsis were not always as sharply drawn as they became during the decades of Belgian colonial rule and especially in the years following Rwandan independence. The people of Rwanda largely spoke the same language, shared religious and cultural traditions, and intermarried across Hutu/Tutsi distinctions.

They shared a common humanity that called for mutual respect. But colonial pressures deepened divisions and turned the difference between Hutu and Tutsi into a distinction between those who deserved to be treated as human and those who did not. The outcome of this division was the atrocity of the genocide that killed nearly a million Tutsi men, women, and children in less than ninety days. Remembrance (*kwibuka*, in Kinyarwanda) warns us of the grave dangers of such us-versus-them divisions. What happened in Rwanda solemnly tells the rest of the world what can happen when in-group/out-group divisions grow deep. This chapter will bring memory of the Rwanda genocide against the Tutsis into dialogue with religious and ethical values that call us to recognize our shared humanity and the human rights of all people.

HUMAN RIGHTS AND THE IMPORTANCE OF MEMORY

The political dangers of sharp divisions between people with different identities are intensified by doubts about the relevance of human rights recently voiced by several influential commentators. As noted in chapter 1, some use dramatic language to declare that we are facing the "endtimes of human rights" or that we have reached the "twilight of human rights.[3] Samuel Moyn, professor of history and law at Yale University, has argued that the drafting of the UN's Universal Declaration of Human Rights (UDHR) had little connection with outrage of the Holocaust of the Jews by Nazi Germany. Moyn's argument reduces the relevance of human rights for our remembrance of what happened in Rwanda. This argument by Moyn has been directly challenged by Johannes Morsink, whose study of the drafting of the UDHR shows that the Nazi genocide against the Jewish people was a key stimulus to its drafting. Morsink's work shows the importance of remembering the reality of genocide, including the genocide in Rwanda, and sustaining a vigorous commitment to human rights.[4] More recently, Moyn has argued that the human rights movement has little to say to the rising economic inequality of our world because it has become too closely allied with free-market neoliberalism.[5] This claim is also relevant to Rwanda because the historic economic relations between Tutsis and Hutus contributed to the pressures that exploded in the genocide of 1994.[6]

In the face of these political and intellectual challenges, remembrance of the genocide against the Tutsis in Rwanda is crucial for the effort to advance human rights today. Protecting human rights requires us to keep alive the memory of the disastrous consequences that can occur when peoples erect walls between "us" and "them." Memory of the consequences of the division between Hutus and Tutsis in 1994 and of the earlier splits between in-groups and out-groups warns us of what can happen when we forget our common humanity. Sustaining a vision of our shared humanity is essential to keeping the commitment to human rights alive. Vivid memory of genocide against the Tutsis is surely called for by the horrible human abuse of humanity carried out in the genocide. It will also be essential to keeping the demands of human rights on the global political agenda. The experience of the atrocity of the Holocaust was at the origins of modern understandings of human rights. Commitment to human rights today will be strengthened by keeping alive the memories of what happened in Rwanda in 1994. Christian religious and ethical support for human rights and social justice will also be strengthened by continuing Christian remembrance of the Rwanda genocide.

This chapter seeks to strengthen Christian commitment by reflecting on several aspects of Christian support for human rights in the past, in light of the atrocities that happened in Rwanda. Remembrance of the Church's historical record shows that Catholic Christians have a mixed record in their support for human rights. In recent decades the Catholic community has become a very strong defender of human rights, with the notable exception of its failure to stand for human rights against the *genocidaires* in Rwanda. Further back in history, there were periods when the Church took a strong stand in defense of human dignity and rights, and other times when it contributed to their diminishment. By recalling the Church's mixed history on human rights while remembering its failures during the Rwanda genocide, we can strengthen Catholic commitment to human rights in the face of human rights challenges of today, both globally and in Rwanda itself.

THE MIXED HISTORY OF CHURCH COMMITMENT TO HUMAN RIGHTS

It is well known that the Christian community and the Catholic Church did not distinguish itself by its defense of human rights during the genocide against the Tutsis.[7] Indeed, it is shocking that genocide took place in the African country with the highest percentage of baptized Catholics in its population. It is also scandalous that some Church leaders, including bishops, priests, and religious, took part in the killing or supported the killers. This behavior led Pope Francis to make a formal apology for the truly scandalous failure of the Church and to ask for "forgiveness for the sins and failings of the Church and its members, among whom [were] priests, and religious men and women who succumbed to hatred and violence, betraying their own evangelical mission." The Rwandan bishops have expressed similar regrets for their failures.[8]

Historical memory reminds us that the Catholic community failed to support human rights earlier as well. At the time of the French Revolution, the Catholic ancien régime resisted the *droits de l'homme* proclaimed by the revolution. In the late nineteenth and early twentieth centuries, Catholic leaders rejected emerging modern human rights standards, such as freedom of religion. They saw modern freedoms as tied to the secularism of the French Revolution. This led Catholic leadership to see human rights as part of an ideology that was seeking to confine religious belief to the margins of society. They also saw human rights as individualistic in inspiration and as a force that would undermine the long-standing Catholic commitment to the common good.[9] Historically, Catholic attitudes to Jews far too often had anti-Semitic and anti-Jewish dimensions, reaching back even to the New Testament, where John's gospel portrayed the Jews as enemies of Jesus. These attitudes led Christians too often to deny basic rights to Jewish people. These were among the factors contributing to the anti-Semitism that culminated in the Nazi genocide against the Jews.

Fortunately, the Second Vatican Council set the Church on a path of strong support for human rights. The council declared that the Church, "by virtue of the Gospel committed to her, proclaims the rights of the human person; she acknowledges and greatly esteems the dynamic movements of today by which these rights are everywhere fostered."[10] Thus, the council linked human rights with the core of Christian faith. The council also revised Catholic thinking on Judaism and committed the Church to full respect for the rights of Jews and to dialogue and interreligious collaboration with the Jewish community.

Due to the developments brought about by the council, the Catholic Church has become an important institutional activist for human rights. As noted earlier, this activism led writers such as the late Samuel Huntington to argue that, since Vatican II, the Catholic Church has become one of the most effective agencies contributing to the global advancement of democracy and to the human rights that support democracy.[11] It is clear, therefore, that in recent decades the Catholic tradition on human rights has developed and grown in important ways. This tradition is very much alive today, both intellectually and in the Church's practical engagement in the struggle for human rights.

What brought about this dramatic change in the Catholic approach? The experiences of suffering due to the Holocaust of the Jewish people and the massive casualties of World Wars I and II that led to the drafting of the Universal Declaration of Human Rights are the same experiences that led the Church to recognize the importance of human rights. These experiences have been reconfirmed by the Rwanda genocide, for disastrous conflicts like the two world wars and the horrors of the Nazi genocide of the Jewish people follow almost inevitably when peoples are divided by attitudes of us-versus-them based on religion, nationality, or ethnicity.[12] These experiences also stimulated dramatic development in the Catholic Church's teaching on human rights.

Following World War II and the defeat of Nazism, Pope Pius XII began the recent developments in Catholic tradition. In 1963, Pope John XXIII's encyclical *Pacem in Terris* moved to full support for human rights as the prerequisite for peace. John XXIII insisted that peace can be obtained only when the order laid down by God is observed and that this order requires respect for human rights as the universal and inviolable requirements of the human dignity of all persons.[13] *Pacem in Terris* has since become the Catholic charter of human rights. The Second Vatican Council reinforced the Church's experience-based discovery of the importance of human rights by drawing on religious and ethical norms contained in the long Catholic tradition. Vatican II's Dignitatis Humanae (Declaration on Religious Freedom) explicitly states that the council was carrying out a *development* of the Church's tradition in light of its social experience (the "signs of the times"). In the declaration's words, "The council intends to develop the doctrine of recent popes on the inviolable rights of the human person and the constitutional order of society."[14] The council's Gaudium et Spes (Pastoral Constitution on the Church in the Modern World) presents the Church's role in society as based on the fundamental duty to promote the dignity of the human person made in God's image. From this theological standpoint the council affirmed that the gospel entrusted to the Church should lead Christians to safeguard human rights. Persons possess a worth that should always be treated with reverence. Made in God's likeness, human beings possess a sacredness analogous to the holiness of God. Because human beings are redeemed and recreated in Christ, believers are called to esteem human dignity even more highly.[15] Thus, mistreating a human person is not only morally objectionable. It is a religious violation as well—a kind of sacrilege. By sharing in the experiences that led to the promulgation of the Universal Declaration of Human Rights, Catholic Christianity came to see that the Church's mission to defend human dignity and rights flows from the heart of Christian faith. The Church's recognition that promoting human rights is essential to its mission should have given it a very different role in Rwanda.

EARLIER HISTORY:
THE HUMANITARIAN REVOLUTION

Remembrance of other experiences of grave violations of human dignity in earlier periods in Catholic and Western history can reinforce the conclusion that the Christian community should have played a very different role when defending human rights in Rwanda in 1994. A major threat to human rights today is the rise of nationalist, ethnic, and religious exclusivisms. These forces generate resistance to the universalist orientation of the human rights ethic. Indeed, the tragedy in Rwanda has led some to the depressing conclusion that neither the human rights movement nor Christianity have anything important to say in the aftermath of the genocide against the Tutsis. However, in a recent study, Steven Pinker has assembled an extraordinary range of evidence to show that over the past several centuries there has been a rising commitment to universal and equal humanity and to the substantial decline in the violence humans have been inflicting upon one another in the modern era.[16] Pinker calls these changes "the humanitarian revolution." In his analysis, this revolution was brought about by a growing moral commitment to the organized pursuit of equal dignity for all persons that began with the American and French Revolutions in the eighteenth century. It contributed to the abolition of slavery and to the restrictions on legitimate actions in warfare formulated in the Geneva Conventions, including requirements that civilians not be directly attacked.

A further expansion of the commitment to equal dignity, which Pinker calls the "rights revolution," occurred in the second half of the twentieth century, with the drafting of the Universal Declaration of Human Rights, subsequent rights covenants and conventions, and the human rights movement that seeks to implement these documents.[17] The data and historical narratives presented by Pinker make a strong case that active commitment to the dignity of all persons, shared across the borders separating national, cultural, and religious communities, has led to a substantial decline in the death and suffering of human beings from violence and oppression. Pinker is certainly not arguing that these revolutions have eliminated all human suffering. Indeed, remembrance of the Shoah and the genocide against the Tutsis in Rwanda, among other tragic events of the past several centuries, show that the human suffering caused by the divisions among peoples remains at tragically unacceptable levels.[18] Nevertheless, rising concern for the dignity of all members of the human family across divisions of race, religion, nationality, ethnicity, and gender has been growing over the past several centuries and has had beneficial effects. As we remember what happened in Rwanda in 1994, we should also remember these positive developments in recent history.

SHARED HUMANITY AFTER GENOCIDE IN RWANDA   37

Despite the importance of Pinker's historical work, he is nevertheless mistaken when he argues that the moral revolutions he applauds were largely due to the diminishment of the role played by religion in public affairs. Other scholars, including sociologist Peter Stamatov and theologian Roger Ruston, show that the Christian community and Christian theology made significant contributions to the humanitarian revolution and to a rising commitment to the equal rights of all persons across national, cultural, and religious borders.[19] Stamatov and Ruston, in distinct ways, trace the modern humanitarian and human rights movements back to the sixteenth century, when Dominican friars Antonio de Montesinos, Bartolomé de las Casas, and Francisco de Vitoria raised their Christian voices against the exploitation and enslavement of Indigenous people in the Caribbean by colonial representatives of the Spanish Crown. Indeed, they directly challenged the idea held by fellow Spanish Catholics close to the Crown that the Native Americans were not fully human because they did not share European ways of life and that they lacked genuine freedom because they were not Christian. These friars affirmed that full human dignity reaches across cultural, national, and religious borders. The duty to respect this humanity is also transcultural, transnational, and interreligious.

Two illustrations will indicate the contributions made by the friars. In 1511, just nineteen years after the arrival of Europeans on the Caribbean island of Hispaniola, Montesinos passionately denounced the Spanish conquistadors for their enslavement of the Indigenous people. Speaking in Christ's name, Montesinos declared, "I am the voice of Christ in the wilderness of this island.... This voice says that you are all in mortal sin and that you will live and die in it for the cruelty and tyranny with which you use these innocent people.... Are you not obliged to love them as you love yourselves?"[20] Here Montesinos called the colonial powers to a major change in their behavior by appealing to the commandment to love one's neighbor that is central to the Christian tradition. A few decades later, in 1537–39, another friar, the major theologian Francisco Vitoria, delivered a set of lectures at the University of Salamanca on "the affair of the Indies" (De Indis). Vitoria, too, insisted that the duty to love all one's neighbors and to respect all for whom Christ died demanded a profound change in colonial practice.[21]

In addition to appealing to Bible-based, distinctively Christian traditions, Montesinos, las Casas, and Vitoria also pointed directly to the humanity of the Indigenous people in challenging colonial practice. The very humanity that the Indigenous people shared with the Spanish called for an inclusive, universalist understanding of the rights and duties they also shared. Montesinos invoked the humanity of the Indigenous in these words: "Tell me, with what right, with what justice do you hold these Indians in such cruel and horrible slavery? . . . Are they not men?"—are they not human? This is a direct appeal to the human dignity of the Indigenous people and to the common humanity they shared with the Europeans. This ethic breaks down walls and opens doors of respect across differences in religion, ethnicity, race, nationality, tribe, and gender.

This appeal to an ethic of shared humanity was given philosophical backing by Vitoria through an understanding of natural law. Vitoria was a learned theologian and philosopher whose thinking on the "Indian question" was strongly influenced by the ethics of Thomas Aquinas.[22] Following Aquinas, Vitoria argued that the demands of the moral law could be discovered not only from the Bible but also through reasoned reflection on human experience. Reflecting on the vicarious experiences that Vitoria gained from communication with fellow Dominicans in the Americas while he taught in Salamanca, Vitoria insisted that the duty to respect the humanity of the Indigenous people meant that the Spanish were treating them in a morally unacceptable way. The basic requirements of morality are universal: wherever human persons are present, the moral requirement to show respect is also present.

Montesinos and Vitoria were advocating a sixteenth-century anticipation of universal human rights.[23] Indeed, Vitoria's De Indis lectures, along with his other works, such as *On the Law of War*, were major contributions to the beginnings of modern international law. The objections raised by Montesinos and Vitoria to colonial domination anticipated the modern insistence that human rights are universal. The humanitarian and human rights revolutions celebrated by Pinker did not unfold through a secularist replacement of religion and Christianity, as Pinker maintains, but were at least partly due to the influence of Christian pastors and theologians like Montesinos and Vitoria.

THE RELEVANCE OF THIS MEMORY TODAY

The Rwanda genocide against the Tutsis shows that the memory of the friars' efforts has relevance to contemporary efforts to protect people against abuse because of cultural or religious differences. Though Montesinos, las Casas, and Vitoria did not appeal directly to human rights as these rights are understood today, they strongly sought to protect the life and dignity of the people of the "New World." They denounced the grave abuses being inflicted upon the Indigenous Americans by the Spanish conquistadors. Their defense of human worth across borders was an important contribution to the rise of the idea that rights and duties are universal.

Indeed, the universalist ethical stance of the friars anticipated important aspects of what in very recent days has come to be called "the responsibility to protect." The recent understanding of this responsibility arose largely as a response to the grave abuses that took place in both Rwanda and Bosnia in 1994. The experience of these abuses led the Canadian government to convene an international commission to determine the legitimacy of intervention across national borders to stop very grave human rights violations. The commission issued a report in 2001 titled "The Responsibility to Protect."[24] The report's core ideas were endorsed by the leaders of most of the world's countries at the 2005 World Summit Meeting of the UN General Assembly, which stated that "each individual State has the responsibility to protect its populations from genocide, war crimes, ethnic cleansing and crimes against humanity."[25] Further, if states fail to protect their people from these grave crimes, the international community has a responsibility to do so, first through peaceful means and then, if necessary, as a last resort by armed force.

This commitment has generated strong support and passionate disagreement. The debate continues to be of great importance today as we consider how to respond to crises such as those in eastern Democratic Republic of Congo, in South Sudan, and among the Rohingya people in Myanmar. Recalling the ideas set forth by Montesinos and Vitoria in the seventeenth century, in the Universal Declaration of Human Rights in 1948, and in the "Responsibility to Protect" report more recently will help energize the moral and political commitment needed to respond effectively to those crises. It is important to keep the efforts of the friars in the seventeenth century and the UN's efforts in the twentieth century in lively memory as we seek to respond to today's political and intellectual pressures that lead to atrocities like genocide, ethnic cleansing, war crimes, and crimes against humanity.

The arguments against providing threatened people with the protection called for by the responsibility to protect (R2P) have taken several forms. Political realists, of course, hold that the actions of states should be determined by the interests of the states' own peoples, not by an alleged moral responsibility to protect people from abuse in other lands. Thus, Henry Kissinger maintained that the appeals to humanitarian values that led the United States and NATO (North Atlantic Treaty Organization) to intervene militarily to protect the Indigenous people of Somalia and Kosovo were misguided. In a different vein, some postcolonial thinkers reject the responsibility to protect people in other lands because they see it as a form of neoimperialism. They see R2P as a twenty-first-century version of what the French called *la mission civilisatrice*, which led France to incorporate large swaths of Africa and Southeast Asia into *la grande France* as colonies. The Ugandan scholar Mahmood Mamdani draws on the sad history of European colonialism in Africa and on the fact that much of the debate about R2P has dealt with crises in Africa, to argue that the alleged responsibility masks "a big power agenda to recolonize Africa."[26] Mamdani roundly rejects R2P as an attempt by strong nations to justify imposing their will on weaker ones.

Still others dismiss R2P because they think it has proven ineffective in obtaining the goal of actually protecting people from suffering. For example, some argue that the intervention to protect some members of the Libyan population from indiscriminate attack by Muammar Gaddafi was ineffective and even made the situation worse.[27] Gaddafi referred to his adversaries in Benghazi as "cockroaches," the very epithet Hutus used for Tutsis during the Rwanda genocide.[28] As a result, the UN Security Council, with the notable support of the Organization of the Islamic Conference and the League of Arab States, called for the use of "all necessary measures" to protect civilians in Libya.[29] NATO intervened with airpower, Gaddafi was killed, and Gaddafi's regime was overthrown. Sadly, Libya has since fallen into political chaos, with armed conflicts among several groups, significant violations of human rights on the basis of religion, and unsafe flight of migrants across the Mediterranean.[30] These consequences confirm some in their conviction that pursuing humanitarian goals not required by national self-interest is likely to do more harm than good.[31] I would argue, however, that the intervention in Libya failed not because it was excessive but because it was incomplete. Following the norms that my colleagues in ethics today call *jus post bellum* (justice after conflict), NATO and the United States should have followed their intervention with action to rebuild and to prevent the chaos that developed.[32] What happened in Libya was an incomplete implementation of R2P, not a simple failure.

The case of Syria has also been invoked to suggest that R2P is dead or irrelevant. The political complexities and moral ambiguities of the Syrian situation go very deep. But these complexities do not discredit R2P. Thomas Weiss has argued that the wisdom of the use of military force to protect people from atrocities is governed by three factors: legality, moral legitimacy, and feasibility.[33] In Syria it is clear that the *legal* prohibitions of war crimes and of other atrocities have been violated, both by the Syrian government and by its adversaries. The *moral legitimacy* of efforts to stop a conflict that has displaced over half the Syrian population and killed hundreds of thousands of civilians is hardly questionable. The *feasibility* of military intervention to alleviate the crisis, however, is unclear. Nevertheless, this does not undermine the reality of a responsibility to protect people from atrocity. Rather, it suggests that the key issue is how to do so. The apparent lack of feasible ways to overcome the crisis in Syria through the use of military force suggests that responsible action should be taken through political and diplomatic initiatives to find a path forward. Not only Syrian president Bashar al-Assad and those rebelling against him but also Russia, Iran, some Gulf States, and others have kept the crisis in Syria alive. There are duties to engage these powers in the pursuit of peace through continuing political and diplomatic engagement.

Therefore, despite the fact that there are some reasons to question the continuing relevance of the responsibility to protect, there are also good reasons to support its relevance. In practice R2P has been invoked on a number of occasions since 2005 and has led to effective protection of people from grave rights violations. For example, when ethnic clashes began to flare in Kenya following the disputed 2007 elections, some saw similarities to the early stages of the Rwanda genocide. As a result, nonviolent diplomatic initiatives were taken by numerous international actors, including the UN, the African Union, and a number of other governments from Africa and around the world, including the United States.[34] One of the leaders of these initiatives, Kofi Annan, stated that he saw the crisis in Kenya through "the R2P prism."[35] As a result, a power-sharing agreement was reached between the opposing forces in Kenya and the downward spiral into civil war and perhaps even genocide was stopped. The Kenyan case illustrates that people can be successfully protected against atrocities like the Rwanda genocide through nonviolent political and diplomatic means.

People have also been militarily protected from atrocities on several recent occasions by invoking the UN General Assembly's affirmation that R2P called for action. In 2012, with UN approval, France and the Economic Community of West African States took military action in pursuit of peace in Mali. In 2013 the Security Council supported the use of force by French and African Union troops to stop the atrocities occurring in Central African Republic that displaced nearly one million refugees and internally displaced persons.[36] Though these conflicts are certainly not fully resolved, and much remains to be done to protect people in Mali and Central African Republic, remembering these cases indicates that the doctrine of the responsibility to protect can prevent grave disasters like genocide. Events in Kenya, Mali, and Central African Republic suggest the kind of steps that could have been taken by the international community in Rwanda, both through diplomacy (as in Kenya) and through more forceful means (as in Mali and Central African Republic).[37]

In addition to these cases where we have experience of some practical success in preventing atrocities, normative arguments continue to be made in support of R2P. The Sudanese scholar and diplomat Francis Mading Deng is well aware of the harms brought by colonialism and racism in Sudan.

Despite this awareness, however, he supports R2P, disagreeing with the Ugandan scholar Mahmood Mamdani. Deng's concept of sovereignty-as-responsibility, which he developed to help respond to the needs of internally displaced people in his country of Sudan, was one of the intellectual resources that led to R2P.[38] The plight of the millions of persons internally displaced by the north-south war in his country before its southern regions became the independent country of South Sudan led Deng to argue that sovereignty of states derives from the sovereignty of their people, not from an abstract immunity from outside intervention. Thus, when a government fails in its responsibility to protect its people, it has to a degree already lost some of its sovereignty. Action by other countries can be justified to protect people whose own government is failing in this regard, and such action should not be seen as a violation of sovereignty. The views of both Kofi Annan and Francis Deng show that important African thinkers support R2P and do not see it as driven by an agenda of Western neocolonialism.

The same is true of several important Christian and Catholic leaders. Pope Benedict XVI explicitly endorsed R2P in his 2008 speech to the UN General Assembly, where he strongly affirmed the centrality of human rights in international politics today. Pope Benedict restated this support in his 2009 encyclical *Caritas in veritate (Charity in Truth)*.[39] In 2017 Pope Francis's ambassador to the United Nations also affirmed support for R2P by the Catholic Church. The papal ambassador declared that this responsibility requires "meeting obligations under international human rights and international humanitarian law, and condemning deliberate attacks against civilians and civilian infrastructures. It means preventing or stopping atrocity crimes and protecting populations from them through greater legal, political and moral accountability."[40] These endorsements of R2P have important theological and philosophical roots in key strands of the Catholic moral tradition, with its long-standing insistence that the common humanity of all persons means that moral responsibility reaches across borders. Indeed, in his 2008 speech to the UN, Benedict explicitly recalled that Vitoria argued that nations can have duties across borders that require protecting the dignity of persons as created in the image of God.

Vitoria's affirmation of this transborder responsibility was further developed by another great Spanish theologian of the early modern period, the Jesuit Francisco Suárez. Suárez recognized that the sovereignty of modern states, which was coming into existence in his time, gave each state a rightful independence and a claim to be free from domination by other states. Nevertheless, Suárez stressed that the human race as a whole possesses a unity that he called quasi-political and moral.[41] No state is ever so self-sufficient that it does not require assistance from other countries. The unity of the human family also binds countries together by a "natural precept of love and mercy." This precept binds people "even to strangers of every nation."[42] The moral unity of people across borders thus gives rise to a law of peoples (*jus gentium*) that applies across borders and calls culturally and religiously diverse societies to mutual respect and care for each other. In our time, it can call nations to provide protection to those who are facing grave abuse of their human dignity in other lands.

The responsibility to protect people from atrocities thus has roots not only in the recent experiences of atrocity like the genocide against the Tutsis in Rwanda. It also has roots in the sixteenth-century experiences of domination of Indigenous peoples of the Americas by colonial powers and in intellectual objections to such domination by theologians like Vitoria and Suárez. It is but a short step from Vitoria and Suárez in the sixteenth century to the endorsement of R2P by Pope Benedict and Pope Francis in our time. The development both of modern human rights and of R2P should lead us to take action to ensure that events like the Rwanda genocide do not occur again.

CONCLUSION: THE IMPORTANCE OF REMEMBERING OUR SHARED HUMANITY

Where does this leave us in our efforts to think ethically and theologically about preventing grave violations of human rights or in remembering the genocide against the Tutsis in Rwanda? Our remembering has surfaced important practical efforts to protect human rights in modern history. It has also identified key normative values that call the human community to work vigorously across all borders to protect human rights and especially to prevent atrocities that gravely violate human dignity. Keeping these practical efforts and values at the forefront of our memories will help energize vigorous action to prevent tragedies like the one that happened in Rwanda in 1994.

The Catholic Church has itself not always been a strong voice for human rights throughout its history. Thus, in the Church, as well as in secular society, it will be important to keep alive the memory of the suffering that occurs when human rights are denied and of the Church's successes and failures in defense of rights. On the practical level, we have pointed to significant efforts by the Catholic community in the sixteenth and seventeenth centuries, under the leadership of pastors and theologians like Montesinos, las Casas, Vitoria, and Suárez, to resist the division of the world into Christian Europeans and Indigenous pagans everywhere else, with the former possessing dignity and rights and the latter seen as not fully human and lacking both dignity and rights. The efforts of these pastors and theologians sadly did not prevent grave mistreatment that ultimately led to the deaths of most Native peoples they encountered. Nonetheless, their efforts are a source of hope, for they contributed in important ways to the development of modern international law, with its insistence that legal and moral obligation does not end at the boundaries separating cultural, national, or religious communities. Remembering their insistence on the common humanity of all human beings and the action they took to defend this shared humanity can help keep alive the hope for human rights today. It can energize action to prevent future Rwandas.

In a similar way, we should remember that the suffering caused by the world wars of the twentieth century and by the Nazi genocide against the Jews contributed to the drafting of the Universal Declaration of Human Rights and to emergence of human rights activism in the Catholic community. The Universal Declaration is itself a sign of hope that the human community is committed to preventing such suffering in the future. The fact that grave atrocities have occurred since the drafting of the declaration could lead us to conclude that the modern human rights movement has failed. Indeed, there have been tragic violations of the UDHR in recent decades, including the Rwanda genocide against the Tutsis and also the grave abuses in Cambodia, in Bosnia, and today in Syria, South Sudan, and among the Rohingya of Myanmar.

Nevertheless, and despite these tragic failures, there is encouraging evidence that normative commitments to shared humanity and human rights across borders have made a real difference and can continue to do so. Steven Pinker presents data that show humans inflicting less violence on one another over the past several hundred years than they did in earlier ages, with a particularly notable decline since the end of World War II.[43] Kathryn Sikkink's book *Evidence for Hope: Making Human Rights Work in the 21st Century* also argues that there has been greater respect for human rights since the mid-twentieth century, when the Universal Declaration was proclaimed.[44] Pinker and Sikkink both stress that data on the decline of genocide since the mid-twentieth century has particular relevance to our remembrance of what took place in Rwanda. Despite the atrocities in Cambodia by Pol Pot, the actions against the Bosniaks in the former Yugoslavia, and the genocide of the Tutsis in Rwanda, the number of genocidal events and the number of people killed in intergroup conflict has been declining in an encouraging way since 1945.[45]

The data thus lead us to question claims that today's political realities mean we are in the "twilight" or "endtimes" of human rights. An argument by two distinguished specialists in international affairs, Bruce Russett and John Oneal, reinforces claims about the positive influence of the human rights movement today. Russett and Oneal argue from empirical data that recent declines in war and conflict have been due to three factors: the advancement of democracy, the growth of global interdependence, and the increasing role of international organizations.[46] Democracy provides institutional protection for key human rights. Global interdependence on the economic level links persons together across cultural, national, and religious borders. An increasing number of international organizations include human rights as part of their agendas. Though the modern human rights movement is not the sole or even the principal cause of less genocide and violence in our day, the data surely suggest that human rights norms and the human rights movement are making an important and positive difference.

Sikkink recognizes that we are far from having reached the ideal, where diverse groups live in harmony and where the human rights of all are secure. But she does not base her hope on a comparison between the present with an imagined ideal situation where all human rights are fully secure and where all violation has been eliminated. Rather, Sikkink's hope for the future of human rights rests on her memory of former abuses and on a recognition that we are doing better today than in the relatively recent past.

Following Sikkink, we can conclude that the memory of things past leads to a non-utopian hope that efforts to protect human rights can make a real difference. Human rights are minimal standards that seek to protect people from the worst violations of their humanity and dignity. The norms of human rights have been called "the morality of the depths," the floor beneath which no one should be allowed to sink.[47] Our remembrance of the genocide against the Tutsis in Rwanda is a memory of the depths to which the human capacity for evil can lead us. But remembrance should also remind us of resistance to such evils carried out by Montesinos, las Casas, Vitoria, Suárez, by the drafters of the Universal Declaration of Human Rights, and by the continuing human rights movement of today. The memories of both the depths to which humans can fall and also of the genuine impact of resistance to atrocity can provide real support for sustained commitment to human rights today. From a Christian point of view, we can acknowledge that the continuing struggle for human rights will not establish the fullness of the reign of God among us today. It will, however, help us avoid the most sinful distortions of humanity and the deepest wounds upon human community. It will bring a few more rays of light into the darkness of our world. Such rays of light can be a source of authentic hope, a hope we very much need today. We can be grateful that there are both empirical and normative grounds for such hope.

4

DIGNITY IN SOLIDARITY

Rights as Relational

This chapter responds to the recent criticism of human rights that claims these rights are built on an excessively individualistic understanding of the human person. If this charge is valid, human rights are unsuitable guides for action in cultures outside the West that are shaped by communitarian values, such as the cultures of many societies in Asia and Africa. This alleged individualism also means that work for human rights undermines the solidarity needed to respond to the economic inequality and poverty that mar the world today. I argue here that the human rights ethic is not individualistic. When understood in a way that adequately reflects the full range of rights affirmed in the UN Universal Declaration of Human Rights, human rights norms support a social and relational understanding of the human person. The declaration itself implies that the dignity of the human person can be protected and enhanced only through interaction with others and through active participation in social life.[1] Human dignity and social solidarity are reciprocally related. Human rights, therefore, are appropriate normative standards, not only in the West but also in more communitarian cultures outside the West. Human rights also require and support the solidarity needed to address inequality and poverty.

The chapter has four parts. The first addresses recent criticisms of human rights as excessively individualistic. The second argues that the Universal Declaration sees human rights as rooted in human solidarity, not as individualistically based. The third makes a substantive argument for what can be called a relational understanding of human rights. The conclusion shows that this relational understanding of human rights can be genuinely universal and can address key issues that arise in today's world where the West and the Global South are increasingly interdependent.

CRITIQUES OF HUMAN RIGHTS AS INDIVIDUALISTIC

Criticisms of human rights as inappropriate moral standards for global interaction have been numerous in recent years. Some critics reject the claim that the Universal Declaration is genuinely *universal*. These critics often insist that human rights arose from the West's eighteenth-century Enlightenment, which stressed individual freedom and autonomy. If the human rights ethic grants priority to an individualistic understanding of autonomy as the freedom to be left alone, a human rights–based ethic will not be compatible with the communitarian values stressed by Confucian, African, and Islamic traditions. Thus, human rights would be unsuitable normative guides for public action in much of Asia, Africa, and Muslim-majority countries.

In the Confucian context, for example, the late prime minister of Singapore, Lee Kuan Yew, proposed this kind of critique. For Lee, the declaration's view of the person implies that "everybody would be better off if they were allowed to do their own thing."[2] This is in strong conflict with the mutual support of community called for by the Confucian tradition. Lee argues that human rights are not suitable normative guides for public action in societies shaped by Confucianism tradition, such as China, Japan, Korea, and Vietnam. These nations recognize the need for limits on a person's individual freedom if community well-being is to be achieved. In Lee's view, their people cannot fully endorse the human rights proclaimed in the UN declaration. The declaration, therefore, is not universally normative despite its title.

In an analogous way, some African thinkers have voiced suspicion of "rights talk" as individualistic and un-African. For example, the Nigerian Chris Mojekwu declared that "African concepts of human rights are very different from those of Western Europe. Communalism and communal concepts of right are fundamental to understanding African culture, politics and society."[3] Mojekwu warns against thinking that the period of Western colonial control eliminated the importance of communal values in African societies today. He suggests that the human rights ethic could lead to a new form of Western colonialism.

Stress on communal values is also prominent in the African Charter on Human and Peoples' Rights adopted in 1981 by Organization of African Unity in Banjul, Gambia. The African or Banjul Charter explicitly calls itself a charter of human and *people's* rights. It proclaims not only that all human beings are equal but that all *peoples* are as well. The peoples who form cultural and national communities as well as individual persons have rights to self-determination and to economic, social, and cultural development.[4] This communal stress leads the Banjul Charter to add a set of duties to the rights it proclaims. These duties include the obligation of individuals to support their national community by placing their physical and intellectual abilities at its service and the obligation not to compromise the security of the state of which one is a national or a resident.[5] More recently, the suspicion of human rights as allegedly Western has been evident in some objections to the International Criminal Court's efforts to enforce the most basic right to be protected from atrocities. For example, Mahmood Mamdani, a Ugandan of Indian ancestry, sees the human rights agenda of the International Criminal Court as an effort to reestablish Western colonial domination in Africa. Some postmodern, postcolonial thinkers within the West also see efforts to enforce human rights as a form of neocolonialism.[6]

In addition to these cultural critiques of human rights, there has been a long-standing economic objection that human rights legitimate economic exploitation because of their allegedly individualistic orientation. Karl Marx objected to human rights for this reason. He insisted that "none of the so-called rights of men goes beyond the egoistic man, the man withdrawn into himself, his private interest and his private choice, and separated from the community."[7] For Marx, human rights give primacy to private or individualistic interests, and thus readily support the results of free-market capitalism. He saw human rights as ignoring patterns of social relationship that are structured by economic institutions and the harmful effects of many of these institutions. Marx insisted that human emancipation must go beyond political emancipation to economic emancipation. He wrote that "right can never be higher than the economic structure of society and the cultural development conditioned by it."[8] A human rights ethic that gives primacy to civil and political freedom will not challenge the economic inequalities that divide society into classes. Such an approach will leave social divisions in place and end up supporting both oppression and poverty.

Samuel Moyn's more recent argument, that human rights are "not enough" to address the inequalities that lead to massive human suffering today, echoes this Marxist critique. Moyn does not endorse a Marxist approach explicitly. He does, however, make his commitment to socialism quite clear. For a generation, Moyn says, we have thought that "human rights are the essential bulwark against atrocity and misrule."[9] But the economic inequalities of today's world show us that the challenge is to make "the older and grander choice between socialism or barbarism." If this choice is made rightly it will make socialism "the global project it has rarely been but must become."

Moyn argues that the human rights movement has gone in the opposite direction from the socialist approach he favors. It has become far too closely associated with "neoliberal" strategies for economic development. Such strategies stress economic liberty and insist on minimal state control of markets. Neoliberals see free markets as engines of economic growth and maintain that when growth takes place, it will trickle down to those at the bottom of society and alleviate their poverty. Moyn insists that, on the contrary, such growth rarely benefits the poor. It usually ends up in the wallets of those at the top of the economic ladder, contributing to economic inequality. Failure to recognize the harmful effects of this inequality is due to a sort of market fundamentalism.

Moyn relies on a reading of recent history to back up his claim that the human rights movement has become destructively allied with a harmful neoliberal development strategy based on the primacy of the freedom of the individual. In his view, the contemporary human rights movement took shape in the mid-1970s, when the Helsinki Accords led to significant Western pressure on the Soviet Union and Warsaw Pact countries to support human rights by reducing state control on both political and economic life. Moyn is correct when he argues that the Helsinki Accords led to a significant growth in the human rights movement. This is evident, for example, from the fact that one of today's most important human rights organizations, Human Rights Watch, began in 1978 under the name Helsinki Watch. Its goal was to monitor rights abuses in countries behind the Iron Curtain that had signed the Helsinki Accords, since the accords included explicit commitment to respect for human rights within the Soviet bloc.[10] The human rights efforts of the mid-1970s, therefore, had significant anti-totalitarian, anti-authoritarian emphases, especially in Europe.[11] Moyn draws on this history to support his claim that the human rights movement is primarily concerned with political repression by authoritarian regimes but uninterested in the harmful effects of economic equality. He thinks that the human rights movement has developed in a way that leads it to "abet" inequality.[12] Efforts to advance human well-being should therefore turn away from the human rights approach to one based on the promise of social justice that has long been part of a socialist commitment. Such commitment will provide an effective alternative to the individualistic neoliberalism that supports unjust economic inequality.

There have been notable replies to the claims that human rights are too individualistic to be relevant to communitarian cultures outside the West and too supportive of market freedom to resist today's inequalities. For example, on the cultural level, Kim Dae-jung, the South Korean human rights activist who became president of his country, vigorously rejects Lee Kuan Yew's claim that the human rights ethos is incompatible with Asian cultures. Kim cites the duty of Confucian scholars to resist erring monarchs as an Asian precedent for democratic procedure that antedates modern democracy in the West.[13] Amartya Sen, who is originally from India, makes similar claims, insisting that solid support for human rights can be found in both Indian and Chinese religious and cultural traditions.[14] In the African context, the Beninese philosopher Paulin Hountondji has defended the importance of human rights in resistance to oppression by African governments that have become authoritarian or corrupt.[15] The Nigerian Nobel laureate novelist Wole Soyinka called human rights the most important idea of the millennium that ended in the year 2000, especially in the face of the kind of oppression that turned him into an exile from his homeland.[16] On the economic level, one distinguished historian of the drafting of the Universal Declaration of Human Rights, Johannes Morsink, has shown that in the Universal Declaration the rights to economic necessities have a status that is just as demanding as the rights to political freedom.[17] Morsink holds that human rights are not individualistic norms but that they are suitable both in communitarian cultures and to address today's economic inequalities.

In what follows I offer further response to the objection that human rights are excessively individualistic and argue that the Universal Declaration sees support for human rights as an expression of solidarity among persons. This will enable us to build on the text of the Universal Declaration in a substantive argument that rights are best understood as grounded in a deeply social or relational understanding of the human person.

RIGHTS AND SOLIDARITY IN
THE UNIVERSAL DECLARATION

The Universal Declaration of Human Rights supports interpreting human rights and social solidarity as closely interconnected. The text of the UDHR itself gives significant emphasis to the importance of human interdependence and solidarity for the protection of human dignity and describes human personhood as embedded in social life and as requiring social solidarity. Thus, I argue, the understanding of human rights in the UDHR is not individualistic.

To be sure, the Universal Declaration includes the rights not to be subject to outrages that "shock the conscience of humanity" such as the Nazi genocide against the Jews and also the freedoms that were central to the anti-totalitarian, anti-communist impulses of the human rights advocates who supported the Helsinki Accords in the mid-1970s.[18] If the declaration were limited to these rights, a case might plausibly be made that it sees rights principally as providing immunity from interference by other persons with one's personal security and freedom—in other words, as rights of individual persons to be left alone. But the declaration clearly goes beyond this immunity when it affirms social, economic, and cultural rights in articles 22 through 27. These social and economic rights include the right to employment, the right to an adequate standard of living for oneself and one's family (food, clothing, housing, medical care), the right to education, and the right to security in the event of unemployment, sickness, or old age. Securing these rights will often require positive action by others, including by government. The need for such action is the reason social and economic rights are often called positive rights. Protecting them requires one to be actively committed to one's fellow citizens in a way that positively supports their economic and social well-being. How much commitment to the well-being of others can reasonably be expected is surely a debatable point. The Universal Declaration insists, however, that "everyone" has a right at least to the food, clothing, housing, medical care, and education needed for her well-being and that of her family. Thus, the declaration's affirmation of social and economic rights requires active support for at least a basic level of well-being for one's fellow citizens. Such support itself requires positive and reciprocal relationships among citizens and will depend on the presence of a kind of social solidarity that is far from the individualistic spirit some critics argue the UDHR presupposes.

It is precisely the fact that social and economic rights require a minimal level of solidarity that leads some to declare that they are not genuine human rights at all.[19] Those who hold this argue that rights require not interfering with other people's activities by just leaving them alone. Civil and political rights are often seen this way. The right to free speech means no one may legitimately prevent me from communicating what I think by destroying my printing press or shutting down my radio station. For this reason, civil and political rights are often called negative rights. They are like fences or walls that protect one against harm or interference that others might inflict. Social and economic rights, on the other hand, are called positive rights since their implementation requires positive action. These civil and political rights are often thought to be easier to protect than rights to food and health care. Thus, some see civil political rights as genuine rights, while they regard social and economic rights as ideals.

This sharp distinction, however, overlooks the need for the larger society to take significant positive steps to protect the civil and political rights of its citizens in an effective way. A verbal guarantee of freedom of speech in a country's constitution will not have real meaning unless the country has created legal and political institutions to prevent others, including the state, from interfering with people's ability to communicate with others as they wish. The effective protection of freedom of speech, of religion, and of assembly requires creating an effective judicial system and other social means to enforce the constitutional guarantee of these rights. As Henry Shue has put it, "the protection of 'negative rights' requires positive measures."[20] Civil and political rights, therefore, depend on positive social action, institution-building, and expenditures that go well beyond just leaving one's fellow citizens alone. It requires both respect for one's fellow citizens and a commitment to their well-being. Both civil and political rights and social and economic rights require a form of commitment to others in positive relationships.

The text of the Universal Declaration, therefore, shows that the drafters were aware that the protection of both forms of rights requires a measure of social solidarity. Article 1 of the declaration recognizes this, proclaiming that "All human beings are born free and equal in dignity and rights. They are endowed with reason and conscience and should act towards one another in a spirit of brotherhood." Here the declaration implies that a "spirit of brotherhood" will be essential to securing human rights for all human beings. Today, our awareness of the importance of gender-inclusive language suggests that the intent of the article would be better expressed by stating that persons should act toward one another with a "spirit of solidarity." Indeed, the *Oxford English Dictionary* tells us that the meanings of "brotherhood" include "care," "comradeship," and "solidarity."[21] Solidarity, of course, is the antithesis of the individualistic spirit that leads some to see the human rights ethic as unsuited to the communitarian cultures of Asia and Africa and as unable to challenge the economic inequalities of today's world. The text of the Universal Declaration does not support this kind of an individualistic interpretation of human rights. It implies that fraternity, sorority, solidarity, and support for others through mutual relationship will be required by the ethic it proposes.

Though the text of the declaration clearly implies that effective protection of rights will require a degree of social solidarity, the drafters went out of their way to avoid endorsing any specific philosophical theory of human rights. They did not endorse a theoretical rationale for what they produced, either individualistic or communitarian. For example, René Cassin, who played a key role in creating the declaration, wrote that the drafting committee sought "to take no position on the nature of man and of society and to avoid metaphysical controversies."[22] The drafters were deeply aware that diverse ideological, cultural, and religious traditions would be unable to reach an agreement if the declaration sought to base human rights on a philosophical understanding of human nature or on ultimate religious beliefs about God and the world. The philosopher Jacques Maritain advised the drafting committee to avoid endorsing any comprehensive vision of the good life since this would prevent agreement on human rights. He recognized that if human rights were grounded in Western Enlightenment liberalism, representatives of the Soviet Union could not support them, and if they were grounded in Marxist social thought, Western democrats would reject them, both dooming the human rights project from the start. Nevertheless, Maritain believed that there was a route to consensus. Some basic agreement across differences could be found by relying on practical reflection on human experience. As noted earlier, Maritain quipped that the drafters could reach agreement, "but on condition that no one asks us why."[23] By drawing on experiences they shared in common, Western liberals and Soviet socialists, as well as Confucians, Muslims, and nonbelievers, could reach agreement that some forms of human behavior whose harmful effects they had all witnessed, such as genocide, should never be permitted to happen again. Shared experience could also show those from very different traditions that some goods, such as freedom of belief and thought, adequate nutrition, health care, and work, should be provided to all persons when such provision is possible.

As argued in chapter 2, the determination of what rights to include in the declaration was an inductive process, drawing on experience of mistreatments of others and failures to assist them that all could see should be avoided. Morsink calls this a process of determining "rights from wrongs."[24] The rights were identified inductively from concrete experiences of human atrocities that all could see as morally wrong and also from shared experience of human needs that all saw should be met. Induction from experience of harms to be avoided and needs to be met, not deduction from philosophic, ideological, or religious principles, led to the Universal Declaration.[25]

The consensus across traditions and ideologies on the rights that were proclaimed in the Universal Declaration was certainly a major achievement. We should continue to recognize its importance today, especially when conflict-generating differences often seem to have the upper hand. Indeed, the World Conference on Human Rights held in Vienna in June 1993 recognized the continuing importance of agreement across diversity when it reaffirmed "the solemn commitment of all States to fulfil their obligations to promote universal respect for, and observance and protection of, all human rights and fundamental freedoms for all."[26] The Vienna conference stressed the continuing importance of agreement across traditions when it proclaimed "the universal nature of these rights and freedoms is beyond question."

54 CHAPTER 4

TOWARD A RELATIONAL
UNDERSTANDING OF RIGHTS

Despite this remarkable agreement across the major traditions of the world, it is certainly possible that the distinctive normative visions contained within these traditions will continue to influence people's approaches to human rights. Richard McKeon, who served as rapporteur for the Committee of Experts convened by UNESCO (United Nations Educational, Scientific and Cultural Organization) to advise the drafting committee on more philosophical issues, expected diverse traditions to continue to have influence in three ways: the traditions could shape the way the human rights agreed to in the declaration are interpreted; they could lead to differing readings of the context within which human rights are pursued; and they could influence recommendations about how to implement rights.[27]

Western Pluralism and Social Solidarity

Due to the continuing influence by differing cultures, religions, and philosophies, it is not surprising that the interpretations of human rights that prevail in the West today are often more individualistic than those seen as desirable in non-Western communities. Nevertheless, there are diverse Western understandings of the appropriate relationship between the individual person and society. The Western tradition is in fact internally pluralistic on this issue. There is not a single Western answer to the question of whether human rights should be grounded in a more individualistic understanding of the person or on one that sees human beings as embedded in social relationships. If the interpretation of human rights is influenced by an individualistic understanding of the person, it is unlikely that Asian, African, and other more communal traditions will conclude that human rights fit with their values, despite the cross-cultural consensus reached by the UDHR drafting committee in 1948. On the other hand, if an understanding of human rights is shaped by a view of the human person that sees social solidarity as essential to the realization of human dignity, non-Western societies will be able to support human rights without abandoning key aspects of their traditions. This will also increase the possibility of genuinely universal support for human rights today. To address these matters, we will have to consider some of the more theoretical, philosophical matters that the drafting committee sought to avoid. Despite the individualism that sometimes prevails in the West, there are important strands in the Western tradition that contain strongly social understandings of the person. Drawing on these strands will

DIGNITY IN SOLIDARITY   55

enable us to give a more theoretical/philosophical grounding for the consensus on human rights reached by the drafting committee.

Many disputes about human rights today, of course, are disputes about who should exercise political power over whom and in what manner this power should be used. Such disputes about power are often driven by the pursuit of the self-interest of ruling persons or groups. Not all disagreements about human rights, however, are driven by pursuit of power and self-interest. Some are rooted in divergent theories of the relation between person and society. When the disputes take this more theoretical form, the possibility of convergence between the West and the communal traditions of the Confucian, Islamic, and African worlds will contribute to the human rights movement in important ways. Thus, the cross-cultural consensus on human rights can be strengthened if those in the West draw upon strands of their own tradition that see social solidarity and interhuman relationships as key dimensions of human well-being. I argue that human dignity can be realized only in community with other persons. The advancement of human dignity and the protection of human rights require interhuman solidarity and supportive social relationships. Human rights, therefore, presume a relational understanding of the person.

The strand of the Western tradition most often associated with the emergence of human rights in their contemporary form is that developed during the eighteenth-century Enlightenment. The political philosophy of the eighteenth century in the West was, of course, immensely rich. Nevertheless, it is not misleading to see the work of Immanuel Kant as a crucial influence on the way human dignity and human rights have been philosophically understood in the West in recent centuries. For Kant, the fundamental standard of morality is that all human beings be ought to be treated with respect for their inherent dignity, as ends in themselves and not only as means to be used for some other purpose.[28] The dignity or worth of human persons is not like the price of things. The value of a human being—the person's dignity— is beyond price. Things with price can be exchanged for each other in the marketplace. But humans, because of their dignity, are valuable in themselves and thus cannot be simply traded one for another.[29] All human beings, therefore, should be treated with unconditional respect.

The response due to human dignity is respect for the inherent worth of the person, not the kind of fairness that is involved in setting a just price for a commodity being exchanged in the marketplace. In support of this stance, Kant argued that the individual person's capacity for autonomous free choice is the source and prime characteristic of human dignity. In his words, "autonomy is the ground of the dignity of human nature and of every rational nature."[30] Kant's stress on autonomy as the principal characteristic of dignity could easily lead to seeing dignity as a characteristic of the person apart from the interconnections of social life. If taken this way, Kant's linkage of dignity with autonomy would easily validate the claims of those who see human rights in an individualistic way and as inappropriate for more communal cultures, such as those that prevail in Asia and Africa.

Kant's ethic, however, can also be invoked to support positive commitment to social interaction as essential to the protection of human dignity. Kant formulated the categorical imperative that is fundamental to his moral philosophy not only as calling for the protection of the autonomy of persons as ends in themselves but also as requiring that the norms which guide one's choices should be universally applicable to all in similar situations across society. Also, Kant stressed that the persons who are to be treated as ends in themselves should be seen not as isolated individuals but as members of what he called a "kingdom of ends." This gives the call to treat persons as ends a notably social dimension.[31] The purpose here is not to outline the relation between Kantian moral philosophy and human rights in a systematic way. Rather, it is simply to highlight that if human dignity is seen as grounded in capacity for autonomous free choice and is understood outside the social framework that Kant supports, this will reduce or possibly destroy the relevance of human rights for more communal cultures.

Indeed, there is empirical evidence that contemporary Western societies, especially the United States, have adopted a strong commitment to autonomy as their overriding moral concern and that they see autonomy as unencumbered by the social support that Kant saw as essential.[32] This is suggested by Alan Wolfe's empirical study of the moral values that are shaping US culture today. Wolfe draws on both quantitative survey research and qualitative interviews of individuals from very diverse sectors of US social life. His data suggest that most Americans today believe that "individuals should determine for themselves what it means to lead a good and virtuous life."[33] Autonomy as freedom to make specific choices and, more importantly, to decide on one's own what values should shape the overall direction of one's life, has become central to the moral orientation by which most Americans shape their lives today. The autonomous freedom that is shaping the moral culture of the United States does not give much attention to the social commitments present in Kant's ethic. Wolfe recognizes that this carries considerable dangers, but he thinks it is not a bad thing overall and that it is likely irreversible.[34]

I share Wolfe's concern that autonomous freedom can bring dangers. However, I think he is too sanguine about our capacity to deal with these dangers effectively within an individualistic ethic. We need to recognize the important ways that freedom is rooted in social and communal relationships. If these relationships are not present and adequately sustained, autonomy is likely to wither. Since freedom is a key dimension of human dignity, the commitment to the dignity of persons must include a commitment to building and sustaining the social relationships needed to support autonomy. Support for both the autonomy of individuals and for the social and communal relationships needed to sustain autonomy go together.[35] Both autonomy and relationship are required to sustain the human rights ethos laid out in the Universal Declaration. Indeed, an understanding of human rights that both reflects the text of the Universal Declaration and leads to policies that protect people in an effective way must recognize how important social relationships are for human dignity. In other words, human dignity and human rights must be understood as embedded in the social interactions needed to sustain dignity and protect rights. We need a relational understanding of human rights.

The Social Person in Western Thought

The fact that humans can flourish only in relationships and social interaction has long had an important place in the Western tradition. Aristotle, whose thought is one of the central sources at the origin of Western ethical reflection, recognized that human relationships are crucial aspects of human flourishing. In his *Politics* Aristotle describes the human person as an essentially social or political animal. In Aristotle's Greek, the person is *zoon politikon*, an animal of the *polis* or city-state.[36] Life in the civic community is essential to the good life. Active sharing in the relationships of society is necessary for one to live well, not an accidental add-on. Indeed, Aristotle saw *speech* and the ability to communicate with others in public debate as a key human characteristic. Through speech, humans are able to interact with each other actively and reciprocally. Speech enables humans to dialogue with each other about how they should live together and about what is just and unjust in their interaction.[37] Thus, the human relationships that speech makes possible bring the civic community into existence. In the absence of such interactive relationships, the polis and political life would not exist. Aristotle's vision thus implies that exclusion from the social interaction that creates the polis leads to a less than fully human life.

Of course, Aristotle's willingness to accept that some human beings are naturally destined to be slaves also indicates that he did not see all humans as entitled to the full freedom that comes with citizenship. Today we rightly reject this aspect of his thought. But just as we can draw on Aristotle to provide a corrective to the individualistic tendencies of Kant, we can draw on

Kant to overcome Aristotle's inadequate approach to human equality. Kant insisted that *all* human persons possess equal dignity as ends and deserve to be treated in a way that takes account of their common humanity. Drawing on Aristotle we can add to Kant that respect for a person's dignity requires us to recognize and support her active participation in the social relationships of the polis. This blending of Aristotle's stress on the importance of social participation with Kant's commitment to equal dignity will lead us to see human dignity and human rights in relational terms.

The relational aspects of human dignity are further clarified by Aristotle's observation that a person who is self-sufficient and has no need of social life "must be either a beast or a god."[38] A beast or brute animal lacks the capacities of consciousness or spirit, such as those that enable humans to know and to exercise freedom. Because humans possess these abilities, they are not passive and inarticulate. Rather, as I argued previously, persons are capable of the kind of self-transcendence that makes them valuable for their own sake. Not being a beast or a thing is thus a marker of the distinctive worth of human personhood. It indicates that persons live in a genuinely human way when they are able to engage in activities of the spirit, such as growing in knowledge and exercising freedom. That humans are not beasts is also indicated by their capacity to move beyond themselves through knowledge of other persons, through appreciation of the dignity of others, and by forming relationships of friendship and solidarity with them. The self-transcendence by which one person respects the worth of another can also be a reciprocal recognition of the value they share with each other together. Human dignity is not realized by a person alone or simply within the self-consciousness of individuals. Rather, dignity is actualized and expressed when persons encounter each other in active relationships and when they affirm and support one another as fellow human beings. The capacity for self-transcendence that is the source of human dignity, therefore, is a capacity for human relationships built on mutual respect. Because humans are neither beasts nor things, each person's capacity for self-transcendence makes a claim on this capacity in other persons.[39] Persons actualize their human dignity in the relationships of a community bound together in mutual respect and moral solidarity.

Aristotle also insisted that human beings are not gods. Unlike a god, who might be imagined as unconstrained by the conditions of the concrete material world, the human spirit is embodied. The human good is that of a bodily being and it has material preconditions. Human dignity can be realized only if the material conditions needed for bodily flourishing are present. Protecting human dignity, therefore, requires securing a person's capacities for knowledge, freedom, and relationship; and it requires guaranteeing access to

DIGNITY IN SOLIDARITY 59

food, shelter, medical care in sickness, and other needed material supports. Not being a god thus reinforces Aristotle's insistence that humans are social beings. Attaining the material goods a person needs requires interaction both with the material world and with other persons. The material support needed for human dignity will not be attainable if a person is cut off from social life. The bodily requirements of human well-being, therefore, reinforce the claim that persons are morally interdependent. This moral relatedness means that persons have legitimate claims on one another to collaborate in ways that make it possible for them to share in the material goods and bodily activities required for living with dignity. Human dignity thus implies the existence of the right to have one's material needs met to at least a basic level and for the social supports that will make this possible.

We can briefly summarize this effort to synthesize some elements drawn from Kant and Aristotle. One person's ability to know and understand ought to be recognized and supported by other persons. One person's freedom places requirements on the freedom of others. One person's material needs for food, shelter, and medical care places requirements on how others share in these resources. The requirement of human dignity in each of these areas of human activity is made explicit as a human right. There are human rights in each of these areas of human life—the capacity for knowledge, the achievement of freedom, and the attainment of material conditions of well-being. Further, since attaining dignity in each of these domains will require the support that comes from active participation in the larger community, human rights should guarantee the social relationships needed for this participation. Human rights, therefore, are relational realities. They are rights to those relationships with others in society that are needed to protect one's dignity in the diverse forms of interaction that constitute social life.

Jewish and Christian Traditions on the Person as Relational

The argument from secular philosophical sources that social relationships are essential to the protection of human dignity and rights can be reinforced by perspectives proposed in the Jewish and Christian traditions. Both Jews and Christians see the covenantal bond they have with God and with other humans as the source of the communal solidarity to which they are summoned. Both Jews and Christians are called to love their neighbors as they love themselves (Lev. 19:18; Mark 12:31). Such love leads to the building up of the community and the solidarity needed to sustain it. The Catholic faith synthesizes such biblical perspectives with Aristotle's more secular understanding of the social nature of the person, leading to a relational understanding of dignity and rights that can be proposed as normative both for Christians and for others in a religiously pluralistic society.

This relational approach to the protection of human dignity is made quite explicit in several normative affirmations in recent Catholic social thought. For example, the US Catholic bishops have insisted that the most basic form of justice requires avoiding patterns of social interaction marked by inequality, domination, and oppression. These should be replaced by social relations based on equality, reciprocity, and solidarity. Social relations marked by these qualities will enable persons to participate actively in social life. Thus, the US bishops conclude that society and its members have an obligation to make such participation possible for all its members and each member has a right to such participation. In the words of the bishops, basic justice "demands the establishment of minimum levels of participation in the life of the human community for all persons."[40]

In this framework, injustice occurs and rights are denied when persons are arbitrarily excluded from the participation in the social relationships they need to live with dignity. The Catholic bishops go on to define human rights as "the minimum conditions for life in community." Human rights set the basic level of social participation that is needed to live in dignity. For the bishops, these minima are required for the community life that the Bible sees arising from God's covenant with the people of Israel and from the resulting covenant of the people with each other. The bishops also see this participation as required by Aristotle's conviction that persons are essentially social animals. These basic levels of social participation are due to people by right. Because human dignity can only be realized and protected in solidarity with others, both dignity and human rights are achieved in interactive relationships with others. Respect for human rights and a strong sense of both personal and community responsibility are linked, not opposed.

An Example: The Right to Participate and the End of Apartheid

This relational understanding of human rights sees both civil/political rights and social/economic rights as protections of different forms of participation in the social interaction needed to live with dignity. We can illustrate this through an example: the systematic violations of human rights in South Africa when the apartheid regime was in still place. Under apartheid, Blacks and those called Colored in South Africa (Asians and people seen as of "mixed race") were denied nearly all civil and political forms of participation in South African public life. They could not vote, which denied their participation in the shaping of the regime and the laws that governed them. They were prevented from assembling as they wished and from speaking and communicating with each other through the press in ways that would inform public opinion and shape public life. They were denied the capacity to live out their religious and moral convictions in public life when the regime saw their participation as a threat to white supremacy.

Being denied even minimal levels of participation of the political dimensions of public life subjected nonwhite people to truly harmful violations of their human dignity. These limits on the participation of people of color in South African life were serious violations of their civil and political rights. Their dignity was denied by their exclusion from social relationships based on equality. Similarly, in the economic sphere, the exclusion of nonwhites from different spheres of South African economic life violated their dignity in harmful ways. Under apartheid, whites in South Africa lived on an economic level similar to that of well-off citizens in Europe and the United States. The severe economic inequality of the country resulted in the deliberate exclusion of Black people and others of color from participation in the highly developed white sectors of the country's economic life. White South Africans could participate in globally linked finance and thus grow in wealth. People of color were excluded from almost all education. They had great difficulty gaining the education needed to enable them to become literate and had no access to the distinguished universities open to whites.

Under apartheid, white South Africans were able to participate in a health-care system that was so advanced that it was able to carry out the world's first successful heart transplant surgery. People of color lacked the most basic forms of primary care and frequently lacked basic public health resources, like clean drinking water and basic sanitation. These harms resulted from the denial of their rights to participate in political, social, and economic life. This exclusion from essential social relationships and forms of social participation denied people of color the most basic requirements of their dignity as persons.

HUMAN RIGHTS AS A UNIVERSAL GUARANTEE OF PARTICIPATION

This South African illustration shows the value of conceiving human rights as guarantees that people be able to participate in the life of the community at the level required by their dignity as persons. Seeing human rights in this relational, participatory perspective shows why civil/political rights and social/economic rights are both essential. The inclusion of both civil/ political rights and social/economic rights in the Universal Declaration was a significant achievement in 1948. A relational, participation-based understanding of human rights sees rights as norms that are neither simply individualistic nor simply collectivistic. Such a relational understanding of human rights can make important contributions to overcoming the divisions that threaten the globe today. It can challenge North Atlantic countries to recognize the importance of the communal solidarity stressed in Asian and African cultures. It could also help North Atlantic countries, especially the United States, recognize that economic and cultural rights must be given more attention, both ethically and in policy, than these rights have often received. The countries of the Asian, African, and Islamic worlds can also benefit from the relational interpretation of human rights suggested here. It could help them recognize that freedom for active political participation by all, if carried out appropriately, will contribute to the communal solidarity they value in an inclusive way. It can help these societies recognize that active participation by all can lead to stronger social union rather than threatening such union. A relational, participation-based understanding of human rights will help advance the human rights agenda in these countries in a way that builds upon their traditional values rather than undermines them.

It is hoped that this sketch of a relational understanding of human rights shows that we are not facing the twilight or endtimes of human rights.[41] Rather, the way is open to advancing the human rights project in a universalist way in today's divided world and to strengthening the relationships needed to support the dignity of all.

PART II

THE RIGHT TO RELIGIOUS FREEDOM

One of the fears that leads some to see religious communities as dangerous for human rights is the conviction that believers are so convinced of the truth of their faith that they cannot respect the freedom of those in other faith communities. Thus, the stance taken by religious communities toward the freedom of those in other faith traditions is a central issue for human rights today. The Catholic tradition has moved from suspicion of the religious freedom of non-Catholics to the Second Vatican Council's resounding declaration that all persons possess a fundamental right to religious freedom. This development in the living Catholic tradition was significantly shaped by the influence of the US Jesuit theologian John Courtney Murray. Despite the initially stiff opposition Murray faced from Catholic ecclesiastical leaders, his work enabled the Second Vatican Council to endorse the right to religious freedom unambiguously. How to implement the right to religious freedom, however, can be difficult to determine in some circumstances. This is particularly true when communities seek to pursue the moral implications of their religious beliefs in public life. Thus, how to deal with moral pluralism as well as with religious pluralism has become an urgent question today. Murray and Vatican II addressed both of these forms of pluralism, and part II highlights their work on these matters and sketches the implications of their work for the broader human rights agenda.

The Catholic bishops of the United States have not dealt with these issues particularly well in the past few years. Indeed, the bishops' recent approaches to the ethics of abortion and same-sex relationships has led some in the United States to see religion as a threat to freedom rather than as a support of freedom as was envisioned by Vatican II. The violations of human dignity brought by failures to respect religious freedom around the world today show the dangers that could arise from such failures, even in the United States. This part presents the contemporary Catholic understanding of religious freedom and some of its implications for the role of the Church in the public life of society.

5

RELIGIOUS FREEDOM, MORALITY, AND LAW

Vatican II and John Courtney Murray Today

In 1965 the Second Vatican Council's Declaration on Religious Freedom brought about a major development in Catholic doctrine when it declared that "the human person has a right to religious freedom" and that "this right of the human person to religious freedom is to be recognized in the constitutional law whereby society is governed and thus it is to become a civil right."[1] The council's words stand in dramatic contrast with Pope Gregory XVI's 1832 encyclical *Mirari Vos*, which saw freedom of conscience as a kind of madness.[2] American theologian John Courtney Murray played a key role in enabling the council to bring about this major shift in Catholic teaching. Understanding how and why this shift took place is important to attaining an adequate appreciation of Catholic approaches to human rights today. This chapter will show the council understood religious freedom and its relation to both morality and civil law. It will also focus on the influence of John Courtney Murray on the council's declaration.

The importance of Murray's influence is suggested by the fact that in December 1960, his portrait appeared on the cover of *Time* magazine. *Time*'s editors saw Murray, along with Reinhold Niebuhr and Karl Barth, as one of the very few theologians with the public influence needed to appear on their cover.[3] Behind Murray's portrait was an enlarged reproduction of the title page of Robert Bellarmine's *De Controversiis*. Few *Time* readers likely noticed this linking of Murray with Bellarmine, as thinkers engaged in significant theological controversy. There is little doubt, however, that Murray was deeply involved in some of the most important controversies in both Catholic and American life in the mid-twentieth century. Despite the controversies that initially greeted his work, Murray's ideas influenced the Second Vatican Council and the ongoing tradition of Catholic thought on human rights in the postconciliar period. In more recent days, however, another topic Murray addressed—the role of the Church in shaping the moral dimensions of political life—has become a focus of new controversy, especially in the United States. Whether and how Murray's thinking on political morality should guide the public ministry of the Church today thus calls for fresh examination.

This chapter addresses the ways both Vatican II's Declaration on Religious Freedom and Murray's thought continue to be influential in shaping Church engagement in public life. It will do so in four steps. First it will sketch the controversy concerning Murray's thought on religious freedom and its reception by Vatican II. Second, some of today's disputes concerning the way the leadership of the Catholic community is addressing the relation between civil law and morality will be explained. Third, an emergent challenge to the efforts by religious communities to address public life will be presented, namely, the polarization of political life in the United States along religious lines. Fourth, it will argue that a deeper appropriation of the approach of Murray and Vatican II to the relation of freedom, morality, and civil law could enhance the effectiveness of the church's role in public life.

MURRAY'S THOUGHT ON
RELIGIOUS FREEDOM AND VATICAN II

The caption to Murray's picture on *Time*'s 1960 cover read "U.S. Catholics & the State." In the 1950s Murray had written innovatively on the way the Catholic Church should interact with the state (or, as he preferred to call it, the government). As a public intellectual Murray had also been deeply engaged in debates with Protestant and secular opinion-makers about the religious role of Catholicism in US public life. Catholics had long been held in suspicion by these opinion-makers, who feared that the Catholic understanding of religious freedom was a threat to American democracy. This suspicion had become very clear to Murray while collaborating with these thinkers in the early 1940s to shape a plan of action that would help make post–World War II international relations more stable and peaceful. Such suspicion was vividly perceptible when the Catholic John F. Kennedy ran for president of the United States in 1960. In that year Murray published *We Hold These Truths: Catholic Reflections on the American Proposition*, a book that argued that Protestant and secular shapers of US culture should get over their fears that Catholicism was a threat to US political institutions. The book eloquently suggested that the United States had much to learn from the long Catholic tradition. Though not directly linked to Kennedy's campaign, Murray's thought provided much of the intellectual background for Kennedy's political breakthrough when he became the country's first Catholic president. This breakthrough occurred only after significant political disagreement and debate, as symbolized by Kennedy needing to reassure the Protestant ministers who were members of the Greater Houston Ministerial Association that his faith did not threaten the well-being of the republic. Kennedy's election broke through the barrier that had long excluded Catholics from full participation in US political life. Murray's theological innovation on religious freedom was the intellectual analog to Kennedy's political breakthrough. The convergence of Kennedy's election and the publication of Murray's *We Hold These Truths* was a key reason for Murray's appearance on *Time*'s cover.

Murray's work also addressed internal discussions within the Catholic community on religious freedom. This line of thinking surely carried personal cost for Murray because of the initial response of Church leadership to his thinking. In the end, however, Murray's theology helped bring about the extraordinary shift in the Catholic Church's stance toward religious freedom that occurred at Vatican II. Murray argued that attention to the historical contexts of the rejection of religious freedom by nineteenth-century popes such as Pius IX and Leo XIII could enable the Church to affirm religious freedom in contexts that were different, such as those prevailing in mid-twentieth-century democracies.[4] When Murray proposed this approach, his views were roundly rejected by his traditionalist theological adversaries. These adversaries saw his defense of religious freedom as encouraging a religious relativism (they called it "indifferentism") that would effectively deny the unique truth of the Catholic faith. Adopting this stance, Murray's critic Francis Connell made the blunt charge that Murray's theological advocacy of a positive Catholic stand on religious freedom could not be "harmonized with revealed truth."[5]

Such opposition and the Vatican pressure that resulted from it led to Murray being effectively marginalized from the discussion of the topic. In 1958 it led his Jesuit superiors to tell him to remain silent on the topic of religious freedom until the climate in Rome had changed. That change came much more quickly than either they or he had a right to expect. Soon after John XXIII's election in that same year, the new pope announced his intent to convene an ecumenical council, which opened in 1962. Murray's arguments were fully vindicated by this council, where he played a major role in drafting the Declaration on Religious Freedom. Indeed, Murray's thought was a major source of the doctrinal development that led Vatican II to declare that "the right to religious freedom has its foundation in the very dignity of the human person as this dignity is known through the revealed word of God and by reason itself."[6] This conciliar proclamation stands in stark contrast with Connell's assessment that Murray's views could not be reconciled with the revealed truth of the gospel.

The continuing influence of Murray's thought on religious liberty, as mediated through Vatican II's Declaration on Religious Freedom, is evident in the recent teachings of the postconciliar popes. Pope John Paul II called religious freedom the "heart of human rights," thus affirming its central place in the Church's larger social mission.[7] Such a papal statement would have been unthinkable before Vatican II. Under John Paul II's leadership the defense of religious freedom assumed a central place, not only in the teachings of the Church but also in the practices of the faith. As was noted previously, the late Samuel Huntington, a Harvard political scientist with much interest in the development of democracy in the modern era, argued that the Second Vatican Council, especially its affirmation of the right to religious liberty, transformed the Catholic Church during the pontificates of Paul VI and John Paul II into one of the leading human rights actors on the world stage. Catholicism played a key role in the move of a number of countries from authoritarianism to democracy in the latter third of the twentieth century: Portugal and Spain in the mid-1970s, multiple Latin American states in the late 1970s and early 1980s, the Philippines in the mid-1980s, and Poland and Hungary in the late 1980s. Due to the influence of the council, Huntington concludes, "roughly three-quarters of the countries that transited to democracy between 1974 and 1989 were Catholic."[8]

Pope Benedict XVI continued strong emphasis on religious freedom as a leading edge of his advocacy of human rights. Benedict's approach to religious freedom had several distinct but related elements. First, in his January 1, 2011, message for the Church's World Day of Peace, Benedict placed religious freedom in a broadly international context, arguing that the protection of this freedom is a precondition for peace within and among nations. He sees religious persecution and acts of violence based on religion as serious threats to peace.

Second, Benedict was particularly concerned that the religious freedom of Christians was being restricted and even denied in a number of countries today. In the pope's assessment, "at present, Christians are the religious group which suffers most from persecution on account of its faith."[9] In his 2011 address to the diplomatic corps at the Holy See, Benedict specifically mentioned limitations on the religious freedom of Christians in Arab and Muslim countries like Iraq, Egypt, nations of the Arabian Peninsula and the Middle East generally, African countries like Nigeria, and Asian nations such as China and Pakistan.[10] The bombings of Christian churches in Egypt and Iraq are deadly signs of such persecution of Christians.

Third, concern for the religious freedom of Christians did not detract from Benedict's commitment to the religious freedom of all persons. He saw religious freedom as rooted in the fundamental dignity of the person, which Jewish and Christian scriptures affirm is grounded in the creation of every person in the image of God. At the same time, the pope argued that scripture is in harmony with human experience and that, through the use of reason, human dignity "can be recognized by all."[11] Thus, *all* persons have a right to this freedom and *all* have a duty to respect it. In Benedict's words, "Religious freedom is not the exclusive patrimony of believers, but of the whole family of the earth's peoples."[12]

Fourth, religious freedom means freedom to exercise one's beliefs in public with others in community, not only in private and not only alone. Drawing on a "relational" or "communitarian" understanding of religious freedom, Benedict argued that secularistic efforts to restrict religion to the private domain of an individual's faith are as serious a threat to religious freedom as is fundamentalist fanaticism.[13] Benedict's stress on the importance of the public and communal dimensions of the exercise of religious freedom was also an explicit teaching of the Second Vatican Council. Dignitatis Humanae had affirmed that free exercise of religion is not only a personal freedom but includes the freedom to seek to influence the institutions and policies that shape and govern public life. In the council's words, "It comes within the meaning of religious freedom that religious communities should not be prohibited from freely undertaking to show the special value of their doctrine in what concerns the organization of society and the inspiration of the whole of human activity."[14] Commenting on this passage from the council, Murray observed, "Implicitly rejected here is the outmoded notion that 'religion is a purely private affair' or that 'the Church belongs in the sacristy.'"[15]

Each of these points about religious freedom shows the lasting impact of Vatican II's Declaration on Religious Freedom and Murray's continuing influence through the declaration. The new thinking on religious freedom has clearly been received into the Catholic tradition on human rights in its contemporary form and it continues to shape the development of this tradition.

CONTROVERSY CONCERNING CIVIL LAW AND MORALITY

The fact that the council and the subsequent popes saw religious freedom as requiring respect for the Church's right to play an active role in public life shows, however, that Catholicism remains in some tension with more secular aspects of the freedom-affirming, liberal traditions of the modern West. Through the influence of Murray and other theologians the Church had learned much from these traditions. But Pope Benedict, like Murray himself, strongly resisted efforts to exclude religious influence from public affairs, seeing such exclusion as an unacceptable secularism. For example, Benedict protested against Europe's unwillingness to acknowledge publicly the Christian roots of its cultural life. The pope objected to philosophies that regard skepticism about the possibility of attaining truth in the religious sphere as a precondition for commitment to religious freedom. Thus, the Catholic understanding of religious freedom since the council stands in sharp contrast to secularizing approaches to public life and interpretations of the place of religion as strictly private.

This contrast is particularly evident with regard to the *moral* dimensions of the Church's role in public life. In several teachings focused particularly on religious freedom, Benedict affirmed that the Church could legitimately exercise its freedom in efforts to protect the right to life through civil law. He also suggested that the Church has a right to call for the defense of the family founded on marriage between a man and a woman, thus rejecting same-sex partnerships and gay marriage.[16] Needless to say, abortion and same-sex relationships are among the most hotly disputed moral issues in Western society today. In the United States they have become particular flash points of moral-political controversy.

The US Catholic bishops have adopted particularly pointed public advocacy positions on the right to life (including opposition to abortion, euthanasia, and embryonic stem cell research) and on resistance to gay marriage and public acceptance of the legitimacy of same-sex relationships. The bishops' 2007 statement, Forming Consciences for Faithful Citizenship, was a formal instruction by the US Catholic hierarchy covering the full range of the public dimensions of the Church's moral concerns. In this document, the bishops placed particular emphasis on abortion and euthanasia. The bishops teach that these actions are "intrinsically evil" and "always incompatible with love of God and neighbor." Thus, they must "always be rejected and opposed and must never be supported or condoned."[17] The US bishops intensified this statement in their 2019 version of this document when they declared that resisting "the threat of abortion remains our preeminent priority because it directly attacks life itself."[18] In a similar way, they echo the affirmation found in the Catechism of the Catholic Church that homosexual acts "are contrary to the natural law" and that "under no circumstances can they be approved."[19] Thus, the bishops insist that "marriage must be defined, recognized, and protected as a lifelong exclusive commitment between a man and a woman."[20]

It is notable that the US bishops link their opposition to same-sex relationships and gay marriage to the exercise of religious freedom. They state that human rights of all persons must be protected but that this "should be done without sacrificing the bedrock of society that is marriage and the family and without violating the religious liberty of persons and institutions."[21] This linkage of opposition to gay relationships with religious freedom echoes recent controversies that have arisen about whether Catholic institutions can be civilly required to provide health-care benefits that would benefit employees who are partnered in same-sex relationships, or whether Church agencies can be required to provide adoption services to gay couples. Though the bishops do not discuss the linkage between such policy matters and religious freedom in an in-depth way, that linkage is explored in a document called the Manhattan Declaration, which has been supported by a number of Catholic, Eastern Orthodox, and evangelical leaders. This document explicitly links opposition to abortion and gay marriage with protection of the religious freedom of Christians who are opposed.[22] It has been endorsed by a number of the leaders of the bishops' conference, including Cardinal Timothy Dolan, former president of the bishops' conference. As is well known, the bishops' positions on these matters have generated much argument and considerable resistance.

Argument and resistance to the way the US bishops have been approaching their role in public life reached high intensity during the debate on the Affordable Health Care Act (ACA), passed by the US Congress and signed into law by President Barack Obama in March 2010. The US bishops intervened vigorously in the legislative debate about this bill. The bishops have long supported affordable and universally available health-care insurance for all Americans. However, in 2010 they opposed the legislation that greatly expanded the number of people covered by health insurance. They saw the bill as "profoundly flawed."[23] This opposition was based on their conclusion that the bill could lead to taxpayers' money being used to fund abortions. In reaching this conclusion, the bishops disagreed with the leadership of the Catholic Health Association and a significant group of leaders of women's religious communities, who argued that the bill would not in fact fund abortions. The action by the bishops has led a number of commentators to conclude that resistance to abortion has come to overshadow other social ethical concerns for the bishops. It also raises questions about whether the bishops have rightly interpreted the relation between moral principles, such as the duty to protect human life, and civil law, such as a complex piece of legislation like the 2010 health-care bill. The questions about the abortion-related consequences of the legislation were not matters of moral principle;

they were prudential judgments about the consequences that would follow if the legislation were passed. Whether the bishops possess the competence and authority to make such judgments about the complexity of public policy is debatable.[24]

The bishops' strong opposition to the 2010 ACA was surely an exercise of the public dimension of their right to religious freedom. It raises the question, however, of how the right to exercise religious freedom relates to other moral concerns, such as the right of all persons to adequate health care. In addition, when religious freedom is exercised to advocate legislative policies that are designed to enforce certain moral standards, such as opposition to abortion, the question of the role of civil law in the enforcement of such moral norms comes to the fore. A similar question arises with regard to the opposition by Church groups to legislation that would civilly recognize same-sex partnerships. The public discussions about policy on both abortion and homosexual partnership raise important questions about whether and how civil legislation is an appropriate means for the promotion of the moral norms taught by the Church's magisterium. The question of the relation of civil legislation to moral norms was treated with theological acumen by Murray. Before addressing these aspects of Murray's thought and its influence on Vatican II, it will be useful to note the growing religio-political polarization in US society today. This polarization is of great importance, for both the ethical quality of public life and the well-being of the Church itself. It shapes the context for a possible further reception of Murray's thought today.

POLARIZATION AS A CHALLENGE TO PUBLIC RELIGION IN THE US TODAY

Murray addressed a number of practical ethical issues that had implications for public policy. Needless to say, this moral aspect of Murray's work was also marked by controversy. He drew on the just war tradition in a way that addressed the threats of the Cold War and the nuclear age. This contribution had strong influence on the US Catholic bishops' 1983 pastoral letter on the ethics of nuclear weapons and strategy, The Challenge of Peace.[25] Murray also reformulated key elements in the Catholic tradition's approach to the relation between morality and civil law in ways that dealt with the pluralism of moral convictions present in the United States of his day. In particular he addressed several issues where Catholic moral convictions were in considerable tension with the stance of non-Catholics, notably regarding free speech, censorship, contraception, and some other aspects of sexual morality.

RELIGIOUS FREEDOM, MORALITY, AND LAW   73

Murray's work on these issues remains highly relevant to analogous controversies occurring today. Serious disputes about the relation between Catholicism and the public life of pluralist America continue on both the religious and moral levels. These contemporary disagreements, however, take a notably different form than they did before Murray made his contribution. The chief difference, thanks to the appropriation of Murray's thinking at Vatican II, is that no Catholic thinker can address the role of religion in public life today without presupposing the existence of the right to religious freedom. How this right is to be interpreted, however, and how religious freedom affects the moral realm, remain highly disputed. The approach of Murray and Vatican II continues to be a fertile resource for reflection on the public contribution of Catholicism in the United States in the face of ongoing disputes about the role of religion in public life.

The religious divisions in US politics today take different forms, including the same suspicions that excluded Catholics from high office before the Kennedy presidency. The role being played by the Catholic Church in American politics today remains a key element in current religio-political division. When another Catholic, John Kerry, ran for president in 2004, his election was not opposed by secular and Protestant leaders who feared his Catholicism as a threat to American freedoms. Rather, Kerry's most visible adversaries were several US Catholic bishops who regarded the senator's pro-choice stance on abortion as a betrayal of the value of human life that Catholics should be advocating in the political domain. Several bishops threatened to deny communion to Kerry, in effect suggesting that he was not a Catholic in good standing. Abortion, along with stem cell research, euthanasia, and gay marriage, have come to be seen by the leadership of the US Conference of Catholic Bishops today as moral matters on which no political compromise is possible. This stance has significant political implications.

The current trends in the interaction of religion with politics in the United States have been studied in depth in the important book by Robert D. Putnam and David E. Campbell, *American Grace: How Religion Divides and Unites Us*. Putnam and Campbell see two outcomes resulting from recent developments in the relation between religion and society in the United States that point to the continuing relevance of Murray's thought today. First, largely because post–baby boomer generations are increasingly alienated from the approach taken by both Catholic and evangelical religious leaders to gay rights and abortion, younger Americans have become increasingly secularized. One survey indicates that many younger persons in the United States have come to view religion as "judgmental, homophobic, hypocritical, and too political."[26] In an extraordinary development, the percentage of young people who say they have "no religion" increased from 5 percent in the 1970s, 1980s, and 1990s, to over 25 percent who describe themselves that way today. Those who respond "none" when asked what religious community they belong to are not necessarily atheists; many of them state that they continue to believe in God. But the data suggest that their divergence from the positions of religious leaders on homosexuality and somewhat less so on abortion are at least part of the explanation of their alienation from any religious community. Putnam and Campbell see this divergence as an important source of the reconfiguration of the relation of religion and society that has occurred in the United States in the first decade of the twenty-first century.[27]

This departure from religious community and religious practice has been particularly marked among Catholics. The Pew Forum on Religion and Public Life's 2008 "U.S. Religious Landscape Survey" concluded that "approximately one-third of the survey respondents who say they were raised Catholic no longer describe themselves as Catholic. This means that roughly 10% of all Americans are former Catholics."[28] Putnam and Campbell reach a conclusion that should be even more disturbing for Catholic pastors: their data imply that among non-immigrant Catholics today, 60 percent who were raised as Catholics "are no longer practicing Catholics, half of them having left the church entirely and half remaining nominally Catholic, but rarely, if ever, taking part in the life of the church."[29]

Second, there is a notable correlation between being actively engaged in a religious community and supporting the Republican Party, and a similar link between not being active in any religious community and supporting the Democratic Party. Thus, there is a growing and correlated religio-political polarization in the US today. Putnam and Campbell's data suggest that the increasing divide between religious Republicans and unchurched Democrats revolves primarily around the issues of abortion and homosexual relationships. The intensity of a person's religious engagement is significantly correlated with that person's stance on abortion or gay rights. Being religiously active is less linked with people's positions on other issues that have significant moral dimensions, such as income inequality or spending on foreign aid.[30] As the Republican Party has increasingly taken a pro-life, anti-gay marriage stance and the Democratic Party has moved in the other direction, we have seen the emergence of the so-called God gap in American political alignment. Those who are pro-life and pro–traditional marriage are likely to be both believers and Republican voters, while those who are pro-choice and pro–gay rights are increasingly secular in outlook and Democratic voters. Thus, a coalition of more religiously active citizens in support of the Republican Party has emerged. Putnam and Campbell suggest that opposition to abortion and homosexuality are "the glue that holds the coalition together."[31]

Such religious-political alignment is, of course, nothing new. Throughout the first three-fourths of the twentieth century the Catholic population was closely linked to the Democratic Party. This was largely due to Democratic support for labor unions and the social policies that aided many immigrant and working-class Catholics to advance economically. The question that arises, however, is whether it is a good thing for the United States today that the divisions that exist between religiously active and more secular people are increasingly linked with a growing political polarization between Republicans and Democrats. This question is particularly important because abortion and homosexuality appear to be overshadowing a large range of other public issues having moral importance. These include the avoidance of war, ending reliance on the death penalty, promotion of greater economic justice through housing, jobs, and just wages, provision of affordable and accessible health care, overcoming racial and gender discrimination, alleviating global poverty, and promoting religious freedom and human rights everywhere.[32]

The alignment of active Catholics with the Republican Party's agenda thus raises the question of whether abortion and same-sex relationships should play an overriding role in shaping where a faithful Christian should stand politically. Should the broader range of other issues play determining roles as well? The US bishops' 2007 statement on political responsibility set the stage for the emergence of this God gap when they argued that abortion and homosexuality are intrinsically evil and thus must *always* be politically opposed, while other political issues such as the justification of war involve prudential judgments concerning concrete circumstances. This left some room for consideration of the overall effect of decisions about policy. The bishops' 2007 statement, perhaps unintentionally, has suggested to many of the most active and devout Catholics that a politician's or a party's stance on public policy regarding abortion or homosexual partnerships are litmus tests for how they should vote. This way of thinking was further encouraged when the US Bishops Conference directly appealed to legislators to vote against the 2010 Affordable Health Care Act because they saw it as placing insufficient barriers to using funds raised through taxes to pay for abortions. As noted previously, other Catholics, and organizations such as the Catholic Health Association, argued that the bill would not lead to the funding of abortion. In the face of this disagreement, the stance of the bishops' conference suggests that some moral judgments, such as the unacceptability of abortion or gay sex, have direct and immediate consequences in the legislative and legal domains. Other concerns, such as the threat to human dignity from a lack of health care or the harm inflicted by war, can be related to the policy domain only through a process of prudential reasoning.

Thus, the question of how normative judgments about the moral status of actions like abortion relate to prudential judgments about the moral impact of complex pieces of legislation like the 2010 Affordable Care Act assume considerable importance. This importance is heightened in the context of the growing political polarization in the United States, where religious-secular splits around the issues of abortion and gay relationships are increasingly pronounced. Mary Jo Bane, former academic dean of Harvard's Kennedy School of Government, has argued that this growing polarization in American politics today is making it increasingly difficult to agree upon or achieve common purposes in national life.[33] Since the Catholic moral tradition shaped by Thomas Aquinas and reshaped by Murray sees the promotion of the common good as the principal purpose of law and politics, one can ask whether such polarization should not raise serious concerns among Catholics.[34] For this reason Bane, who is an active Catholic, expresses worry about the apparent contribution by religious leaders to the growing inability to work for common purposes and the common good in US politics. Though religious leaders seem not to have direct impact on the political views of their church members through preaching or organizing, they do indirectly influence these views through the environment they create within their congregations. Thus, Bane is dismayed that religious leaders have become "complicit" in the political divisions that make the common good increasingly difficult to attain. Indeed, Bane suggested that encouraging such polarization contributes to what may be a social form of "sin" in America today.[35]

Even if Putnam, Campbell, and Bane are only partly right about what is happening at the intersection of religion and politics in the United States today, the stakes are very high when we consider how people should exercise their religious freedom and express their religious convictions in public life. The religiously based activity of at least some Americans appears to be deepening the political divisions that make the pursuit of the common good increasingly difficult. It also seems that the activities of religious leaders, including the US Catholic bishops, have led to a notable rise in the percentage of young people who are alienated from active participation in religious life.

It is true, of course, that neither the unity of society nor the percentage of the society who are religiously active should override all other values as the Church determines its pastoral agenda. There may well be some moral questions that have such high importance that pursuing them justifies pastoral actions that lead to social conflict and the departure of some from active involvement in the Church. For example, it could be argued that the abolition of slavery would not have been successful if some religious leaders had not been willing to cause conflict and risk losing some of their followers because of their uncompromising stand against it. A similar argument could be made concerning the willingness to risk conflict and alienation of some churchgoers in the later civil rights struggle for racial equality. Fortunately, the issues of abortion and gay rights may not threaten American political life with the armed civil conflict that occurred in the 1860s. Nevertheless, religio-political polarization can threaten efforts to work for the common good in less dramatic ways, and the sharp decline in active participation in religious community by the younger generation is surely a genuine loss for the Church. Careful consideration of Church positions on public policies toward abortion and same-sex relationships is surely needed.

VATICAN II ON FREEDOM, LAW, MORALITY

The Second Vatican Council's treatment of the appropriate relation between civil law, moral norms, and religious conviction, developed with the help of Murray, can help us address some of these controversial matters today. In a chapter in *We Hold These Truths* titled "Should There Be a Law," Murray drew on the thought of St. Thomas Aquinas to present an overall framework for how morality should be related to human or civil law.[36] Murray argued, as did Aquinas, that civil law should be founded on moral values but that civil law need not seek to abolish all immoral activities in society. De facto, such a goal is impossible to attain. The demands made by civil law should be compatible with the level of virtue that has been attained by most of the people the law regulates. It is very unlikely that the majority of people in a particular society will be fully virtuous. Civil law, therefore, should not try to coerce people to move beyond the level of virtue they have already attained. Efforts to coerce people to move dramatically beyond their existing level of virtue is likely to produce resistance, bringing civil law into disrepute and leading to an outcome that may be worse than pursuing more modest moral goals.

Murray observed that efforts to promote virtue in the sexual area through civil coercion are particularly unlikely to succeed. For this reason governments influenced by the Catholic tradition have rarely sought to enforce the Church's sexual code in a rigorous way. A rather tolerant approach to a moral issue like prostitution has often been found in Catholic states. For example, Murray noted that in late sixteenth-century papal Rome, under the rule of the otherwise quite strict Pope Sixtus V, nine thousand prostitutes practiced their trade among a population of seventy-thousand. Needless to say, Murray held prostitution to be morally unacceptable. He called it "debauchery." Nevertheless, like both Aquinas and Saint Augustine before him, he maintained that an effort to abolish prostitution through the coercive police power of the state is not required by a Catholic understanding of the moral power of civil law.[37] Indeed, such an effort could be counterproductive.

In a similar way, Murray argued in the mid-1960s that trying to prevent the use of contraception through civil legislation is also unlikely to be successful. He recommended, therefore, that Cardinal Richard Cushing of Boston not oppose a change of law that would permit the sale of contraceptives in Massachusetts by reversing legislation linked with the Protestant-influenced Comstock Laws of the 1870s. Here Murray drew on Aquinas, distinguishing between public and private morality. Aquinas argued that civil law has as its goal the promotion of *public* morality. This public morality seeks the common good of the civil multitude. It does not extend to coercively promoting the full virtue of each citizen, including the virtues that govern behavior in private interactions such as friendships or personal relationships.[38] Murray acknowledged that the question of whether contraception was a matter of public or private morality was disputed among Catholics. He also argued, however, that the case for holding it to be a matter of private morality was "sufficiently conclusive."[39] Since civil law should seek to use coercion only in matters of public and not private morality, Murray recommended to Cardinal Cushing that the Church not advocate the continuation of the Massachusetts law that prevented the sale of contraceptives.

Murray further argued that the case for not seeking to prevent the use of contraception through the power of civil law was reinforced by the fact that many people not only rejected the argument that contraception was immoral but that some, including some religious leaders, held that it could be morally required as a means to responsible parenthood. Murray did not accept this argument in his mid-1960s memo to Cardinal Cushing, which presumed as a starting point the Catholic teaching that birth control was morally objectionable.[40] Still he argued against seeking to translate the Catholic moral objection to contraception into a civilly enforced ban because many citizens, including many religious citizens and clergy, saw it as morally acceptable. In Murray's words,

> It is difficult to see how the state can forbid, as contrary to public morality, a practice that numerous religious leaders approve as morally right. The stand taken by these religious groups may be lamentable from the Catholic moral point of view. But it is decisive from

the point of view of law and jurisprudence, for which the norm of "generally accepted standards" is controlling.[41]

Respect for the religious convictions of those not sharing the official Catholic rejection of contraception thus led Murray to judge that civil law should not attempt to prevent all citizens from using contraceptives by preventing their distribution. Though the Church could teach its members that birth control is morally unacceptable, the role of civil law was limited in this domain.

Nevertheless, Murray certainly did not maintain that the existence of moral disagreement on a particular matter of public policy should *always* lead to the rejection of the use of civil legislation on that matter. He noted that civil law can sometimes play an "educative" role that helps to shape the consciences of members of the public. The civil law can sometimes be "ahead" of the public consensus on the moral standards that should govern society.[42] He noted that this was the case on the matter of racial equality, where civil law was clearly ahead of public opinion in southern states when Murray wrote in the mid-1960s. He was ready to support the use of civil law to seek to reshape the values of those who were ready to accept racial inequality because fundamental standards of justice were at stake, and these standards are matters of public rather than private morality.

The central importance of justice in determining the proper reach of civil law also appears in Vatican II's Declaration on Religious Freedom, no doubt due to Murray's influence. As already noted, the right to religious freedom not only requires the protection of private belief and practice but also guarantees that persons and religious communities may seek to influence public affairs in accord with their religious convictions. Thus, churches legitimately seek to influence legislation in ways that reflect their convictions about what makes a society a good society. This is an essential aspect of the free exercise of religious freedom, and as the council put it, this freedom is to be "respected as far as possible, and curtailed only when and in so far as necessary."

This is directly relevant to how a society should frame civil laws regarding matters about which there is considerable moral and religious disagreement. Should the government use civil legislation and coercive regulation to prevent abortion and same-sex relationships? If so, how should it do so? Or are these matters where the Church and other moral educators such as the family should seek to develop the kind of virtue in people that will lead them to do what is right in these domains without being compelled to do so by threat of the government's police? The council's declaration states directly that the presupposition of how the government should respond to matters on which moral or religious disagreement exists is a presupposition in favor of freedom. As the council put it, "the freedom of man is to be respected as far as possible, and curtailed only when and in so far as necessary."[43] In analyzing this text, which was clearly dear to his heart, Murray added that this means freedom should be limited only insofar as necessary to preserve society's very existence.[44]

Both the council and Murray went on to specify a set of criteria that should be used to determine when such a threat to society exists and when it does not, and thus when coercive limitation of freedom is legitimate and when it is not. They called these criteria the standards of "public order."[45] Public order, as Vatican II and Murray understood it, has three components: justice, which secures the rights of all citizens; public peace, which itself is grounded in justice; and the standards of public morality on which consensus exists in society.[46] Understood this way, public order is a moral concept. It is not, however, the rich reality of the full common good that citizens would be able to achieve in their lives together if they were entirely virtuous. Rather, it is a more minimal level of morality that includes the protection of the most basic prerequisites of social life. These prerequisites include protection of the levels of justice and peace that are required if a society that is civil is to exist at all. When such requirements of public order are endangered, the use of the coercive power of the state is justified.

Drawing on this analysis, we can conclude that the question to be faced in addressing the matters of same-sex relationships and abortion in the United States today is whether permissive stances toward them threaten social life and whether the justice and public peace that sustain social life require that they be civilly prohibited. Clearly some religious leaders, including the leadership of the US Conference of Catholic Bishops, believe that abortion and same-sex relationships do threaten the justice required in social life. They hold that homosexual relationships, especially civil recognition of same-sex partnerships, are threats to the family bonds that hold society together and that abortion is unjustified taking of innocent human life. Therefore, the bishops argue against laws granting civil recognition to same-sex partnerships and advocate for laws that will prevent or restrict access to abortion. They also stand against public policies that they see as providing financial or other support for abortion, as they argued that the 2010 Affordable Health Care Act would do. Thus, the US bishops suggest that the standards of justice and public morality that the council saw as setting appropriate limits to freedom can be invoked to support the use of coercive governmental power to limit same-sex partnerships and prevent abortion.

However, a significant number of US citizens do not agree with the bishops on these issues. They do not see same-sex relationships or all abortions as violations of the justice and public morality required to hold society together. Some of those who disagree with the position of the US bishops do so on religious grounds. One could argue, of course, that those who disagree with the bishops are simply in error when they hold that homosexual partnerships based on mutual love and commitment can be morally justifiable or when they conclude that in some tragic circumstances abortion could sadly be justified. This is not the place to engage in examination of the theological and natural law arguments on which the positions of Church teaching on homosexuality and abortion are based. The question that is urgent in the present context, and to which Vatican II and Murray make a valuable contribution, is whether it is appropriate to use coercive civil restraint when there is significant disagreement in society about the ethical values at stake in the domains of homosexual relationships and public policy on abortion. This is especially true when some of these disagreements are related to religious conviction.

One might argue that the use of civil law on these matters of moral disagreement can be justified by appealing to the educational role of civil law. Indeed, civil law in a number of European countries does seek to discourage abortion in what could be seen as an educational way by setting conditions for its legality that are notably stricter than the standards legally in effect in the United States.[47] Similar civic education through statutes regarding divorce could also surely reinforce the social importance of marriage and family stability better than they do now in the United States. To appeal to the educational role of civil law as a basis for criminalizing behavior on which there is substantial moral and religious disagreement in society, however, moves dangerously close to affirming that those in moral error regarding homosexuality and abortion simply have no rights in these areas because of their error.

The position that "error has no rights" was the position of those who rejected Murray's argument for religious freedom in the 1950s.[48] They believed that when Murray supported the civil right to religious freedom for all persons he was effectively saying that persons were free from any obligation to seek and hold the truths about God, Christ, and the Church. Murray repeatedly had to make clear that his argument for religious freedom was not based on a relativistic stance toward religious truth that held that all religions are equally true or equally false. His argument had an entirely different basis. He justified religious freedom by arguing that it is not the role of government to reach decisions about religious truth and to enforce decisions about which religious beliefs are true and which are false. The government and its officials are simply "denied all competence" to make judgments regarding religious truth or error.[49] Murray's argument for religious freedom, therefore, was based on the limited power of the government to determine and enforce truth in the religious sphere. Vatican II supported this position as well.

This argument for limits on the power of government has implications for moral issues when there is significant pluralism in society. Government's coercive power does not extend to the full scope of the moral life, just as it does not extend to the regulation of religious truth. Attaining the fullness of the moral life, which encompasses the entire scope of the common good, is the responsibility of civil society, including the Church and the broader components of cultural life. As Murray put it, "there are circumstances in which human authority has neither mandate nor duty nor right to use its coercive power against error and evil."[50]

We are thus led to ask where this line of reasoning leads on some key issues facing the Catholic community in the United States today. For example, can we establish that same-sex unions have such negative effects on the stability of family life that they undercut the justice required for society to sustain its necessary unity? Can we clearly show that the Affordable Care Act in fact supports abortion or that a strict ban on abortion is a requirement of justice? If so we could rightly argue that laws against same-sex unions are called for by the standards of public morality and that the US bishops were right to urge members of Congress to vote against the 2010 health-care bill in the name of justice. But if we cannot clearly establish that homosexual relationships so threaten the continued unity of society by undermining the family bonds that are important to this unity, then we ought not maintain that coercive use of state power to prevent such relationships is called for or legitimate. Similarly, the appropriateness of the bishops' recommendation that members of Congress vote against the 2010 health-care bill depends on showing that the bill's support for abortion was so clear that it outweighed its contribution to justice by the provision of greater access to health care.

If the standards of justice do not lead to these conclusions, this does *not* mean all same sex-relationships and all abortions should be simply accepted. They could be civilly regulated to prevent abuses that are clearly unjust. In addition, the Church itself should work vigorously to improve the level of virtue among both its members and in society at large in ways that significantly improve the level of sexual morality in society and reduce the number of abortions. The Church, the family, educational bodies, and many other groups have formative moral influence in the broader culture, and resorting to the coercive power of the state is not the only way to work for moral improvement.

It should be noted that suggesting that the government may not be the appropriate agent for pursuing the advancement of moral values in the domain of homosexuality and abortion is *not* an argument that homosexuality and abortion are morally insignificant or morally acceptable. Murray clearly maintained that attaining and holding to religious truth is of the highest importance. But he also maintained that it is not the role of the government to compel people to hold the right beliefs. Similarly, we might extrapolate from Murray's argument and suggest that when there is the kind of moral disagreement that we have in the United States today on committed and stable same-sex relationships and on abortions that occur in situations of grave distress, it is not the role of government to resolve these disagreements through the use of its police power. Indeed, the use of coercive law in these areas is likely to be ineffective, may well have negative consequences such as increased social division, and could lead to a disrespect for the law that makes society less worthy overall.

Whether such negative effects flow from efforts to control homosexual activity and eliminate abortion by law calls for careful attention to what can be known about the consequences of such efforts. But if the interpretations of what is happening at the intersection of religion and American public life offered by Putnam and Bane are correct, the approaches of a number of religious leaders, including the US Catholic bishops, seem to be leading to social divisions that make the common good increasingly difficult to attain. Such divisions seem to be making it more difficult to attain justice in addressing matters such as the reduction of poverty and unemployment. These strategies are also alienating a sizable segment of the younger generation of Americans from religious community. This loss of the young will itself make it more difficult in the future for the Church to influence the larger culture in light of moral values.

The analyses presented by Vatican II and John Courtney Murray did not answer all questions concerning how we should relate religion, morality, and the civil law in the third decade of the twenty-first century. They did, however, lead the Church to a transformative discovery that human freedom is essential to the relation of human beings to God and to moral life. They certainly understood that freedom might need to be limited in some social situations. But the council's great insight was what it called the principle of the "free society." Through Murray's influence this principle was enshrined in Vatican II's Declaration on Religious Freedom. In words that Murray himself likely wrote, the council declared, "The usages of society are to be the usages of freedom in their full range. These require that the freedom of the human person be respected as far as possible, and curtailed only when and insofar as necessary."[51] The question today is not whether restriction of freedom is sometimes necessary to protect social unity but whether some of the efforts by the Church to secure such restriction in the areas of sex and reproduction have themselves become threats to social unity and to the common good. If the latter is the case, it suggests that a different approach to same-sex relationships and the links between abortion and health care is called for.

As I have suggested elsewhere, it will likely be more fruitful for the Church to seek first to influence the moral values held in the larger culture, and only then, when a greater agreement has been reached on those values, seek to embody them in civil law.[52] Indeed, considering the dialogue and public argument that is needed to shape cultural values, it is at least imaginable that the Church will itself gain some new insights into the issues that cause so much controversy today. It was Murray who helped the Church at Vatican II reach new and deeper insight on the matter of religious freedom, thus enabling the Church to become a stronger force for human rights, justice, and public morality. Perhaps a fuller reception and deeper appropriation of the council's position can help the Church address the controversies of our time with greater effectiveness.

6

RELIGION IN PUBLIC

The Challenge of Freedom

This chapter explores the role of religious communities, especially the Catholic Church, in the public, political life of society. Since Vatican II the Catholic community has recognized that its public role is supported by the respect others have for its religious freedom. It also recognizes that when the Church seeks to influence public life, it must itself respect the religious freedom of other communities. This chapter highlights some of the key issues concerning the right to religious freedom as this right was understood by the Second Vatican Council and by John Courtney Murray. Thus, what is said here builds on the discussion of religious freedom in the previous chapter.

In recent decades religion has been playing an increasingly public role in world affairs.[1] The interaction of religion and politics sometimes leads to injustice toward religious minorities and, too often, to conflict and even war. Vatican II, in its Gaudium et Spes (Pastoral Constitution on the Church in the Modern World), devoted major attention both to the public role of the Church and to the Church's possible contribution to human rights. Indeed, this document declared that the Church, "by virtue of the Gospel committed to her, proclaims the rights of the human person; she acknowledges and greatly esteems the dynamic movements of today by which these rights are everywhere fostered."[2] Thus, the promotion of human rights has become a central emphasis of the Catholic Church's social engagement. Efforts to promote human rights must surely respect the religious freedom of others, and thus tensions can arise between the Church's effort to influence the shape of public life and its duty to respect the rights and freedom of others. This chapter seeks to clarify several dimensions of this tension and make a contribution to the ongoing conversation about the role religion should play in helping to promote the full range of human rights, form the values that shape public life both in the United States and more globally, and build a more just and peaceful world.

85

Regrettably, this conversation about the public role of religion is not always well guided, especially in the way the right to religious freedom is typically understood. In the United States it is not uncommon to hear religion called a strictly private matter. Seeing religion, and indeed all value commitments, as private affairs is one of the results of the individualism that is such an important current in US culture.[3] This individualistic approach to religion can highlight the intimate relation between one's religious beliefs and one's deepest identity as a person and thus belief's high importance. Seeing religion as a purely private affair, however, can also reduce religion to an insignificant level that verges on triviality. In addition, those who see religion as a strictly private affair are likely to want to marginalize religious contributions to public life, thus reducing the influence of faith communities on public matters such as the promotion of the full range of human rights and the advancement of peace and justice. When this happens, religious freedom comes to be identified with the privatization of religion.

Vatican II, of course, did not see religion as a strictly private affair. Indeed, it declared the growing split between faith and the affairs of life in society was among "the more serious errors of our age."[4] The council certainly appreciated the deeply personal aspects of faith and wanted to preserve the crucial role religious freedom plays in enabling individual persons to shape who they themselves are. But it also saw freedom, including religious freedom, as achieved in society and in public life. Religious freedom has important public dimensions that depend on the political and juridical institutions that shape both society and its members. Strictly private or individualist understandings of religious freedom do not have the tools needed to help faith communities envision their roles in public life in ways that help build up the common good of individual countries and of the larger international society. Vatican II saw religious freedom not only as an essential protection for the personal act of faith but also as a social, public reality with important political implications. Here I will draw upon both the work of the council and the thought of John Courtney Murray to help clarify how religious freedom is particularly important today because of its essential contributions to public life in the United States and in the world.

RELIGIOUS FREEDOM AS A PERSONAL REALITY

Our concern with the connection between religious freedom and matters of public life such as global peace and social justice, of course, should not lead us to overlook the fact that religious freedom is a personal reality that reaches into the heart of each individual. Before considering how religious freedom is important for public issues, therefore, it is important to make a few comments about how the Second Vatican Council saw religious freedom as a deeply personal reality. A person's religious beliefs or lack of such beliefs shapes her identity in paramount ways. Thus, the protection or violation of religious beliefs has effects that could hardly be more personal.

Dignitatis Humanae argues for the human and civil right to religious freedom by noting several ways the protection of this freedom is important to the innermost identity of persons. First, the council appealed to the long-standing Catholic conviction concerning the high importance of freedom of conscience. It is a basic affirmation in Catholic tradition that every person has an obligation to follow the dictates of his or her conscience. This obligation binds not only in the moral sphere but the religious domain as well. As Dignitatis Humanae puts it:

> The human person sees and recognizes the demands of divine law through conscience. All are bound to follow their conscience faithfully in every sphere of activity so that they may come to God, who is their last end. Therefore the individual must not be forced to act against conscience nor be prevented from acting in accord with conscience, especially in matters religious.[5]

Freedom of conscience thus implies the existence of a personal right to religious freedom. The exercise of conscience is a profoundly personal activity. This was made clear by the council's Gaudium et Spes, where it is written that "conscience is people's most secret core, and their sanctuary. There they are alone with God whose voice echoes in their depths."[6] The council saw conscience, and thus religious freedom, as exercised in the intimacy of each person's heart, where they encounter God. The language could hardly be more personalist. However, despite the tone of this statement, the council did not hold that religious belief is a private reality, nor that religious freedom is protected by keeping religion in the private sphere.

Second, the council stressed religious freedom's personal dimension when it argued that the right to this freedom is based on the fact that a person can come to a conviction that a belief is true only through personal deliberation conducted in freedom. Some of the more conservative bishops at the council, such as the head of the Holy Office, Cardinal Alfredo Ottaviani, feared that such an affirmation of religious freedom rested on an indifference to truth. This suspicion had led to the effective silencing of John Courtney Murray on the issue of religious freedom just a few years before the council was convened.[7] To counter this concern, Dignitatis Humanae unambiguously affirmed that its understanding of religious freedom presumed that all persons have a duty to affirm the truth: "All persons should be at once impelled by nature and bound by a moral obligation to seek the truth, especially religious truth. They are also bound to adhere to the truth once they come to know it, and to direct their whole lives in accordance with the demands of truth."[8] This duty, however, can be followed only in freedom. Human beings can seek and come to hold the truth about God and the human condition in relation to God only through free deliberation and freely given personal assent. The declaration thus affirms that all persons should be free from coercive interference with their duty to fulfill this obligation, and therefore have a right to religious freedom.

Third, the council grounded religious freedom on that fact that the act of faith must itself be free if it is to be a genuine act of faith: "The act of faith or its very nature is a free act. The human person . . . can assent to God's self-revelation only by being drawn by the Father and through submitting to God with a faith that is reasonable and free."[9] Because of this essential connection between authentic faith and freedom, the civil protection of personal religious freedom is closely associated with the advancement of freedom more generally understood. Securing religious freedom is thus closely linked with the institutions of democracy that protect freedom more broadly conceived.

John Courtney Murray synthesized these personal dimensions of religious freedom by arguing that they are all expressions of the essential connection between the freedom of faith and the fundamental dignity of the human person. In one of his final writings on the declaration, Murray eloquently explained the council's understanding of human dignity as the ontological foundation of the right to religious freedom. This freedom is not only the freedom of choice by which persons decide among various options that appear on a kind of menu of specific religious alternatives. The religious freedom that is a deep expression of human dignity is the freedom of the person to decide who she is and what she will become. It is a decision about the ultimate meaning of one's life. It is the kind of freedom through which a person puts at risk her whole existence. In Murray's words,

> The primordial demand of dignity, then, is that man acts by his own counsel and purpose, using and enjoying his freedom, moved, not by external coercion, but internally by the risk of his whole existence. . . . Human dignity consists formally in the person's responsibility for himself and, what is more, for his world. So great is his dignity that not even God can take it away.[10]

Human dignity, therefore, comes to expression in human freedom, and the deepest meaning of one's dignity as a person is shaped by the use of one's religious freedom.

The council, therefore, makes a philosophical claim about the nature of the human person as free and self-determining when it argues for the right to religious freedom. It further makes a theological claim when it affirms that freedom—including religious freedom—is one of the key characteristics that constitute a human being as created in the image of God. Through these theological and philosophical arguments the council set forth why the right to religious freedom is of such high personal importance to every human being. These arguments are the basis of the council's affirmation that religious freedom is an essential expression of personal dignity "as known through the revealed word of God and by reason itself."[11]

Vatican II and Murray had clear secular philosophical warrants for their affirmation that the protection of religious freedom is essential to treating humans as what they are, that is, as free, self-determining beings. They also had strong Christian theological warrants for affirming this right. Both kinds of warrants set the council and Murray at odds with the currents in modern and postmodern thought that affirm the importance of religious freedom because of skepticism about religious or even secular philosophical truth claims about what it is to be human. At the same time, the council did not hesitate to affirm that those who rejected its reasons were nonetheless still entitled to respect for their religious freedom. Though the council argued that religious freedom is grounded in the truth about the human person, it also maintained that this freedom must be respected "even in those who do not live up to their obligation of seeking the truth and adhering to it."[12]

PUBLIC RELIGION, CONFLICT, AND PEACE: SOME EXAMPLES

The council's strongly personalist understanding of the importance of religious freedom did not lead it to hold that religion should be kept private, as do some other modern and postmodern understandings of religious liberty. Far from it. The council argued that the right to religious freedom means not only that individual persons ought not to be forced to act against their convictions but also that they should be free to act in accord with those convictions "in private or in public, alone or in association with others."[13] Indeed, the right to free exercise of religion, to borrow the US constitutional term, includes the right of religious communities to free exercise of their beliefs, including efforts to form social organizations that aim to influence public life by "demonstrating the special value of their teaching for the organization of society."[14]

The council, therefore, was strongly committed to the importance and legitimacy of public activity by the Church for justice and peace. The council, and even more so John Courtney Murray, were aware that in a pluralistic society, public religious action can lead to considerable tension. Indeed, in our day the public action of religious communities has sometimes led to significant conflict in global politics. At the same time, the impact of faith communities in public life has also often been positive, with religious leaders and believers at large making significant contributions to justice and peace. To set the stage for a consideration of dimensions of religious freedom that go beyond the protection of individual freedoms, we now turn to a description of several examples of both negative and positive social influences of religion in public life. This will enable us better to clarify how the council understood the relation between religious freedom in public life and the Church's role in the promotion of social peace and justice.

Vatican II holds that the liberty to exercise religion in public includes the freedom of a faith community to seek to shape public policy and otherwise influence public affairs. A quick overview of the recent historical record shows that such a public role of religion can have both negative and positive effects. This public role can generate conflict and lead to the violation of the requirements of justice for some members of the communities affected. Or this public role can be a source of enhanced social unity, reconciliation, peace, and justice. One need only contrast the roles played by Osama bin Laden and by Archbishop Desmond Tutu of South Africa to see that the effects of public religion can be quite diverse. These multiple kinds of influence of religion in the affairs of the larger society have led Scott Appleby to speak of the "ambivalence of the sacred."[15] Before turning to the way the council proposed that faith communities, including the Catholic Church, should seek to influence the institutions of public life, it will be useful to note some recent examples of both the negative and positive influences of religious communities in public life. Doing so will help show that religious freedom is not simply a personal reality, much less a strictly private affair, but that it has important public, institutional dimensions.

On the negative side of the ledger, Brian J. Grim and Roger Finke have noted several regrettable twentieth-century cases in which religious communities have denied religious freedom to people of other faiths, leading to grave injustice and conflict.[16] They note that in the early 1900s more than three million Christians lived in Turkey, about 20 percent of the population. Today there are but three hundred thousand, or about 2 percent. Most of the difference is due to the large number of Armenians who perished in what can appropriately be called genocide. Better known is the Shoah in the 1930s and 1940s, in which anti-Judaism and anti-Semitism led to the genocide of the Jewish people at the hands of the National Socialist regime in Germany, taking the lives of about two-thirds of all the Jews living in Europe when the Nazis came to power. During the cultural revolution in China in the 1960s and 1970s, religion was a particular focus of state persecution; all religious practice was banned and many religious leaders faced prison and even death.

The record in the first years of the twenty-first century is also deeply distressing. Drawing upon data gathered by the US Department of State, by the Pew Forum on Religion and Public Life, and by several other sources, Grim and Finke have concluded that at least some cases of people being abused or displaced from their homes because of their religion have occurred in 86 percent of the world's countries. Religious persecution is today so widespread in much of the Middle East and South Asia that Grim and Finke conclude it has become the norm in those regions and that the injustice of such persecution is one of the principle causes of conflict and bloodshed in those regions.[17] There are severe cases of religious persecution and conflict in Africa as well.

Persecution because of religion is less present in Europe and the United States, but it is certainly not absent. Martha Nussbaum has made a strong appeal to resist what she calls the "new religious intolerance" directed at Muslims in Europe and, to a lesser degree, in the United States. Nussbaum cites European legislation banning Muslim women from wearing head scarves in certain public settings and the US controversy over the proposal to construct a mosque near the "ground zero" of the September 11, 2001, attacks on the World Trade Center in New York.[18] A particularly vivid illustration of the rise of "Islamophobia" in the West is the recent case of remarks made by Marine Le Pen, head of the National Front in France and member of the European Parliament. Le Pen compared the presence of veiled women and of Muslims at prayer in the streets because of insufficient space in mosques to the Nazi occupation of France during World War II. Le Pen and the National Front are significant political actors in France. Though the European Parliament has rejected Le Pen's views, the fact that she received 41.5 percent of the vote in the French presidential election in 2022 indicates she cannot be ignored.[19]

Failure to respect those who are religiously different has also led to violent conflicts. For example, the commitment of the ruling family of Saudi Arabia to exclusive state support for the Wahhabi school of Islam has led to resistance by other schools of Islam. It has helped generate jihadist movements, including Al-Queda. The resulting conflicts in Afghanistan and Iraq have been grave. Buddhist control of the government in Sri Lanka led to resistance by the minority Hindu community and generated a bloody civil war. In India, the Hindu nationalist convictions of the Bharatiya Janata Party was one of the sources of the rise of Lashkar-e-Taiba, a Muslim group with ties to Pakistan, that in 2008 carried out terror attacks in Mumbai, killing many.

The role of religion in the civil wars of recent decades is similarly discouraging and has been rising. Nineteen percent of the civil wars begun in the 1940s were fought at least in part over religious issues. This percentage rose to 41 percent in the 1980s, to 45 percent in the 1990s, and to 50 percent of the sixteen civil wars underway in 2010. In 2023 civil wars were underway in Iraq, Syria, Libya, Yemen, Chad, Nigeria, and elsewhere. A number of these current conflicts have religious dimensions. These religiously linked civil wars are of concern not only to the countries in which they occur but to the international community as well. Intrastate wars almost always produce serious effects on neighboring regions, through the disruption of economic activity, the displacement of refugees, and the effects on the balance of power and ideological alignments. When civil wars are religiously based the international consequences are likely to be magnified because religious identity is almost always tied to membership in a community that reaches across national borders. Thus, when conflicts have religious dimensions they easily flow over into the affairs of other countries.[20]

These are examples of the negative effects religious communities can have if they pursue their public roles without attending sufficiently to the rights of other religious communities, including others' rights to religious freedom. Vatican II was well aware of the ways that faith communities, including Catholicism, have engaged in behavior that has led some to see religion as a threat to human well-being, peace, and justice, leading to a distorted picture of religion and indeed of God.[21] The attaining of peace and justice calls for protecting society from such social misuse of religion. (A further consideration of how religious conflict shows the importance of religious freedom appears in the following chapter.)

Fortunately, public activity by religious communities also often has positive results as well. Religious leaders like Mahatma Gandhi, Martin Luther King, the Dalai Lama, Pope John Paul II, and Desmond Tutu have played significant roles in the pursuit of social justice, peace, and reconciliation. Gandhi's nonviolent campaign for India's independence from British rule was grounded in his Hindu beliefs, interpreted with the help of his reading of Christian authors such as Leo Tolstoy. Gandhi's nonviolence has inspired movements for justice and peace among Christians, such as King's campaign for racial justice in the United States and Tutu's participation in the antiapartheid movement that led to the nonracial democracy in South Africa that elected Nelson Mandela its first president in 1994. John Paul II was deeply involved in Poland's struggle for freedom from control and domination by the Soviet Union. The pope's support for the Solidarity Movement in Poland contributed in very important ways to tearing down the Berlin Wall in 1989 and to the collapse of the Soviet Union and its empire in 1991. The Dalai Lama has been a powerful Buddhist voice raised on behalf of the people of Tibet in the face of their oppression by the People's Republic of China. His voice, like that of many other religious people engaged in campaigns for justice, has appealed for significant change through nonviolent means. One of the most notable developments in recent international affairs has been the significant rise of nonviolent movements for political change, and many of these movements have been religiously inspired. Despite the conviction of many political realists that nonviolence is an ineffective political strategy, many of these movements have been successful.[22] The commitment to respecting those who are different, including those who are religiously different, has enabled these movements to seek greater justice in public life in vigorous ways while remaining committed to the use of peaceful means.

The efforts of religious communities to contribute to greater justice in society by promoting democratic political processes and institutions have also been visible in recent years. Particularly notable among these efforts have been the contributions made by the Catholic community to the advancement of the human rights that support democracy. Samuel Huntington concluded that the post–Vatican II Catholic Church had become one of the strongest worldwide forces for democracy and human rights. He saw the modern rise of democracy occurring in three waves. The first wave was the American and French Revolutions in the eighteenth centuries, the second was the democratization of the former Axis powers of Germany, Italy, and Japan following the Second World War, and the third wave has been underway since the early 1970s. This third wave included the coming of democracy to Spain and Portugal, the decline of military and authoritarian rule in Latin America, South Korea, and the Philippines, and the end of communism in the Warsaw Pact nations. From his analysis of the data, Huntington concludes that, "in its first fifteen years, the third wave was overwhelmingly Catholic.... [R]oughly three-quarters of the countries that transited to democracy between 1974 and 1989 were Catholic."[23]

Monica Duffy Toft, Daniel Philpott, and Timothy Samuel Shah have reinforced Huntington's conclusion about this dramatic contribution by the Catholic community to democracy and the human rights on which democracy depends. They have noted that between 1972 and 2009, seventy-eight countries in the world experienced substantial democratization. Religious communities played a role in advancing democracy in forty-eight of these countries, and religious communities took the leading role in advancing democracy in thirty of these countries and a supporting role in eighteen of them. In nations such as India, Indonesia, and Kuwait, Islam was a leader in support of democracy. Hinduism was a leader in India, Eastern Orthodoxy was in Serbia, and Protestantism played a leading role in several African countries as well as in South Korea and Romania. Catholicism showed stronger leadership. Toft and her colleagues conclude that between 1972 and 2009 the Catholic community helped promote democracy in thirty-six of the seventy-eight countries that experienced substantial advances for democracy and that the Catholic community had a leadership position in the democratization of twenty-two of these countries.[24]

This move of Catholicism from its more traditional alignment with authoritarian modes of political organization to support for democracy was certainly dramatic, perhaps even revolutionary. There seems little doubt that this shift can be attributed to the innovations of the Second Vatican Council, and especially to the council's strong support for human rights, including the right to religious freedom. The transition was brought about by the Church's experience-based recognition of the dangers of authoritarian regimes such as Nazism and Stalinism several decades before the council was convened. These dangers threatened both the freedom of all in society and also the Church's own freedom. The Catholic tradition of commitment to the freedom of the Church in earlier historical periods helped Vatican II to recognize that endorsement of the right to religious freedom was in continuity with important dimensions of the larger Catholic tradition.[25] At the same time, the broad range of the violations of human dignity by Adolf Hitler and Joseph Stalin showed that more than the Church's own well-being and freedom was a stake. The experience of the multiple kinds of abuse by authoritarian rule thus led Pope John XXIII to strongly support the full range of human rights in his encyclical *Pacem in Terris,* which was issued in 1963, during the council. This broader human rights agenda had been earlier developed with the drafting of the UN's Universal Declaration of Human Rights immediately following World War II.[26] When Vatican II followed the lead of *Pacem in Terris* in its endorsement of the full range of human rights articulated by the United Nations, the council moved the Church to the forefront of the struggle for human rights and democracy. Further, both the Universal Declaration and *Pacem in Terris* explicitly stated that respect for human rights is essential to the protection of peace.[27] In a similar way, Vatican II's commitment to human rights and religious freedom supports the Church's strong encouragement of its mission in the public life of society. Thus, Vatican II's teaching on religious freedom led the postconciliar Church to establish important new initiatives for a broad effort to promote human rights, democracy, social justice, and peace.

CHURCH CONTRIBUTIONS TO PUBLIC LIFE

The council's affirmation of the right to religious freedom had important consequences for the Church's engagement with issues of human rights, social justice, and peace. Thus, securing this right has significant implications beyond a private zone of personal faith. Support for religious liberty has important effects for social life and for social institutions, both within nations and globally. Clarifying how Vatican II understood the larger public requirements of religious liberty will help show why support for religious freedom had significant consequences for the Church's social engagement with public issues of social justice and global peace.

Drafts one and two of the council's Declaration on Religious Freedom stressed the personal dimensions of religious freedom, which might suggest that these drafts viewed this freedom as a largely private matter. These drafts based the right to religious freedom on the personal foundations of the duty to follow the dictates of one's conscience and on the fact that the act of faith must be free if it is to be authentic faith. In Murray's view, however, these personalist arguments were insufficient to show that there is a right to free exercise of religion in the midst of society, especially when a cogent argument can be made that the religious beliefs being exercised have morally objectionable public consequences. The existence of a right necessarily implies a correlative duty that others should respect this right. This raises the question of whether others in society have a duty to respect my conscience when it is in error, that is, when my conscience leads me to action that can be seen as morally wrong. To be sure, other persons have a duty not to try to coerce me to act in a way that would violate my convictions. But do they also have a duty to permit me to act on my convictions if acting upon those convictions can be reasonably judged to be harmful to others, perhaps in serious ways? Murray maintained that the arguments of those who answer this question negatively "are not negligible. . . . Another's error of conscience can create no duties in me."[28] Thus, Murray argued that the council needed to go beyond an appeal to freedom of conscience in order to develop an adequate understanding of the public dimensions of the right to religious freedom and how respect for freedom should be expressed politically and legally. This is a matter of clarifying the way political and legal institutions should deal with religion when it exercises public influence.

The limits of the appeal to freedom of conscience and the need for a consideration of the roles of political and juridical institutions in protecting religious liberty can again be illustrated by the South African case. The apartheid regime, which legally required that different racial and ethnic groups live apart from one another, had been developed by some Afrikaner Dutch Reformed Christians on the basis of their interpretation of the Bible, particularly the story of the Tower of Babel (Gen. 11). They understood the story to reveal that separation of diverse peoples is the will of God. Following this belief, after apartheid had been abolished in 1994, some Afrikaners continued to hold, on conscientious religious grounds, that racial separation was their religious duty. They sought legal approval of their right to act on this conviction and to create white "homelands" within South Africa based on racial and ethnic separation. Those who are convinced that such Afrikaner beliefs are morally objectionable will need a theory of religious freedom that goes beyond appealing to respect of conscience if they are to affirm *both* the right to religious freedom *and* the new South African constitution's refusal to grant these Afrikaners the freedom to continue racial separation.

This South African example comes from a time well after the end of Vatican II and the death of Murray. But it shows why the council needed to rely on grounds other than freedom of conscience in order to present an adequate understanding to the right to exercise religious freedom in public life. Murray argued this very point with several progressive, Francophone, pro-religious freedom theologians who were advising the bishops at the council.[29] The argument appears in imperfect form in the later drafts of what became Dignitatis Humanae. But Murray also introduced into the conciliar declaration the idea that religious freedom depends on the institutional relationship between the state and other bodies in civil society. The state and its juridical institutions should have limited power to implement the fullness of the common good. Murray's key argument, in other words, was political—it concerned the power of the state and the laws implemented by the state.[30] The state is essentially limited in power, especially in relation to religious faith and the Church.

This argument for a limited state has theological grounds. It goes back to the apostles' statement that "we must obey God rather than any human authority" (Acts 5:29, NRSV). It also has roots in the medieval investiture controversy in which the popes defended the freedom of the Church by resisting attempts by princes to appoint bishops. Both of these arguments presuppose that the spirit of the human person transcends politics. This transcendence, which Jacques Maritain called "the primacy of the spiritual," means there is more to human beings than can be encompassed by politics and the state.[31] This transcendence of the person sets definite limits to the exercise of state power.

The relevance of this theological argument for the political realm comes from the fact that protection of the religious transcendence of the person and of the freedom of the Church require the freedom of society from any form of absolutist control by the government. Society and state are distinct from one another. Just as there is more to the person than can be controlled by the state, so there is greater richness to life in society than politics can encompass. A misguided effort to bring the totality of society under state control is the very definition of totalitarianism, and it should be opposed both in the name of the right to religious freedom and in the name of human rights more generally. Citizens should be free from state control in their religious belief, which grounds the civil right to religious freedom. Analogously, citizens should also be free in other broader ranges of their social life. The right to religious freedom is thus linked with the full range of civil and political rights that are guaranteed by constitutional democracy and democratic self-government. In political life, the person "is fully citizen, that is, not merely subject to, but also participant in, the processes of government."[32] The Catholic community's engagement in struggles for human rights and democracy in the decades since the Council has been an effort to live out this insight.

The approach to religious freedom taken by the council also had important implications for the relation between juridical and legal institutions and the broader domain of the ethical or moral. Because the state is limited, its reach does not extend to the promotion of the full moral reality of the common good that should be achieved in society. The role of state action is limited to the most basic moral requirements of social life that both the council and Murray called public order. Public order includes genuinely moral values, including public peace, justice, and those standards of public morality on which consensus exists in society.[33] These minimal moral standards are the concern of the government. On the other hand, promotion of the fullness of virtue and the totality of the common good is the vocation of the Church, of families, and of the many educational and cultural bodies that form civil society. The state's moral role is more limited: the protection of the basic requirements of peace, justice, and human rights that make life in society possible at all. This is the basis on which the council affirmed that when public order is at stake, law may legitimately limit human freedom, including religious freedom.[34]

This specification of when legal restraint is called for shows why the Afrikaners mentioned in the example above could be legally prevented from continuing with their racially separatist practices despite the fact that they claimed these practices were required by their religious beliefs. Religious freedoms, like all human freedoms, are fundamental values, but they are not absolute. They are to be restricted only when and insofar as such restriction is necessary to secure peace and justice. Murray called this the principle of the "free society," which affirms that each human person "must be accorded as much freedom as possible, and that this freedom is not to be restricted unless and insofar as necessary."[35] Through his influence, this principle was enshrined in the Declaration on Religious Freedom. There the council declared, "The usages of society are to be the usages of freedom in their full range. These require that the freedom of the human person be respected as far as possible, and curtailed only when and insofar as necessary."[36]

Both the council and Murray were very much aware of the link of the right to religious freedom with the full range of other freedoms. It was certainly not an accident, therefore, that the development of Church teaching on religious freedom that occurred at the council stimulated new public engagement by the Church on the broader global agenda of social justice, including the promotion of democracy. Recent experience has also shown that the promotion of freedom for religious communities removes the sense of oppression that often leads these communities to feel that resorting to armed struggle is the only way to protect themselves and to bring their vision of society to the public realm. Protection of religious freedom is often a precondition for greater peace in society, both within countries and among them.[37] The council's commitment to religious freedom, therefore, enabled the Church to take new and creative action to influence the shape of public life. It made possible the movement of the Catholic community to greater engagement with issues of social justice and democratization, and helped deepen the Church's engagement in the promotion of peace.

The Catholic Church's strong engagement in the promotion of these broader issues of justice, democracy, and peace in the decades since Vatican II, of course, was not brought about solely by this new commitment to religious freedom. Additional factors surely include the council's encouragement of deeper pastoral engagement with poverty in the developing world, its suggestion that the dangers posed by nuclear weapons require "a completely fresh appraisal of war," and its new support for interreligious dialogue and cooperation.[38] Nevertheless, the development of the Church's understanding of religious freedom brought about at the council set the Catholic Church on a course that enabled it to make important contributions to justice and peace in society. It can be hoped that movement in this direction will be renewed in vigor in the years ahead. The world is in great need of such a contribution to religious freedom and to the justice and peace that is often linked with this freedom. By continuing on the path blazed by the Second Vatican Council, the Church can continue and, one hopes, deepen the council's contribution in the years ahead.

7

GLOBAL LESSONS FOR THE UNITED STATES

The right to religious freedom has long been a hallmark of culture and politics in the United States. Today it has become the focus of considerable controversy, with a few who regard themselves as progressive even stating that the country ought to move "beyond religious freedom."[1] This chapter will sketch some aspects of the disputes about religion in public life in the United States today. It will suggest how several crises involving religious freedom on the global stage can shed light on the approach needed in the United States. It concludes that greater dialogue and pursuit of the common good across the divisions generating conflict is essential to the continuing strength of religious freedom in the United States and to religious contributions to human rights globally.

CURRENT QUARRELS IN THE UNITED STATES

Religious freedom has long been a central American value. Commitment to it is enshrined in the first of the amendments to the US Constitution, which has led some to call religious liberty America's "first freedom." When the US Catholic bishops launched their campaign for religious freedom, they called it the county's "first, most cherished liberty."[2] The fact that the right to religious freedom appears in the first of the Constitution's amendments may not have been of set purpose. Nonetheless, Michael W. McConnell agrees it should be called America's first freedom because of its importance in the life of the country.[3] Following Brian Tierney, McConnell argues that religious freedom has played a key role of the advancement of democratic self-government because the institutional distinction between *sacerdotium et regnum*, church and state, is an important historical root of the limits on the power of government. The freedom of the Church from control by the state contributed to the freedom of the people to govern themselves democratically.

The late John T. Noonan did not hesitate to call the right to the free exercise of religion "an American invention."[4] Noonan also believed that this American invention had broad impact in other countries. It became a model gradually adopted by many societies around the world. Noonan borrowed a laudatory phrase from James Madison to characterize the role of religious freedom in the United States when he titled his book on the topic *The Lustre of Our Country*. Noonan's book both explores the American idea of religious freedom and sketches its global influence. Noonan also shows that at Vatican Council II the American idea helped the Catholic Church discover the compatibility of religious freedom with its own deeper tradition. As both historian and judge, Noonan knew that religious freedom is imperfectly safeguarded in the United States. He was also fully aware that the protection of religious freedom in a society as diverse as the United States is a social experiment not guaranteed to succeed. Nevertheless, Noonan believed that the experiment has made genuine progress. The pioneering American approach to religious freedom has been remarkably successful in the United States and has had positive effects in other lands as well.[5]

In the years since Noonan published his work, however, issues have arisen that lead some to question whether the American experiment in religious freedom will continue to succeed and whether other nations will find it attractive as some did in the past. Historically, the protection of religious freedom has helped the US deal with differences among its people in a peaceful way. Today, however, appeals to religious freedom have become central in the culture wars currently underway.[6] For example, the US Catholic bishops invoked religious freedom when they objected to the mandate to provide contraception to all women, which was covered by President Barack Obama's Affordable Care Act and health insurance plan.[7] Until the Obama administration found a way to accommodate their objection, the bishops opposed "Obamacare," despite their long-standing call to guarantee health insurance to all Americans. The contraception issue was also at the focus of the US Supreme Court's decision in *Burwell v. Hobby-Lobby* (2014).[8] This judgment held that closely held, privately owned companies could be exempt from the mandate to provide health insurance that covered providing contraception for their employees if the owners of those companies have religious objections to providing forms of contraception they see as possibly abortifacient. On July 8, 2020, in *Little Sisters of the Poor v. Pennsylvania* (2020), the court concluded that because the mandate was not written into the health care law passed by Congress but was an administrative regulation, the exceptions to it could also be determined by a decision of the administration.[9] Technically, therefore, the Little Sisters' victory in this case was not based on religious freedom but on the court's interpretation of administrative law. But because the Little Sisters had claimed exemption from the contraception mandate on religious freedom grounds, popular opinion will likely see the outcome as an implication of religious freedom.

The case has already intensified public controversy over the implications of religious freedom in US politics today. Similar controversy was generated in 2018 by the court's decision in *Masterpiece Cakeshop v. Colorado Civil Rights Commission* (2018) to protect on narrow legal grounds a baker's refusal for religious reasons to sell a wedding cake to two men planning to celebrate their same-sex marriage.[10] Though both the *Little Sisters of the Poor* and the *Masterpiece Cakeshop* decisions had quite narrow legal bases, the controversies they have generated have been broad-ranging and intense.

On the other hand, in the more recent case of *Bostock v. Clayton County, Georgia* (June 15, 2020), the court interpreted Title VII of the 1964 Civil Rights Act to mean that employment discrimination "based on homosexuality or transgender status necessarily entails [unlawful] discrimination based on sex."[11] Justice Neil Gorsuch's majority opinion in this case relied on his "textualist" approach to the interpretation of law. Gorsuch did not draw on the increasingly positive moral assessment of same-sex relationships or transsexual identity that many Americans have recently adopted, but on a reading of the literal meaning of the Civil Rights Act itself. Due to the narrow grounds of his judgment, Gorsuch predicted that some faith communities would make appeals to their right to religious freedom to justify forms of discrimination against gay or transgender persons. Justice Samuel Alito went further in a dissenting opinion on this case, suggesting that the decision will leave the federal judiciary mired in controversy for years to come.

The view that faith communities are exempt from laws banning discrimination in their employment decisions has been affirmed by court decisions concerning what has come to be called "ministerial exception." In both *Hosanna-Tabor Evangelical Lutheran Church and School v. Equal Opportunity Commission* (2012) and *Our Lady of Guadalupe School v. Morrissey-Berru* (July 8, 2020) the court ruled that the questions of who a religious community employs and whether their work should be regarded as a "ministry" should be decided by that community itself in light of its religious convictions.[12] In order to keep government from infringing upon a faith community's freedom to carry out its ministry, therefore, those with a ministerial function in a church are not covered by the nondiscrimination requirements that apply in secular decisions about employment. The scope of these rulings, of course, has remained disputed. In the *Lady of Guadalupe* case, for example, Agnes Morrissey-Berru, who was not a practicing Catholic and who lacked certification in catechetical training, was dismissed from her position based on the school's negative judgment of her teaching qualifications and performance. She claimed, however, that she was fired because of illegal discrimination based on her age. In a parallel case, *St. James School v. Biel*, Kristen Biel, who had previously had some difficulties with what the school called her "classroom management," was eventually dismissed when she informed the school that she had breast cancer and would need to stop teaching to undergo therapy. She saw this as a violation of her rights under the Americans with Disabilities Act. The US Supreme Court, however, ruled that both Morrissey-Berru and Biel fell under the norms granting their employers a "ministerial exception" to the legal prohibition of discrimination, especially because of the court's reluctance to become involved in settling internal Church disputes.

Thus, conflicts between religious freedom and the prevailing legal and cultural norms in the United States will continue into the future. These conflicts are likely to be particularly intense when they concern sex and reproduction, where cultural divisions run especially deep. For example, Archbishop José Gomez of Los Angeles, when he was president of the US Conference of Catholic Bishops (USCCB), denounced the *Bostock* decision that outlaws discrimination based on sexual orientation and transgender status. The archbishop called this decision "an injustice that will have implications in many areas of life."[13] Conservative Catholics and evangelicals in the United States had been counting on conservatively oriented judges like Gorsuch to use the law to reverse cultural trends on issues that include gay and transgender rights. Now they feel betrayed. In the words of Rod Dreher, cases like *Bostock* should make "the scales fall from the eyes of religious conservatives. We have been the Republican Party's useful idiots."[14] On the other hand, some with more progressive stances toward gay and transgender people fear that the traditionalist objections to the *Bostock* decision will stimulate efforts to appoint more judges who are conservative. Those who seek change will therefore continue to vigorously resist such appointments. Disputes about the intersection of religious freedom with matters of sexuality are likely to continue in animated and perhaps dangerous ways.[15]

The dangers are evident from the way such cases have led some opinion leaders in the United States to voice fears that religious freedom is becoming an enemy of the requirements of justice: justice in providing women what they need to protect their health and justice in enabling same-sex couples to live in accord with their sexual orientation. One critic asserted that "it's time to speak out against religious freedom. . . . For the ardent religious believer and the organized hierarchical religious organization, 'religious freedom' often refers to the right to restrict the freedoms of others, or to impose one's religion on the larger world."[16] Indeed, when the US House of Representatives banned discrimination based on sexual orientation in its 2019 Equality Act, it sought to prevent judgments like the one reached by the Supreme Court in *Masterpiece Bakeshop*. The act declared that no exception to its ban on discrimination against LGBT people could be made to protect religious freedom. With the same goal in view, just a few days after the Bostock decision banned exactly this kind of discrimination, Democratic members of the US Senate fell just three votes short of approving a version of the Equality Act. Similarly, when Rep. Beto O'Rourke was seeking the Democratic nomination to run for the US presidency in 2020, he called for the abolition of tax-exempt status to religious institutions that oppose same-sex marriage.[17] Both the provision in the Equality Act and O'Rourke's stance are clear signs of the cloud of suspicion that has fallen over claims to religious freedom in the United States today.

To make my own position clear, I do not agree with objections to the contraception mandate in the Affordable Care Act, and I oppose discrimination based on sexual orientation, as do nearly seven in ten Americans today, including religiously active Americans.[18] Nevertheless, I also think that some of the recent proposals to restrict religious freedom are both misguided and dangerous. We need to find an alternative approach that protects justice in women's health, justice regarding sexual orientation, justice for those who work in religiously affiliated institutions, and justice that simultaneously protects the religious beliefs and practices of those with whom one may disagree on these matters.

Douglas Laycock, a leading expert on religious freedom in the United States today, has highlighted the dangers of the current situation. Laycock notes that many of the controverted issues in the culture wars over religious freedom relate to sex. They have been brought on by changes in sexual ethics that are often called the sexual revolution. Laycock sees an analogy between the impact of the French Revolution of 1789 on the public role of religion in France and the possible impact of today's culture wars over sexual ethics on the public role of religion in the United States. In France, the Church sided with the ancien régime against the revolution, leading many to conclude that religion was and still is an opponent of freedom. This led in turn to a view of religious freedom that sees religion as a strictly private matter and to tight, even hostile, regulation of the exercise of religion in public. Thus, in the name of *laïcité*, French law today prohibits wearing any visible sign of religious affiliation in schools, such as the hijab some Muslim girls believe their faith requires. Laycock points out that in the United States, on the other hand, religious communities largely supported the American Revolution in 1776 and faith and freedom came to be seen as natural allies.[19] Laycock fears that the way the Catholic bishops and many evangelicals are dealing with issues of sexual ethics today is leading a growing number to see religion as an enemy of liberty. In Laycock's view, the outcome could be "to permanently turn much of the country against religious liberty—or at least to turn public opinion toward a very narrow, more French-like understanding of religious liberty."[20] There is a risk that efforts to restrict the free exercise of religion in public could lead to a privatized view of religious freedom that excludes all religious influence in public affairs. This could have quite negative consequences for both the religious and political life of the country.

More recently, however, Laycock was encouraged by the compromise written into the Respect for Marriage Act signed by President Joe Biden on December 13, 2022. This act supported both the legitimacy of same-sex marriage and the religious freedom of those who oppose same-sex marriage. Laycock argues that such compromise is needed for future protection of human rights on both sides of the debate. Nevertheless, Laycock does not seem very hopeful that this kind of compromise is likely in future cases.[21] Indeed, his pessimism is supported by the fact that the chair of the US Bishops Committee on Religious Liberty, Cardinal Timothy Dolan, declared that the Respect for Marriage Act "stacks the deck" against religious freedom and is "a new arrow in the quiver of those who wish to deny religious organizations' liberty to freely exercise their religious duties, strip them of their tax exemptions, or exclude them from full participation in the public arena."[22] Achieving the compromises urged by Laycock seems unlikely when major religious leaders take a stand like Cardinal Dolan's.

SOME GLOBAL LIGHT ON US CONTROVERSIES

The status of respect for religious freedom around the world today is also disturbing. The violence of some disputes that threaten religious freedom on the global scene is a warning to the United States of the dangers that arise in controversies over religious freedom. The resistance to pluralism evident in some of these global conflicts can shed light on the risks the US is facing today.

As noted in chapter 6, Brian Grim and Roger Finke have shown that in 2011 people were abused or displaced because of their religion in 86 percent of the world's counties.[23] Two of the most visible cases of religious persecution happening today are against Muslims: the attacks on the Rohingyas in Myanmar and the severe restrictions placed on the freedom of the Uighurs in the Xinjiang region of western China. In Myanmar (Burma), since August 2017 the Buddhist majority has driven over nine hundred thousand Muslim Rohingyas from their homes into neighboring Bangladesh. There is little likelihood that the Rohingyas will be able to return home in the near future.[24] A nationalist desire to maintain traditional Buddhist culture leads many Burmese to want the Rohingyas to leave. This nationalism is likely a stronger cause of the displacement than is Buddhism per se.[25] Nevertheless, persecution on religious grounds and the denial of the right to religious freedom is an important dimension of what is happening to the Rohingyas. Indeed, the persecution has been so severe that the International Court of Justice at The Hague has charged the government of Myanmar with genocide against the Rohingyas. The court will not reach a final judgment on the genocide charge for some time. It has, however, imposed emergency "provisional measures" on the government of Myanmar, ordering it to "take all measures within its power" to prevent its military or others from carrying out genocidal acts against the Rohingyas who are facing "real and imminent risk."[26]

Muslims also face severe persecution in the Xinjiang region of western China. The government of the People's Republic of China has interned a million or more Uighur people and other Turkic Muslims, supposedly because they pose terrorist threats to the security of the region and to the PRC more generally. Human rights agencies, however, report that the Uighurs have been detained for "reeducation" simply for practicing their Muslim faith.[27] In an extraordinary set of documents leaked from inside the Chinese government to the *New York Times,* President Xi Jinping is quoted as urging that the Uighurs be treated with "absolutely no mercy" in order to stamp out what he sees as the threat of Islamic extremism.[28] A group of twelve United Nations human rights experts, however, have insisted that the treatment of Muslims in China is "neither necessary nor proportionate."[29] It may "contribute to further radicalization of persons belonging to the targeted minorities, creating major and growing pockets of fear, resentment, and alienation." The *Times* also reports that in western China a half million Muslim children have been separated from their parents to "break the impact of the religious atmosphere on children at home."[30] Both the China scholar Adrian Zenz and the Associated Press have recently reported that the Chinese government is imposing a ruthless program of involuntary insertion of IUDs, compulsory abortion, and forced sterilization on Uighur women to limit the growth of the Muslim population in Xinjiang.[31] The confinement and mistreatment of so many

Uighurs and other Muslims is a sign of the tight restriction on the practice of all faith traditions in China today. Though the number of religious believers in China has grown significantly in recent years, so has government restriction of religion. A recent Freedom House report argues that under Xi the government increasingly uses both violent and nonviolent methods to curb the growth of religious communities and to restrict belief and practice.[32] Such developments in the world's most populous country do not bode well for religious freedom on the global stage.

Nor does the treatment of Christians around the globe. Though this is not well known by many Americans, Christians are persecuted and subjected to severe limitations on their religious freedom in many parts of the world today. The International Society for Human Rights, a secular agency, estimated that in 2009 Christians were the targets of 80 percent of the religious discrimination occurring in the world.[33] The Pew Research Center reports that between 2007 and 2014, Christians were harassed in more countries than any other religious group.[34] The German Catholic organization Aid to the Church in Need regularly provides updated information on the persecution of Christians around the world, and Pope Francis has recently endorsed the agency's work, which is available in its two biennial reports, "Religious Freedom in the World" and "Persecuted and Forgotten?"[35] Up-to-date information on the threats to Christians is provided by the US-based evangelical organization Open Doors, through its World Watch List of locations where such persecution is occurring and how it takes place.[36] Several very useful books also examine the scope and nature of the persecution of Christians.[37] These include John Allen's *The Global War on Christians*, Daniel Philpott and Timothy Shah's *Under Caesar's Sword: How Christians Respond to Persecution*, and Paul Marshall, Lela Gilbert, and Nina Shea's *Persecuted: The Global Assault on Christians*. All of these sources agree that Christians are facing assaults on their freedom in many parts of the world.

For example, Christians have suffered greatly due to the conflicts in the Middle East. The struggles in Iraq following the 2003 US invasion hit Christians in a very damaging way. The breakdown of the Iraqi state after the invasion enabled radical Islamicist groups to proliferate and to launch attacks on their ethnic and religious adversaries. Matthew Barber describes the grim effect on Iraqi Christians: "Attacks on Christians occurred across the entire breadth of the country, from Basra to Mosul. Christians were routinely terrorized with bombings of churches, targeted vandalism of Christian businesses, bomb and mortar attacks on Christian houses, and frequent instances of kidnapping and rape."[38] The result was that large numbers of Iraqi Christians were forced from their homes. At the time of the US invasion, there were

1.5 million Christians in Iraq. As ISIS gained strength, in 2014 the number of Christians in Iraq had declined to about 500,000, and more recently the number has fallen to between 100,000 and 300,000. The suffering of Iraqi Christians is further indicated by the fact that many of those still in their homeland were internally displaced to the Kurdish region of northern Iraq, and many who had fled to another country ended up in Syria, a country that was becoming similarly inhospitable to Christians. These severe threats have led Kent Hill to declare that Christians in the region are "on the brink of extinction."[39]

There have also been severe cases of religious persecution against Christians in a number of African countries. In Sudan, the long civil war between the Muslims of the north and the Christians and traditional African believers in the southern region, which is now the independent country of South Sudan, had religion as an important driving force. The desire to control South Sudan's oil and to wield straightforward political power were also factors in causing this conflict. Nevertheless, attacks by Muslims from the north on Christians in the south took over 2 million lives and created over 5 million displaced persons before the Comprehensive Peace Agreement of 2005 ended the conflict.[40] Since the independence of South Sudan in 2011, Christians in the north, including the 300,000 living in the capital, Khartoum, have faced arrest, detention, and deportation.[41] Though religion is not the sole source of Sudan's bloodshed and displacement, it has played a significant role in generating the tragedy that has caused deep suffering to the Christians there and to those holding traditional African religious beliefs as well.

There have also been significant threats against the freedom and wellbeing of Christians in other parts of Africa. In Nigeria, for example, Boko Haram, an ally of the radical Islamic State of Iraq and the Levant, has killed and kidnapped numerous Christians over the past two decades. Though Boko Haram's deadly activities have declined somewhat since their high point in 2014, the Global Terrorism Index ranked it the world's fourth-deadliest terrorist group in 2018 and the deadliest in sub-Saharan Africa. It has been responsible for 35,000 combat-related deaths since 2011, 18,000 of them from attacks that were clearly terroristic.[42] Christians have been Boko Haram's prime targets, though it has also attacked some Muslims who do not share its commitment to a radical interpretation of Islam. In northeast Nigeria, over two hundred Christian churches have been destroyed. Nigeria's National Emergency Management Agency estimates that the Boko Haram insurgency has created 200,000 refugees and 1.5 million internally displaced people. Most of the displaced have been Christians.[43] In the Middle Belt region of Nigeria, Christians also face violent persecution by Fulani herdsmen who follow a radicalized version of Islam. A Catholic-sponsored agency concerned with persecution of Christians, Church in Need, reports that Church leaders on the ground in Nigeria have seen a notable rise in attacks on Christians, both in the north, where Boko Haram is especially active, and in the Middle Belt region, where Fulani Muslims are present. Some advocates of human rights, including the right to religious freedom, argue that the attacks on Christians in Nigeria meet the legal definition of genocide. Others see the violence as a conflict between farmers and herders over resources, but with religious dimensions. The rising strife between Muslims and Christians is surely the result of a complex blend of religious animosity, ethnic rivalry, and the effects of climate change on the availability of the pastureland needed by herdsman.[44] De facto, Christians have suffered rising attacks on their freedom and well-being.

Paul Marshall argues that the persecution of Christians arises largely due to the Christian conviction that the church and state are two separate bodies. This belief leads Christians to object to the idea that the state should be the encompassing arbiter of all human life. This in turn leads Christians to support social pluralism. It thus generates tension between Christians and regimes that "have a monistic conception of the social order" and that see the state as the controlling authority over all of society.[45] Marshall thinks that this tension is the root of the persecution of Christians in authoritarian settings such as remaining Communist regimes like China, in nationalist states that seek to repress minorities, in countries where Muslims have exclusive access to political influence, in regimes that make state security politically preeminent, and in secularist regimes that simply want religion marginalized. The hostility to Christianity by regimes of these types arises from their desire to achieve social unity through the administrative power of the state. The use of state power to enforce a single system of values will lead to conflict between church and state because of the Christian conviction that the deepest values transcend the state. When it is true to itself, therefore, Christianity will stand opposed to regimes that aspire to enforce a single value system across the whole of society. Because there is a significant number of monistic or antipluralist regimes on the political scene today, Marshall thinks it is no accident that the political persecution of Christians is widespread.

WHAT THE UNITED STATES CAN LEARN FROM GLOBAL RELIGIOUS CONFLICTS

Marshall's view of what leads to persecution of Christians sheds light on an important matter the United States should remember as it grapples with the challenges it faces today concerning religious freedom within the US and also in the larger world. Both domestically and globally, denials of religious freedom often occur due to pursuit of a kind of social unity that is incompatible with respect for religious pluralism. The United States has a long historical record of respect for pluralism. Nevertheless, in some areas of American life today, especially where there has been rapid cultural change (such as regarding gender roles and sexual behavior), pluralism has become uncomfortable enough for some people that they seek to resist it with help from the state. Indeed, some religious leaders appeal to religious freedom in ways that go beyond protection of the right of their communities to practice their own beliefs, especially their beliefs regarding morality. They seem to want all of society to practice *their* beliefs.

In the case of *Zubik v. Burwell* (2016), for example, attorneys for the Little Sisters of the Poor appealed on religious freedom grounds to argue that because the sisters viewed contraception as contrary to their religious beliefs, they should not have to pay for it through the health insurance they provide to their employees.[46] The Little Sisters' attorneys went further, however, when they argued that the sisters' insurance company should not be permitted to provide independently funded coverage for contraception to employees who had no moral objection to it. In an amicus brief to the court on the case, Douglas Laycock argued that this seems to imply a religious liberty claim that the Little Sisters' insurance company should not be permitted to cover the costs of contraception for anyone at all.[47] To do so would extend the scope of the Little Sisters' conscientious claim to be religiously free to a claim that their convictions should control the behavior of everyone in society.

Similarly, some evangelical groups appeal to their right to religious freedom not only to protect themselves from all direct participation in gay marriages but also to argue that same-sex marriage should not be recognized in civil law for anyone. They seem to suggest that because they hold a religiously based conviction that same-sex marriage is morally unacceptable, no one should be permitted to engage in it. In her dissent to the court's majority opinion in *Little Sisters of the Poor v. Pennsylvania*, Justice Ruth Bader Ginsburg argued along these lines.[48] She insisted that while a religious person is surely entitled to have her religious rights protected, this does not mean she is entitled to insist that others conform their conduct to her beliefs. Such approaches would implicitly adopt the kind of antipluralist or "monist" stance that Marshall sees as leading to the persecution of Christianity on the global level. It not surprising that Laycock sees trends of this sort as endangering religious liberty in the US context.

To be sure, some moral convictions held by religious communities are appropriate norms for the behavior of everyone in society. Jews and Christians see the prohibition of murder as a moral requirement of their distinctive religious traditions. This does not mean, however, that only Jews and Christians can be required by civil law to avoid murder. In addition, Christians did not hesitate to invoke biblical narratives such as the Exodus story in the abolitionist and civil rights movements of the past. There are generally accepted secular warrants for universally binding prohibitions of murder, slavery, and racial discrimination. Due to evolving understandings of the moral dimensions of human sexuality, however, there is no agreement today on the moral unacceptability of contraception, gay marriage, or even abortion. Failure to recognize the reality of this moral pluralism could, if carried to the extreme, lead to a kind of authoritarian politics.

The question that arises, therefore, is when religious communities should respect not only the rights of those in other communities to hold different convictions about God but also to hold different understandings of the requirements of morality. The challenge raised by moral pluralism becomes particularly urgent when it intersects with the question of when government should get involved in enforcing moral standards. Many of the disputes about religious freedom today overlap with disputes about the relation between civil law and morality. Thus, reflection on the relation between freedom, civil law, and morality will help clarify some issues concerning the protection of religious freedom today. It will be useful to again consider how the Second Vatican Council's Declaration on Religious Freedom and the thought of John Courtney Murray can shed light on these disputes about religious freedom in the United States and on the global crises of religious persecution.

Early drafts of the Vatican II declaration based the right to religious freedom on the personal duty to follow one's conscience. In Murray's view, this conscience-based argument was certainly true, but it was an insufficient basis for understanding the scope and limits of the free exercise of religion when free exercise has consequences for public life that are morally objectionable to some in society. Addressing this matter requires clarifying the scope and limits of freedom of conscience. Vatican II, with Murray's help, addressed this challenge through a political argument about the limited power of the state.[49]

Theologically, the council argued that the spirit of the human person transcends all earthly relationships, including politics. This sets definite limits to the exercise of state power. The transcendence of the person and the freedom of the Church both imply that civil society is distinct from the state and should be free from absolute control by government. Paul Marshall has called regimes "monistic" if they seek social unity by bringing the whole of society under state control. Such regimes can also be called totalitarian because they put the state in charge of the totality of social life. Christianity opposes such regimes because of persons' relation to God, who far transcends the power of the state. These regimes should also be opposed in the name of religious freedom and of human rights more generally.

The approach of the council also has important implications for the relation between civil law and moral law. Following Thomas Aquinas, the council affirmed the importance of promoting the common good of society.[50] Aquinas, however, held that civil law should be suited to the condition of the people it governs. He realistically recognized that many people, perhaps the majority, are not fully virtuous. Thus, law should not try to coerce them to a level of virtue that exceeds their imperfect condition. In addition, Aquinas recognized that the law should be compatible with the customs of the people it governs. Though civil law can help promote the common good and can encourage people to become more virtuous, it should not coercively seek to forbid all vices or to implement the full common good. Its aim should be to prevent the most grievous vices and to promote those basic goods that support the maintenance of human society.[51] Work for the totality of the common good and the fullness of virtue is the vocation of the Church, of families, and of the many other bodies that form civil society. The state's role is limited to the basic moral requirements of social life that can be called public order. In the council's understanding, public order is itself a moral concept, not the false social unity that a repressive government might try to impose by keeping the lid on all dissenting opinion. Public order includes the important moral values of public peace, justice, and the standards of public morality on which consensus exists.[52]

The role of the state and civil law, therefore, includes the promotion of the very important but limited moral values of public peace and justice. Indeed, when public peace and the norms of justice require it, the state can legitimately limit human freedom, including religious freedom. Vatican II's great contribution regarding religious freedom was unambiguous affirmation that "all men are to be immune from coercion on the part of individuals or of social groups and of any human power, in such wise that no one is to be forced to act in a manner contrary to his own beliefs, whether privately or publicly, whether alone or in association with others."[53] This very passage from the council, however, concludes by saying that religious freedom must be exercised "within due limits." Religious freedom, like all human freedoms, is a fundamental value, but it is not an absolute one. Public order, understood as the moral requirements of public peace and basic justice, can legitimately set limits to the exercise of human freedom, including religious freedom.

The civil law, therefore, can legitimately seek to prevent murder, slavery, and discrimination based on racist values, or to protect the fundamental human rights of all in society. The right to religious freedom is affirmed along with the council's support for the full range of other human rights and freedoms. Thus, during the council Pope John XXIII had affirmed the Church's support for all the rights affirmed in the UN's Universal Declaration of Human Rights: both the civil and political rights that include freedom of religion, the social and economic rights to adequate nutrition, housing, education, and other basic needs.[54] In light of these developments, the council's breakthrough on religious freedom led to deep engagement by the Catholic community in the broader global effort to promote human rights, to support democracy, and to reduce poverty around the world.[55]

This surely means that church ministry should strongly support all people's right to practice their faith. The Christian community should be a vigorous advocate for the religious freedom of Christians throughout the world, of persecuted Muslims such as the Rohingyas in Myanmar and the Uighurs in western China, and of anyone else whose religious freedom is under attack. These global issues are also relevant to the culture wars surrounding religious freedom in the United States, including, for example, the conflicts over what public norms should govern gender roles in relation to marriage and whether health insurance should provide coverage for contraception or abortion. Insistence by the Catholic bishops or by evangelical leaders that others should follow Catholic or evangelical moral convictions on such matters will be appropriate only if they can make a cogent case that justice requires it. Only if insurance coverage of contraception or the freedom to form a same-sex partnership violate justice can it be persuasively argued that these practices should be limited by civil law. Some evangelicals and Catholics do in fact believe that forms of contraception, abortion, and same-sex relationships do threaten the justice required in social life. They hold that homosexual relationships, and especially the civil recognition of same-sex partnerships, threaten the family bonds that hold society together, that abortion is unjustified taking of innocent human life, and that some forms of contraception are abortifacient. However, a significant number of US citizens do not see same-sex relationships, contraception, or all abortions as violations of the justice and public morality required to hold society together.

Where does this lead us? One could argue, of course, that people are simply wrong when they support homosexual partnerships based on mutual love or when they sadly conclude that abortion can sometimes be justified in tragic circumstances. This appears to be the stance of some of those on the more conservative side of the culture war issues, when they insist that their positions should be enforced on everyone by civil law. On the other hand, some on the progressive side are saying something similar when they argue that religious freedom does not justify conscientious objection by Catholic hospitals to providing abortions or by counselors or cake bakers to providing their services to gay couples. Both sides of the culture wars seem to be adopting a kind of antipluralist view that calls on the state to enforce a monistic or single understanding of the values that should be allowed full public presence. This echoes the position that prevented the Catholic community from supporting religious freedom until Vatican II, namely, an insistence that "error has no rights." This is not the place to examine all of the theological and philosophical arguments for diverse moral positions on contraception, homosexuality, or abortion. The question that is urgent in the present context, however, is whether it is appropriate to use coercive restraint by the state when there is significant disagreement about such matters, especially when religious convictions are the source of some of these disagreements.

Murray's reflection on this issue can be of some help here. As noted earlier, in the mid-1960s Murray recommended to the archbishop of Boston that he not try to prevent changing civil law so that the sale of contraceptives would become legally permitted in the state of Massachusetts. Following Aquinas, Murray noted that civil law seeks the basic requirements of justice and *public* morality, not the full virtue of each citizen, including the virtues that govern behavior in private interactions such as friendships or personal relationships.[56] Though Murray acknowledged that the question of whether contraception was a matter of public or private morality was disputed among Catholics, he held that the view that it was private morality was persuasive.[57] Thus, civil law ought not seek to forbid its use.

Murray argued that this conclusion was reinforced not only by the fact that many people rejected the immorality of contraception but that some, including a number of religious leaders, saw it as morally required for responsible parenthood. Therefore, he argued against seeking to translate the official Catholic moral objection to contraception into a civilly enforced ban because many citizens, including many religious citizens and clergy, saw it as morally acceptable. He argued that "it is difficult to see how the state can forbid . . . a practice that numerous religious leaders approve as morally right.[58] In the face of the pluralism of moral and religious opinion on the issue, Murray held that civil law should not attempt to prevent all citizens from using contraceptives by continuing to prevent their sale and distribution. He took this position in 1965, well before the vast majority of US Catholics came to see contraception as morally acceptable.

The work of Murray and his influence at Vatican II over fifty years ago do not answer all questions concerning how we should deal with today's controversies about religious freedom in the United States and globally. However, the council did lead the Catholic Church to a transformative recognition that freedom is an essential element in the links between human beings and the truth about God and their life together in society. The council certainly understood that freedom might need to be limited in some social situations. However, Murray's great insight was about what he called the principle of the "free society."[59] This insight was affirmed in the Declaration on Religious Freedom of Vatican II, where the council declared, "The usages of society are to be the usages of freedom in their full range. These require that the freedom of the human person be respected as far as possible, and curtailed only when and insofar as necessary."[60]

This principle is relevant both to the culture wars surrounding religious freedom in the United States today and to the religious persecution taking place against the Rohingyas in Myanmar, against the Uighurs in western China, and against Christians in a number of countries. Social unity is a genuine moral value. But such unity grows in a humanly authentic way when it arises from human freedom. As the Vatican's International Theological Commission put the matter in its recent study of religious freedom, "Freedom to search for . . . the truth of God, and the passion for the brotherhood of men, always go together."[61] Only when requirements of the justice that holds society together are at stake should human freedom, including religious freedom, be limited.

The social unity in Myanmar and in China certainly do not require the creation of nearly a million Rohingya refugees or the internment of over a million Uighurs. Indeed, genuine social unity requires the restoration of freedom to these displaced and interned people. In the United States, Christians rightly pursue the common good and their shared well-being by strengthening relationships and families and by protecting human life. However, the bias of the free society is to pursue these goals by appealing to human freedom and by restricting freedom only when it is essential to do so. The question today is not whether the restriction of freedom is sometimes necessary but whether some of the efforts by the churches to obtain social unity through legal enforcement of traditional moral norms in the areas of sex and reproduction have themselves become threats to freedom, justice, and the common good. If this is the case, it suggests that a different approach to same-sex relationships and to provision of contraception or abortion through health insurance are called for. At the same time, respect for freedom implies that the conscientious convictions of those who oppose such changes should be protected so long as this can be done without imposing injustice on others.

The legal issues that arise in our pursuit of the right balance between individual freedom and the moral requirements of social life are complex. In the midst of this complexity, we should seek an appropriate balance between what the courts call a compelling state interest, which includes the requirements of justice, and the substantial burden that is placed on persons when their freedom is restricted. It will require wisdom and prudence on the part of the law and its agents. Such wisdom and prudence will also be required of believers and especially of Church leaders when others hold conscientious religious and moral convictions that differ from their own. Finding such a wise and prudent balance will be advanced by dialogue and public debate rather than immediate appeal to the coercive power of civil law. As I have suggested elsewhere, dialogue on the controverted questions of religious freedom could enable each side to gain new insights into the issues that cause so much controversy today.[62] It might even lead to the discovery of common ground among those on different sides of today's culture wars and toward a society that is both more peacefully united and in which people remain free to live in accord with their convictions.[63] The pursuit of a balance between the church's own rights, its respect for the rights of those with other convictions, and its contribution to the common good is central to the Christian vocation. As Cathleen Kaveny suggests, responding to this challenge calls Christians to both seek to discover what they owe others as a matter of civic friendship in a pluralistic society and also how to use their power in accord with the Golden Rule.[64]

Such a balance of benefits and burdens, along with dialogue about what is at stake, could help the United States remain faithful to the American invention of the free exercise of religion. It would also strengthen US efforts to contribute to the advancement of religious freedom across the globe. Even imperfect realizations of these goals would be significant achievements today.

PART III

ECONOMIC RIGHTS
AND EQUALITY

The Universal Declaration of Human Rights proclaims a set of rights that are called social and economic rights. These include rights to food, clothing, housing, medical care, and necessary social services. Indeed, pursuing these rights is a legal obligation for all countries who have ratified the UN Covenant of Social, Economic, and Cultural Rights. Since the drafting of the universal declaration there has been a dispute about whether human rights should be limited to civil and political rights, such as freedom of belief and freedom of speech, or should also include economic rights to goods like nutrition, housing, and employment. The universal declaration includes both, and a number of commentators argue that both sets of rights—civil/political and social/economic—are in fact interdependent and that one cannot attain one type of rights without the protection of the others. Others have recently argued that the human rights movement places such strong emphasis today on civil and political rights that it has lost its ability to address the poverty and economic inequality that so mars the global scene today. The Catholic tradition insists that the human rights movement must work vigorously to overcome poverty and reduce inequality. Indeed, the Catholic community viewed poverty, unemployment, and fair wages as human rights issues well before it came to affirm the civil rights of democratic governance and religious freedom. Of course, the Catholic stance toward the equality of rights has itself been evolving, a living reality. This part gives an overview of the development of the Catholic understanding of human equality as the basis of all human rights, including rights in the economic sphere, and that the implementation of these rights requires the efforts of multiple agents. These many agents include states themselves plus a wide range of nongovernmental organizations and international agencies. The multiplicity of agents needed to secure social and economic rights is particularly important in today's globalizing world.

8

EQUALITY, INEQUALITY, AND JUSTICE

This chapter presents some key aspects of the approach to equality and inequality in the Catholic tradition. These Catholic approaches, of course, have analogies in other Christian communities. The chapter is neither a full history nor a systematic overview of the Christian stance toward equality and inequality. Rather, it highlights several aspects on the issue of equality that are relevant to the promotion of human rights, particularly to several violations of human rights such as extreme poverty, slavery, and religious persecution.

The chapter has several parts. First, it sketches some of the inequalities in recent social life, particularly in the economic domain. Second, it presents some important theological and philosophical reasons why Christians affirm the basic equality of all persons. Third, it notes how the moral standard of justice can help specify when strict equality is required and when certain forms of inequality may be acceptable. Fourth, it addresses past Christian support for slavery and religious persecution, both of which are today recognized to be serious violations of equal human rights. Finally, it considers the question of how a religious tradition can change and develop; such development, in fact, enabled Christianity, especially Catholicism, to move from a stance of opposition to equal human rights and democratic equality to a position of leadership in the promotion of equal human rights and democracy today. This shift raises the question of what new developments in the stance of believers toward contemporary inequalities may be required. It is hoped that what is said here may suggest some helpful future directions.

INEQUALITY IN TODAY'S WORLD

Several forms of inequality mark our world today. Among these are the inequalities in the distribution of income and wealth. We cannot, of course, measure human well-being simply in dollars, euros, dinars, or convertible marks. Income and wealth are means, not ends. A pursuit of these means for their own sake can distort the quest for higher values, such as greater care for one's fellow humans, support for a sustainable environment, or the deepening of one's relation to God. Nevertheless, money very often helps people obtain goods that are valuable in themselves, such as health, longevity, and education. Today a lack of income or wealth prevents many people from attaining the health or education they need to live with basic human dignity. Inequalities in the distribution of income or wealth are among the sources of severe deprivation. Distorted distribution can impede the moral and spiritual growth of some it affects. It is useful, therefore, to begin our discussion of the inequalities that mar the world today with some facts about inequalities of income and wealth.

There was an encouraging decline in the worldwide number of poor people over the several decades leading up to 2020. Figures from the World Bank tell us that the number of extremely poor people—those living on less than $1.90 per day—declined from 1.87 billion in 1990 (35.3 percent of the world's population) to 769 million in 2013 (10.7 percent); the number continued to decline into 2019. This thirty-year decline can surely be considered progress.[1] It shows that attaining the UN's Sustainable Development Goal of ending extreme poverty in our time is a realistic hope. Nevertheless, recent pressures from the pandemic and the war in Ukraine have reversed this encouraging trend. As the World Bank reports, the pandemic led to a major setback. In 2020 the rate of extreme poverty rose to 9.3 percent, an increase from 8.4 percent in 2019. Seventy million additional people were pushed into extreme poverty by the end of 2020, increasing the world total to over 700 million. During the pandemic income losses of the world's poorest were twice as high as for the world's richest, and global inequality rose for the first time in decades. The very poorest also faced large setbacks in health and education.[2] Far too many people continue to face severe deprivation, and poverty is significantly greater in some regions of the world than in others. Severe poverty is greatest today in sub-Saharan Africa, where 389 million people, or 41.0 percent of the African population, are poor. This means there are more severely poor people in sub-Saharan Africa than in all other regions of the world combined, a significant change from 1990, when half of the world's poor were living in East Asia and the Pacific. Today only 9.3 percent of the global poor live in those regions.[3]

Inequality of income and wealth is one of the causes of continuing poverty. By conventional economic measurements, the inequality among all the people of the world, no matter where they live, has been declining.

EQUALITY, INEQUALITY, AND JUSTICE   121

However, several forms of inequality are moving in the opposite direction. The inequality *between* countries has been declining, while the inequality *within* many countries has been increasing, again by conventional measures.[4] For example, in 2016 the top 10 percent of earners in Europe took home 37 percent of Europe's total income; in China the top 10 percent of earners took 41 percent of the total income; in Russia, about 46 percent; in the United States and Canada, about 47 percent; in sub-Saharan Africa, Brazil, and India, around 55 percent. The Middle East is the world's most unequal region, where the top 10 percent of earners took home 61 percent of national income.

Not all is well in the United States and Canada. Since 1980 inequality has been increasing rapidly in North America, especially in the United States.[5] The US and Western Europe are on different tracks. In 1980, in both regions, the people in the top 1 percent income bracket took home about 10 percent of the total income of their countries. By 2016 the top 1 percent group in Western Europe had increased its share slightly, to 12 percent of the total, while in the United States the share of the top 1 percent had doubled, to 20 percent of the country's total income. In the same time period, the share of national income going to the bottom 50 percent in the United States declined from 20 to 13 percent. In addition, from recent data, Nobel Prize–winning economist Angus Deaton has concluded that an unexpectedly large number of people in the United States live in extreme poverty today. At the $1.90 per day used by the World Bank to measure extreme poverty, there are 3.2 million extremely poor persons in the United States and 3.3 million in all other high-income countries combined. If this measure of extreme poverty is adjusted to reflect the need for warm clothing and housing in the United States, Deaton estimated in 2018 that there were 5.3 million extremely poor people in the United States. The severity of their poverty accounts for the fact that in the US regions of the Mississippi Delta and Appalachia, life expectancy is lower than in Bangladesh and Vietnam.[6]

Whether one is poor is clearly influenced by race, class, and gender. Racial inequality has a significant impact on the well-being of Black people, both within the United States and in comparison to some parts of the developing world. Amartya Sen notes that Black Americans are notably poorer than white Americans. Black American men live to about age 67, while white men live to age 83; Black women survive to age 78, while their white sisters live to age 90. It is somewhat surprising to learn that both Black men and Black women in the United States have shorter lifespans than do all people in India's Kerala state, and Black men in the US do not live as long as their brothers in China.[7]

Class inequalities are also important. In the United States today, class, as measured by the level of education attained, influences survival in a significant way. Anne Case and Angus Deaton have shown that white US citizens with no more than a secondary education have declining life spans and increased mortality due to drug and alcohol abuse and suicide. Many of these people have given up hope because of the barriers to well-being their lack of education creates. They end up living in ways that cause them to succumb to what Case and Deaton call deaths of despair.[8]

Sen has also shown that gender inequalities have a significant influence on who is poor and even who survives. He vividly illustrates the inequalities between men and women through his discussion of "missing women," or those women who have perished because they are not treated equally to men, particularly as children. Drawing on biologically determinable predictions of male and female birth rates and on ordinary survival rates in regions where gender equality is present, Sen concludes that there are about 100 million fewer women alive on the earth today than would have been predicted in the absence of female disadvantages. These millions of women are "missing" chiefly because of the neglect of female nutrition and health, especially during childhood. In South Asia and East Asia, many young girls receive less food and less health care than their brothers, so their survival rates are lower and their lives are shorter.[9]

It could be argued, of course, that from a religious and ethical point of view the central concern in the economic sphere should be the well-being of each person, not inequality per se. Such well-being requires providing the basic needs, central freedoms, and supportive relationships, including relationship with God, that persons need to live with dignity. This might suggest that the issue of inequality is a distraction from the more basic task of overcoming poverty, oppression, isolation, or other conditions that make attaining more important values difficult. Indeed, it has occasionally been argued that concern with inequality is a sign that one has succumbed to the vice of envy.[10] Some data on recent economic trends, however, suggest that this worry is quite misdirected. A growing body of research shows that reducing inequalities and overcoming poverty go hand-in-hand. Reducing inequalities in income and wealth contributes to economic growth, helps reduce poverty, and enables more people to attain stronger education and fuller human development.[11] High inequality undermines sustained economic growth, which in turn makes it more difficult to reduce poverty. In addition, higher initial levels of inequality make it more difficult for poor people to share the benefits that economic growth can bring. A rising tide often does not raise all boats; the poor are frequently left out. Inequalities in income have particularly bad effects on the availability of goods such as education, health care, and social protection. Low levels of education, health care, and social protection are among the defining elements of poverty, and they prevent people from contributing to society in ways that both promote growth and enable people to share the benefits of growth. Thus, there can be a vicious circle in which inequality, poverty, and low growth are reinforcing phenomena.

These considerations lead us to consider the values that should shape our response to the inequalities of our world today. Religious traditions play an important role in shaping these values. We now turn to a consideration of the contributions Christianity can make to overcoming these inequalities.

BASIC EQUALITY IN CHRISTIAN TRADITION

The Christian tradition is strongly supportive of the equality of all persons. The first book of the Bible, Genesis, affirms that "God created humankind in his image, in the image of God he created them; male and female he created them" (Gen. 1:27). Thus, every human being possesses a sacredness and dignity that requires respect and social support. There are, of course, differences in human capacities and different levels of merit and achievement among people. But no person lacks the sacredness of being created in the image and likeness of God. Human beings have a worth that deserves to be treated with the kind of reverence shown to that which is holy. In the thirteenth century Thomas Aquinas expressed this biblical perspective in a way that has notable parallels to Immanuel Kant's eighteenth-century affirmation that persons are ends in themselves. Aquinas wrote that of all the creatures in the universe, only humans are "governed by divine providence for their own sakes."[12] Creation in the image of God confers on each person what can be called basic equality—a worth or dignity that demands equal respect despite secondary differences in talents or levels of achievement.[13] On the most basic or fundamental level, then, all persons are deserving of the respect and care required for them to live in accord with the dignity God has given them. Since God has given this worth to all persons equally, all persons are equal in this basic way, no matter what other differences may exist.

This basic equality is also supported by the Christian conviction that each person is called to an eternal destiny with God, a destiny that goes beyond historical and earthly realities and that has transcendent significance. The transcendent worth of persons as images of God is reinforced by this vocation to union with God, a union they can attain with the help of God's grace. Christianity also draws on the further belief that, despite failures and sin, God offers humans redemption and recreation in Christ.[14] The grace of redemption and recreation is offered to all because of God's love for all, and this love gives worth to all. It is not surprising, therefore, that the Second Vatican Council (1962–65) taught that a commitment to defend the equal human dignity of all persons flows from the gospel itself and from the heart of Christian faith.[15]

These explicitly religious bases for Christian support for basic equality are reinforced by the way many branches of Christianity also support equality by drawing on more secular, philosophical reflection. The Catholic tradition holds that human dignity can be recognized by all human beings and makes claims upon all, both Christian and non-Christian. This is in line with Catholicism's long-standing natural law–based conviction that ethical responsibilities can be grasped by human reason and by philosophical reflection on what it is to be human. Thus, in addition to its explicit theological grounding for human dignity, the Catholic tradition recognizes that there are secular warrants for its affirmation of human dignity and basic equality. The Second Vatican Council invoked the theological theme of creation in the image of God as the basis of dignity and also argued that this dignity can be seen in the transcendent power of the human mind. Through their intellects, human beings transcend the material universe. The mind's capacity for wisdom gives humans a worth that reflects the presence of God's wisdom within them. For the council, human dignity is also manifest in the capacity of the human conscience to search for moral truth and to adhere to it when it has been found.

The council called conscience the deepest core and sanctuary of a person and affirmed that obedience to conscience "is the very dignity of the human person."[16] The council further held that dignity is evident in the excellence of human liberty by stating that freedom is "an exceptional sign of the divine image within the human person." The dignity of freedom requires that persons act with free choice and that they seek to direct their freedom through knowledge of the true good. These three secular warrants for human dignity—the transcendence of the mind, the sacredness of conscience, and the excellence of liberty—are all aspects of the power of human reason, which is a prime manifestation of the likeness of humans to God. At the same time, because these human characteristics can be rationally discovered through reflection on experience, appreciation of human dignity has a certain autonomy from the explicitly religious beliefs of Christianity. This opens the way for Christians to work together with those who are not Christian in the effort to promote greater respect for equal human dignity.

EQUALITY, INEQUALITY, AND JUSTICE   125

Although all persons are equal on this most basic level, it is clear that not all persons can or should be treated identically in all domains of activity. Equal regard does not require identical treatment, whether equality is considered from a Christian theological or a secular philosophical point of view.[17] Therefore, we need to clarify when basic equality requires treating people the same way and when it calls for treating them differently. The question of when equal treatment is required and when differential treatment is acceptable is frequently a matter of justice. It will thus be helpful to consider what the norm of justice calls for in the Christian response to today's inequalities.

EQUALITY AND JUSTICE

Christian thinkers have long recognized that there is a close relation between equality and the moral standard of justice. Thomas Aquinas, for example, observed that justice "denotes a kind of equality."[18] Following Aristotle, Aquinas distinguished two types of equality. The first he called arithmetic equality, in which the shares of the good being distributed are numerically or arithmetically equal. Arithmetic equality exists when a pie is divided into identically sized pieces and each person at the table is given one slice. Aquinas does not hold that justice requires arithmetically equal shares for everyone in all areas of life, however.[19] For example, neither Aquinas nor most others in the Christian tradition would argue that justice requires that everybody's incomes should be the same amount. However, many do hold that this kind of strict arithmetic equality is required by justice in other spheres of life. For example, "one person, one vote" is a form of arithmetical equality that was strongly advocated by the Christians who resisted apartheid in South Africa and advocated that no one should be excluded from voting because of their race, ethnicity, or gender. Democratic societies hold that this kind of strict numerical equality among all citizens in their voting is necessary for political participation to be just.

Aquinas, again following Aristotle, called a second type of equality proportional. As Aquinas put it, there should be a proportion between the thing being distributed and the person to whom it is distributed.[20] In Aristotle's words, "the ratio between the shares will be the same as that between the persons. If the persons are not equal the shares will not be equal."[21] A maxim that illustrates this kind of proportional equality calls for "equal pay for equal work." The pay should correspond to the amount or difficulty of the labor undertaken. If one person works twice as many hours at the same job as another does, the first person's pay should be double that of the second, thus maintaining an equality in the proportion between wage and work for the two. Similarly, one could maintain that a person's share of some other good should be proportional to need. For example, Catholic social thought and a number of other ethical traditions hold that every person's access to basic health care should be proportionate to each person's need for such care, when society has the resources to meet these needs. Still other goods, such as praise for one's achievements or punishment for one's crimes, should be proportionate to what has actually been done.

The key question, of course, is which standards of proportionality should determine what justice requires in a particular situation. Michael Walzer argues that the criterion of proportionality will be different for different kinds of goods.[22] For a democracy, justice in the distribution of votes in the election of government officials should be governed by arithmetic equality, but sentences handed down in criminal court should be proportioned to the severity of the crime committed, not to the size of the payment the defendant is willing to offer the judge as a bribe. Justice in the courtroom should not be for sale. Similarly, although the wages paid to a worker should be proportional to the hours worked and the contribution made by the work done, the justice of income and wages cannot be measured solely by the agreement the worker has made to accept a certain wage. If a worker has no alternative but to accept the wage offered, the need to earn at least some income can lead to what Walzer calls an "exchange born of desperation."[23] Workers should not be driven by desperation to accept a wage so low that it does not enable them to live with basic human dignity. Similarly, justice in the distribution of health care ought to be proportional to need, not to the ability to pay. Health care is not simply a commodity to be bought and sold in the market; it can be a matter of life or death.[24] The question of what standard of proportionality should be invoked in determining what is just thus becomes very important. The standard of proportionality one relies on will determine whether one sees a given inequality as either just or unjust.

REGRETTABLE INEQUALITIES
IN CHRISTIAN TRADITION

Despite strong support for the basic equality of all persons, Christian tradition has sometimes supported inequalities that many see as objectionable today. Thus, we need humility in our approach to what basic equality requires. To illustrate this need, it will be useful to note several regrettable forms of inequality seen as legitimate in past periods of the Christian tradition that

EQUALITY, INEQUALITY, AND JUSTICE   127

are recognized to be unjust today. Some seminal writings of John T. Noonan, a distinguished historian of Christian and especially Catholic moral thought, provide useful reminders of past Christian support for inequalities that Christians now see as moral deviations.[25] Noonan indicates the nature of the problem by sketching how the Christian tradition has changed its moral teachings on several questions related to inequality, including on slavery and on the denial of religious freedom to non-Christians.

On slavery Noonan is blunt: "Once upon a time, certainly as late as 1860, the church taught that it was no sin for a Catholic to own another human being."[26] It was held that enslaved persons should be treated humanely and that manumission was good. However, from Saint Paul, through Saint Augustine, Henry de Bracton, and Juan de Lugo, down to the American bishop Francis Kenrick in 1841, many of the practices associated with chattel slavery went unchallenged by ecclesiastical authority. More recently, however, "all that has changed. . . . In the light of the teachings of modern popes and the Second Vatican Council on the dignity of the human person, it is morally unthinkable that one person be allowed to buy, sell, hypothecate, or lease another or dispose of that person's children." It should be noted that Pope John Paul II reiterated this condemnation of slavery, citing the Second Vatican Council. The pope, however, made no mention of the eighteen centuries during which slavery was tolerated, if not fully endorsed by the Church. The reality of slavery was seen as compatible with the creation of all in the image of God because the equality called for was judged to be a proportional equality. People could have their freedom limited in proportion to certain qualities, such as being members of "lesser races" with lesser capacities for freedom or having been legitimately defeated in war.

Equality of the proportional type was also invoked to justify limitations on religious freedom. One's right to religious freedom was seen as proportional to the truth of one's religious belief. In Noonan's words: "Once upon a time, no later than the time of St. Augustine, it was considered virtuous for bishops to invoke imperial force to compel heretics to return to the Church."[27] For a period of more than twelve hundred years, "the vast institutional apparatus of the Church was put at the service of detecting heretics, who, if they persevered in their heresy or relapsed into it, would be executed at the stake. Hand in glove, Church and State collaborated in the terror by which heretics were purged." As late as 1832, for example, Pope Gregory XVI declared that the right to freedom of conscience is an "insanity" (*dileramentum*).[28] Gradually, however, the religious wars in post-Reformation Europe and, definitively, the persecution of Jews, Christians, and others by fascist and communist regimes in the twentieth century led to a shift in this teaching.

Dramatic change on this issue is evident if one juxtaposes Gregory XVI's condemnation of freedom of conscience with the Second Vatican Council's declaration that "the right to religious freedom has its foundation in the very dignity of the human person, as this dignity is known through the revealed word of God and by reason itself."[29] Indeed, Vatican II linked its support for human rights with the very core of Christian faith when it declared that "by virtue of the gospel committed to it, the Church proclaims the rights of the human person."[30] The basic equality of all persons and the fact that freedom of belief is now seen as an essential dimension of human dignity, replace the idea that freedom should be proportionally distributed according to the truth of one's beliefs. Indeed, John Paul II saw religious freedom as the "foundation" of all human rights.[31] Regrettably, the fact that the Church had denied the fullness of the right to religious freedom through much of its history, in both solemn teaching and institutional practice, was passed over by the pope.

Noonan's account of these dramatic shifts provides a sobering perspective on aspects of the Christian understanding of the meaning of equality and equal human rights that we cannot accept today. The historical Christian responses to slavery and religious freedom call us to reflect on whether further shifts in our approach to the equality of rights may be called for today, both in Christianity and in other religious-moral traditions as well.

DEVELOPMENT OF THE TRADITION ON EQUALITY TODAY

These dramatic shifts raise the question of the possible scope and limits to legitimate change in Christian tradition regarding the equality of persons and their fundamental human rights. Noonan addresses this issue with the help of ideas he draws from John Henry Newman's influential *An Essay on the Development of Christian Doctrine*. For Newman, in a living tradition the process of "tradition-ing" is not simply a matter of citing and applying classic texts and authorities from the past, even though these texts and authorities must certainly be central in any tradition that expects to remain intact. Newman proposed "conservative action upon its past" as one of the criteria that distinguishes authentic developments of the Christian tradition from corruptions of it.[32] But he also held that a living tradition is marked by its power to assimilate ideas originally discovered elsewhere. In Newman's words, ideas about human existence "are not placed in a void, but in the crowded world, and make way for themselves by interpenetration, and develop by absorption."[33]

Thus, living traditions can learn what fidelity to their own identity requires not only by looking to texts and examples from the past but also by attending to new experiences and to the ideas learned from encounter with those who are different from themselves. It was in this way that Catholicism learned that its conviction that persons are created in God's image required the abolition of slavery and a new commitment to the religious freedom of all persons. New experiences and new encounters with other traditions helped Catholic thinkers recognize that the biblical and doctrinal belief that all persons possess an equal dignity as images of God meant that all persons must be granted full equality in all their fundamental rights. These new experiences and encounters led to the recognition that the gospel itself implies that persons have equal rights to religious freedom and rights not to be discriminated against because of religion, race, nationality, ethnicity, or gender. Equal dignity before God is thus seen to require equal human rights in social, political, and economic life.

The examples of slavery and of past limits on religious freedom show that religious communities and their traditions can have negative effects on basic human equality. Vatican II was well aware of the ways that faith communities, including Catholicism, have engaged in behavior that has led some to see religion as a threat to human well-being, including the equality of human rights needed to sustain such well-being. The council acknowledged that this behavior has led to a distorted picture of religion and indeed of God.[34]

Fortunately, public activity by religious communities also has achieved very positive results in the advancement of equality. Religious leaders such as Mohandas Gandhi, Martin Luther King, the Dalai Lama, Pope John Paul II, and Archbishop Desmond Tutu have played significant roles in the pursuit of peace, justice, and greater respect for human equality. Since we have taken note of some ways that Catholic Christianity has limited and threatened human equality in the past, it will be helpful to conclude by again highlighting some ways that the Christian tradition has made important contributions to the equal dignity of all persons in recent years.

The Catholic community's contributions to the protection of human rights and the promotion of democratic equality have been particularly notable. There is substantial evidence that the post–Vatican II Catholic Church has become one of the strongest worldwide forces for the protection of equal human dignity, human rights, and democracy.[35] Catholicism has played an important role in the global advancement of democracy since the council ended in 1965, beginning with work in Portugal and Spain in the late 1960s, in numerous countries in Latin America and the Philippines and South Korea in the 1970s and 1980s, and through the role played by the Church in Poland, which contributed to the collapse of the Soviet Union in the late 1980s and early 1990s. It can be argued, therefore, that since Vatican II the Roman Catholic Church has become highly effective in promoting basic equality, human rights, and democracy. Between the years 1972 and 2009, seventy-eight countries in the world experienced substantial democratization. Monica Duffy Toft, Daniel Philpott, and Timothy Shah have concluded that the Catholic community played a role in advancing democracy in thirty-six of the seventy-eight countries that made substantial democratic advances during this period and was a leader in the democratization of twenty-two of them.[36] Other religious communities also contributed to the advancement of democracy in some regions. Catholicism's contribution, however, was particularly strong.

The move of Catholicism from its more traditional alignment with authoritarian modes of political organization to support for democratic equality was certainly dramatic, perhaps even revolutionary. There is little doubt that the shift of the Catholic stance from a tendency to support authoritarian government to a quite unambiguous commitment to democracy can be attributed to the innovations of the Second Vatican Council, and especially to Vatican II's strong support for human rights, including the right to religious freedom. This shift was brought about by recognition of the dangers of authoritarian regimes, such as Nazism and Stalinism in the several decades before the council. These dangers threatened the Church's own freedom, so the deep Catholic tradition of commitment to the freedom of the Church itself led the bishops at Vatican II to recognize that the right to religious freedom was in continuity with important dimensions of Catholic tradition.[37] At the same time, the broad range of the violations of human dignity by Hitler and Stalin showed that more than the Church's own well-being and freedom was at stake. The experience of the multiple kinds of abuse by authoritarian rule led Pope John XXIII in his 1963 encyclical *Pacem in Terris* to strongly support equal human rights for all persons, including the equal right to religious freedom.[38] When Vatican II followed the lead expressed in *Pacem in Terris* with its endorsement of the full range of human rights articulated by the United Nations, the council moved the Church to the forefront of the struggle for equal human rights and democratic equality.

We can conclude here with a necessarily brief word on the Christian tradition's stance on the economic implications of basic equality. Once again: the Christian tradition does not hold that a flat arithmetic equality in income or wealth is required by the gospel. However, when inequalities lead to the severe deprivation of those at the bottom of the scale, both love of neighbor and a recognition of the common humanity of all requires challenging such

EQUALITY, INEQUALITY, AND JUSTICE   131

inequalities. The Second Vatican Council affirmed that God wants all people "to live together in one family" as brothers and sisters.[39] Both Christian revelation and secular reason indicate that persons are interdependent and can survive and thrive only with one another's assistance. Thus, we are called to a life that is shared with each another and not divided by inequalities that exclude many from the resources God has created for all. This interdependence is achieved in intimate communities like families, in larger communities like the nation, and globally in the human family as a whole. As Saint Paul teaches us, "From one single stock [God] . . . created the whole human race so that they could occupy the entire earth" (Acts 17:26). All men and women have a common origin; all have a common destiny; all are linked together in interdependence on our one earth. Inequalities that create deep divisions in the human community, leaving many millions desperately poor, go against both God's plan for humanity and the very meaning of our common humanity. Pope Francis has called such inequalities "the root of social ills."[40] He argues that addressing these ills will require a rejection of "the absolute autonomy of markets and financial speculation" and overcoming "the structural causes of inequality."

In light of these teachings and the long tradition on which they are based, the Christian community is challenged to work vigorously to overcome the economic inequalities that wound our world. When such work is effective, it will both help overcome poverty and strengthen the common good that should be shared among all. On the other hand, when divisions deepen and inequalities grow, the weakest members of society suffer most. In fact, many among the very poor have their lives cut short. Pope Francis is very blunt in the words he uses to describe the kind of economic life that is generating the inequalities that mark the world today: "Just as the commandment 'Thou shalt not kill' sets a clear limit in order to safeguard the value of human life, today we also have to say 'thou shalt not' to an economy of exclusion and inequality. Such an economy kills."[41] Indeed, Francis sees poverty as a sad result of inequalities that exclude far too many people from their rightful share in the goods God has created for the benefit of all.

In a similar way, the US Catholic Bishops see the exclusion of the poor as radically unjust. The bishops have written that "basic justice . . . *demands the establishment of minimum levels of participation in the life of the human community for all persons.*"[42] Negatively put, the US bishops see "the ultimate injustice" in activities that lead to a person or group being "treated actively or abandoned passively as if they were nonmembers of the human race." Inclusion based on equality, therefore, is a mark of justice in society, while exclusion due to inequality is an injustice that mars society deeply.

It is clear from this overview that the Christian tradition supports a strong commitment to the basic equality that requires respect for the dignity and human rights of all. It also calls for resistance to those forms of inequality that divide the human community such that some people are deprived of what is required for them to live with basic dignity. Basic human equality should override differences among persons when these differences prevent people from obtaining their most basic needs, restrict their freedoms without justification, or exclude them from essential social relationships. The Christian community has not always lived up to what the central thrust of its tradition requires, and the Christian tradition has not always affirmed what was later discovered to be essential to Christian life. The Christian tradition on equality and inequality remains a living tradition today. We can expect, therefore, that this tradition will continue to develop new insights into what equality requires.

9

CHALLENGES OF GLOBALIZATION

Many Agents of Justice

When the US Catholic bishops drafted their influential pastoral letter "Economic Justice for All" (EJA) in the mid-1980s, the situation of the developing world, especially for its poorest people, was very much on their minds. The chair of the drafting committee, the late Archbishop Rembert Weakland, had been abbot primate of the Benedictine order, a religious community with monasteries around the world. This role had given Weakland some firsthand experience of the economic challenges faced by people in all five continents. Bishop William Weigand, also a member of the drafting committee, had served as a pastor in Cali, Colombia, for nearly ten years and had a deep concern for the plight of the poor in Latin America. Another drafter, Bishop Peter Rosazza, had extensive engagement as a pastor in inner-city New Haven, Connecticut, exposing him to the economic forces pushing many poor men and women in Central America and the Caribbean to seek a better life by migrating to the United States.

Thus, is it not surprising that early in the drafting process the bishops decided to make the international economic links between the United States and the developing world one of the practical areas to be addressed by "Economic Justice for All," along with poverty and unemployment in the United States. Several of the hearings that were influential in shaping the document focused on these international links, with one hearing hosting economists from diverse parts of the developing world and another hosting bishops from South America and Central America. Though the pastoral letter's discussion of poverty and unemployment in the United States probably received most of the public discussion and debate during the drafting process, the letter's international emphases were equally important in the eyes of the drafting committee and perhaps more important in stimulating response by the global Catholic Church. The pastoral letter was published in German, French, Italian, Spanish, and Portuguese translations and was widely discussed abroad, especially in Europe and Latin America. It drew on the vigorous developments in Latin American theology that had stressed the Church's special duty to work with and for the poor.[1] It was a stimulus for similar efforts to address issues of economic justice and economic rights by episcopal religious leaders in England, Germany, and Australia, among other countries.

In his 2009 memoir Archbishop Weakland noted the strong stress on these international dimensions in "Economic Justice for All." When he listed topics not adequately treated in the document, however, the question of globalization topped the archbishop's list of lacunae.[2] In the early 2000s the phenomenon of globalization was seen as one of the most important signs of the times. In very recent years it has been argued that the COVID-19 pandemic and the Russian war in Ukraine have disrupted the international order, increased resistance to international interdependence, and intensified the rise of nationalism. Some have seen this as the decline or even the end of the phenomenon of globalization.[3] These developments shape international affairs in ways that can have harmful effects on both countries in the Global North and those in the Global South. Thus, the changing shape of the global order calls for a deepened understanding of the common good shared across borders. In particular we need to pay attention to how the common good and the closely linked notion of solidarity should shape the way we view the pursuit of justice and human rights in a globally interconnected world.

This chapter presents a four-part argument. First, a brief clarification of the meaning of *globalization* will be offered. Second, several key ideas about the links between the common good, solidarity, and justice developed in Catholic social thought that are relevant to the challenge of global interdependence will be outlined. Third, some suggestions will be offered on the many institutional agents that have a duty to respond to the demands of justice in the face of global interdependence. Finally, a brief reflection will be presented on how a solidarity-based understanding of justice can respond to some of the challenges of economic development that have arisen since the US bishops' pastoral letter on economic justice was written. These include the need to link aid for alleviating poverty with policies that promote good governance and peace-building. This reflection shows the need to attend to both the capacities and the limits of markets in the promotion of economic justice in the context of the global interaction that is occurring today.

THE MEANING OF GLOBALIZATION

The increasing interdependence of the human family that has been called globalization is subject to considerable intellectual and political controversy. In the midst of such controversies, and before deciding that globalization is ending, the term "globalization" needs to be defined. Some time ago Robert Keohane and Joseph Nye provided useful precision by defining globalization as "the increase in networks of interdependence among people at multicontinental distances."[4] This description points to the fact that globalization involves complex networks of interdependence, not single strands of interconnection. Global interdependence is occurring on multiple levels of social life: economic (including the diverse dimensions of trade, finance, investment, production, and consumption), technological (e.g., new forms of electronic communication), environmental (climate change), cultural (the spread of Western dress and music to other parts of the world and the increasing interest by Western students in the study of non-Western cultures), political (the rise in importance of intergovernmental organizations, both regionally, e.g., the European Union, and globally, e.g., the World Trade Organization [WTO]).[5]

These different dimensions of global integration have mixed consequences: some are good, some are bad, some helpful, some harmful. For example, the economic aspects of globalization in the first decades of the twenty-first century were accompanied by not only a decline in the global percentage of people living in extreme poverty but also a continuation of large numbers of extremely poor people. Figures from the World Bank indicate that the number of extremely poor people—those who live on $1.90 a day or less—fell from 1.9 billion in 1990 to about 656 million in 2018, the last year for official estimates.[6] This was surely progress. Indeed, more optimistic thinkers point to this decline in global poverty to argue that integration into global markets through trade and finance can lead to positive economic outcomes. This pro-global integration argument often invokes the example of the so-called East Asian tigers (Hong Kong, Taiwan, Singapore, and South Korea), which grew rapidly in the last decades of the twentieth century as they became linked to global markets. More recently, China and Vietnam are offered as similar examples of how domestic free markets and links to the global marketplace can lead to rapid development. The identification of globalization with such desirable outcomes can give the term a strongly positive meaning.

Global markets, however, have certainly not had uniform or sustained positive effects. Though the number of poor people in the world has declined since the early 1980s, it continues to include most people on the African continent. In 2015 more than half of the extremely poor were in Africa and by 2030 it is forecast that nearly nine in ten extremely poor people will live in sub-Saharan Africa.[7] The Structural Adjustment Programs of the International Monetary Fund (IMF) and the World Bank of the 1980s and early 1990s constrained economic decisions made by governments of developing countries through the conditions they set for obtaining loans, debt relief, and other forms of financial assistance. This approach, known as the "Washington consensus," invoked the East Asian model and called for a shrinking governmental role and increasing openness of markets domestically and internationally. In many African countries, however, this approach led to declining investment in education, health care, and social infrastructure such as roads. With less education and poorer health, the vulnerable segments of the population of these counties were less able to participate in markets, and the lack of infrastructure linking rural agricultural regions with urban and international markets meant they were left further behind. Though markets can generate growth, people who are illiterate, sick, or without the roads needed to participate in markets can be left out of the benefits altogether. As Pope John Paul II put it, "if not actually exploited, they are to a great extent marginalized; economic development takes place over their heads."[8] Thus, in some African countries the paradoxical result of integration into global markets was simultaneous growth both in GDP and in the number of poor people. In hindsight, several economists who had been highly placed within the World Bank wrote strong critiques of the policies followed by the major international financial institutions in the 1980s and early 1990s.[9] In their view, these policies have not alleviated and may even have contributed to inequality, poverty, and suffering in parts of the developing world. Since such developments are often identified with globalization, it is not surprising that in Africa the process has acquired a bad name.

In addition, since the outbreak of the COVID pandemic, the positive effects of greater global integration have declined significantly. The global spread of the COVID infection, combined with the effects of the war in Ukraine, has caused unprecedented economic reversals and increasing poverty. The World Bank estimated that these two crises would add 75 to 95 million people to the number living in extreme poverty in 2022, compared to the time just before the pandemic.[10] Interconnections among nations enabled COVID to spread rapidly and made many people vulnerable to the economic setbacks caused by the Ukraine war. Thus, it is not surprising that the pandemic and the war have caused declining support for global integration and the rise of nationalist sentiments.

These developments have led to some significant proposals on the need to address the continuing reality of poverty. The Sustainable Development Goals, which were adopted by the governments of all the member countries at the UN General Assembly in 2015, set targets that included eradicating extreme poverty for all people everywhere by 2030.[11] These goals have been subsequently taken up as policy objectives by both the World Bank and the IMF. It remains an open question, however, whether these goals will be reached, especially in the aftermath of the crises of very recent years.

CATHOLIC SOCIAL THOUGHT
AND GLOBAL INTEGRATION

This mixture of positive and negative outcomes led Pope John Paul II to state that "globalization, *a priori*, is neither good nor bad. It will be what people make of it."[12] What people make of it will in turn be determined by the values that guide their decisions on specific economic choices, policies, and institutions. John Paul was clear that these decisions should simultaneously "be at the service of the human person" and "serve solidarity and the common good."[13]

The link between service of the human person on the one hand and promotion of solidarity and the common good on the other hand is a central theme in Roman Catholic social thought. It played a major role in shaping the moral argument of "Economic Justice for All" and is central in the more recent teachings of the Holy See on economic issues, particularly in Pope Benedict XVI's *Caritas in veritate (Charity in Truth)* and in the teachings of Pope Francis. Clarifying this connection between human dignity and solidarity is important for the development of a normative, ethical approach to global integration.

We can begin by noting that human interdependence is a fact of life. We interact in a host of ways, with both those nearby and those at great distances. Ethical reflection on economic justice should begin by noting that some of these factual connections serve the human good, while others lead to human harms. In considering the impact of globalization, we need to pay careful attention to the quality of economic interdependence across borders. John Paul II distinguished the de facto interdependence that is inevitable in human life from a *moral* interdependence that respects the dignity of persons in a reciprocal way.

De facto interdependence can have negative or positive value from a moral point of view. Morally negative patterns of interdependence are marked by inequality and exclusion from resources necessary for the realization of human dignity. Such negative interdependence is evident between groups whose interactions are marred by domination or oppression or by conflict or war, or among those who are living under economic institutions that exclude some people from relationships that are prerequisite for decent lives. Morally positive interdependence, on the other hand, is marked by equality and reciprocity; those interacting show respect for each other's equal human dignity and relate to each other in ways that reciprocally support each other's dignity and freedom. Catholic social thought holds that morally positive forms of interdependence are based on respect for the equal dignity of persons and enable persons to share in the common good.[14] Such equal reciprocity, or reciprocal equality, can be called solidarity; this solidarity leads to forms of interdependence that are just. On the other hand, interconnections marked by inequalities that lead to the domination of one person or group by another or to the exclusion of some from active participation in the economic interactions are unjust. The injustice is due to the fact that such patterns of domination or exclusion undermine the dignity, freedom, agency, and rights of those who are in the subordinate positions or who are altogether excluded.

Therefore, if we adopt Nye and Keohane's definition of globalization as the increase in networks of interdependence among people at multicontinental distances, an ethical assessment of globalization becomes a question of determining whether the diverse strands in the network of interdependence are marked by equality and reciprocity or by inequalities that lead to domination and exclusion. Morally positive patterns of globalization exhibit a solidarity among participants that is based on reciprocal respect for their equal dignity. In John Paul's words, such patterns are marked by "a solidarity which will take up interdependence and transfer it to the moral plane."[15] Benedict has echoed John Paul's call to move factual interdependence in a moral direction by steering globalization toward forms of interaction based on "communion and the sharing of goods."[16] Benedict's rich theological concept of communion thus has direct ethical implications. It requires reciprocity in social relationships, and such reciprocity requires respect for the equal dignity of the partners to the relationship.

In the face of the differing aspects of global integration, therefore, one of the chief contributions of the Church's ministry today will be to support movement from patterns of global interdependence that are marked by inequality, domination, and oppression to patterns based on equality, reciprocity, and solidarity. This will be a ministry that continues to pursue what "Economic Justice for All" called "basic justice"—that form of justice that "*demands the establishment of minimum levels of participation in the life of the human community for all persons.*"[17] In negative terms, it will be a ministry that resists all forms

CHALLENGES OF GLOBALIZATION   139

of what "Economic Justice for All" called "the ultimate injustice"—activity in which "a person or group [is] treated actively or abandoned passively as if they were nonmembers of the human race." Inclusion and participation based on equality, therefore, are the fundamental marks of patterns of globalization that are just. These values should be shaping the social, economic, and political institutions of our globally interconnected world.

This is especially relevant to the assessment of the economic dimensions of globalization. For example, as the interconnections of global markets have had increasing impact on wider segments of the global population, one can ask whether these markets have benefited all in reciprocal and proportionally equal ways or whether some have benefited notably more than others. Some sub-Saharan African countries experienced economic growth not too long ago, in part due to the intensification of global trade and transnational investment. Nevertheless, poverty in sub-Saharan Africa has been increasing and remains unacceptably high. The interconnection of African countries with the developed world through trade and financial markets, therefore, has not addressed poverty in an adequate way. Nor are sub-Saharan African countries equal and reciprocal participants in shaping the policies of the institutions that significantly influence world trade and finance, such as the WTO and the IMF. This has been called "globalization's democratic deficit," and it continues today despite some increases in the voting power of developing countries at the World Bank.[18] In addition, though the current economic setbacks affect nearly all people in harmful ways, the effects have been more harmful in poor countries than in rich countries. The impact of the recent two crises are also internally unequal within developing countries. The poorest countries paid the biggest price and bore a disproportionate burden of the negative consequences. These unequal effects on poor nations and on the poorest within them cannot be considered just.

INSTITUTIONAL DIMENSIONS

This ethical perspective has institutional implications as well. In light of these unequal and nonreciprocal effects of the global marketplace, Catholic social thought continues to insist that though free markets can contribute to growth and thus the advancement of human well-being, markets alone are not enough to assure the attainment of justice in the global economic sphere. Neither the individualistic pursuit of self-interest, central to many models of free market capitalism, nor the subordination of personal initiative, characteristic of centrally planned economic systems, is ethically acceptable.

Freedom and solidarity are interconnected and mutually dependent. Justice requires the inclusion of those being excluded from the benefits of global markets and assistance to those negatively affected by these markets.

In some circumstances, therefore, markets will need social and political guidance. In light of the challenges raised today by poverty and by the current financial crisis, Benedict stressed the need for more effective institutional mechanisms to regulate markets. He began a 2010 address to the Pontifical Academy of Social Sciences by stating directly that "the worldwide financial breakdown has . . . shown the error of the assumption that the market is capable of regulating itself, apart from public intervention and the support of internalized moral standards."[19] The ethical requirements of the dignity of the person and of the common good must guide the decisions, policies, and institutions that shape global economic interaction if they are to be just. In particular, respect for the demands of human dignity and commitment to the common good together point to "the urgency of strengthening the governance procedures of the global economy, albeit with due respect for the principle of subsidiarity."[20] In other words, stronger structures of global governance that also respect the need for national and local initiatives are needed to secure justice.

This Catholic willingness to consider limits on the market is reinforced in the context of global markets by the conviction that the advancement of the global common good in an increasingly integrated world calls for stronger structures of transnational governance. Pope John XXIII's 1963 encyclical *Pacem in Terris* (*Peace on Earth*) drew a strong conclusion about the inadequacy of the international political institutions of his day. He wrote that these institutions were "unequal to the task of promoting the common good of all peoples."[21] In response, he called for a "public authority, having worldwide power and endowed with the proper means for the efficacious pursuit of its objective," namely, the worldwide common good. He gave particular endorsement to the United Nations.[22] Benedict went even farther in his encyclical *Caritas in veritate* when he wrote that "in the face of the unrelenting growth of global interdependence, there is a strongly felt need, even in the midst of a global recession, for a reform of the *United Nations Organization*, and likewise of *economic institutions and international finance*, so that the concept of the family of nations can acquire real teeth."[23]

John XXIII's call for a "public authority" capable of enforcing the global common good and Benedict's desire that such authority have "real teeth" suggests the Catholic Church is envisioning something like a world government that will oversee the dynamics of global interaction in the interest of justice, much as national governments have responsibility for the basic requirements

CHALLENGES OF GLOBALIZATION   141

of justice domestically. Both popes, of course, carefully qualified their discussion with a call for full respect for the principle of subsidiarity, that is, respect from national and local initiative.

The particular contribution of subsidiarity would be clearer, however, if these Catholic Church teachings gave more attention to the fact that today's global order is being shaped neither by nation-states alone nor by global organizations such as the UN. The dynamics of global interaction are increasingly the result of a complex network of institutions, some private and some public, and some national, some regional, and some global. For example, the extent of poverty in developing countries is affected by the actions of private entrepreneurs and by development and financial institutions such as the World Bank and the IMF. The extent of poverty is also shaped by the activities of regional agencies like the African and Inter-American Development Banks, by country-to-country bilateral assistance, by direct foreign investment or loans from private corporations and banks, and by the activities of numerous nongovernmental organizations dedicated to promoting development. We must note especially the activities of Church-related and other faith-based organizations, such as Caritas Internationalis and WorldVision, and of secular development agencies like Oxfam. Some of these agencies seek not only to provide development assistance but also to influence development-related policies of governmental and other private sector agencies.

The roles played by these diverse actors make it clear that individual nation-states and global political bodies like the UN are far from the only important actors with significant influence on development. Anne Marie Slaughter has noted that the global order that is emerging is composed of multiple networked agencies, some being parts of governments that are horizontally networked with their counterparts in other countries, some being governments that are vertically networked into global and regional intergovernmental organizations, and still others being private sector companies, nongovernmental organizations (NGOs), and faith-based organizations, all of which are linked in various ways with governmental and intergovernmental agencies.[24] In an earlier work I describe this picture of the emerging global scene as "a network of crisscrossing communities."[25]

This picture of global networks suggests that advancing the institutional framework for greater justice in our interconnected world will not simply be a matter of establishing a new worldwide layer of governmental authority whose mission is to control transnational economic actors from above. Despite their endorsement of the principle of subsidiarity, both John XXIII's and Benedict XVI's calls for a "public authority" with worldwide power and "real teeth" suggest that something like a world government is the precondition for greater justice today. While national sovereignty should be limited when it leads to injustices, the many different kinds of actors that comprise this global web today mean that the needed response will have to be made on multiple levels and by a variety of institutions. A more effective UN, though needed, will be but one institution that must contribute to more just global economic interaction based on equality and reciprocity. Other agencies that have key roles to play will include global and regional intergovernmental bodies such as the IMF, the World Bank, the European Union (EU), and the African Development Bank. Private sector corporations and banks will also play crucial roles, as will nongovernmental development agencies, certainly including the Catholic Church and its development arms such as Caritas and Catholic Relief Services (CRS).

Just as globalization is a thickening web of many strands of transborder interconnection, moral responsibility for economic justice falls on many diverse actors that are spinning this emerging web of interdependence. Respect for equality and reciprocity needs to occur throughout this growing multidimensional web of transnational connections. It will not be achieved solely by superimposing a new institutional layer of power or control above the level of the nation-state. Some brief concrete reflections can help illustrate this needed respect.

OVERCOMING POVERTY— SOME PRACTICAL REFLECTIONS

Addressing a complex, practical issue like global poverty today is necessarily a complex undertaking; if efforts are distorted through oversimplification, results could be counterproductive. With the hope of avoiding such distortion, let us conclude with just a few words about the general implications of the ethical position presented here for the challenge of overcoming poverty. These suggestions concern programs of aid and their relation to good governance and peacemaking. In addition, a brief suggestion is made regarding the challenges faced by governments, private corporations and banks, nongovernmental agencies, and the Catholic Church in their efforts to respond to the reality of poverty in our world.

The US bishops' pastoral letter "Economic Justice for All" strongly advocated the importance of assistance for the poor of the developing world. It saw such assistance as a way to live out the option for the poor that is close to the heart of the gospel, which should be "the central priority for policy choices" in our interdependent world.[26] The bishops noted that although the

United Sates had been a leader in development assistance in the years following World War II, more recently the United Sates has been contributing a smaller percentage of its GNP to development assistance than almost all other industrialized countries in the Organization of Economic Cooperation and Development. The bishops saw this as "a grave distortion of the priority [that] development assistance should command."[27]

There are voices in the contemporary discussion of efforts to overcome the poverty of the developing world today that continue to support the pastoral letter's call for aid as an effective way to address global poverty. For example, Jeffrey Sachs, who has advised the secretary-general of the United Nations on the implementation of its Sustainable Development Goals, strongly supports increased aid from rich countries.[28] In 2002, heads of state from the world's nations gathered at Monterrey, Mexico, for a UN conference on financing development. A consensus was reached that developed countries should continue to set 0.7 percent of GNP as their target for development aid to poor countries.[29] Implementing this consensus today would demand a considerable increase in aid funds contributed by the United States.

In recent years, however, the effectiveness of aid as a remedy for poverty has been challenged by some analysts. William Easterly, formerly of the World Bank, has argued that all of the grand development schemes of recent decades have failed, including those advocated by Sachs.[30] A provocative challenge came from Dambisa Moyo, a Zambian woman who is a Harvard- and Oxford-trained economist and who worked at Goldman Sachs for eight years. Moyo's provocative thesis was that, at least in Africa, aid has not only failed to alleviate poverty but has actually made poverty worse. In her words, "the problem is that aid is not benign—it is malignant. No longer part of the potential solution, it is part of the problem—in fact aid *is* the problem."[31] Moyo argues that aid creates a cycle of corruption by giving corrupt leaders resources they need to say in power, which leads to continuing poverty and, in turn, the need for further aid. Because aid puts large pots of money at the disposal of the government in power, it also increases the incentive to use violent force to keep power or, if one is out of power, to seize it, thus making civil war more likely. Aid also removes incentives for creative initiatives that might enhance development through increased investment and trade. Moyo proposes that to overcome poverty through development in Africa, aid should be replaced by market-based initiatives such as trade, enhanced foreign direct investment, and support for micro-finance that enables the poor to participate in the market.[32]

Moyo's analysis contains some elements of truth. For example, there is no doubt that corruption is a major obstacle to development in many of the world's poorest countries, especially in Africa, that this corruption has been linked with civil conflict in some countries, and that such conflict only deepens poverty. For example, Kenya's former anticorruption minister, John Githongo, faced threats to his life when he challenged the deep divisions in society which were rooted in economic differences between ethnic groups and that led to governmental corruption and to tribal conflicts like the postelection violence that took place in Kenya in 2007.[33] However, Moyo's analysis overlooks the failure of the market-oriented structural adjustment programs instituted by the World Bank and the IMF during the 1980s and early 1990s. Also Moyo seems overly confident that, in the face of the present global financial crisis, African countries will be increasingly attractive sites for direct foreign investment and will be able to enter into global trade markets if incentives to do so are increased by the abolition of aid. Indeed, Moyo's teacher at Oxford, Paul Collier, counters that in recent years, "aid agencies look to be more important as sources of finance for investment than at any time in the past two decades."[34]

Moyo also fails to credit adequately the way that aid that was aimed at alleviating the effects of HIV/AIDS played an important positive role in African countries such as her own Zambia.[35] Without such aid, more people would have fallen victim to AIDS and been made unable to contribute to any form of economic advancement. The same can be said of aid that effectively targets other health needs and that supports effective educational programs among the poor. People who are sick or illiterate are unlikely to be able to participate in markets in ways that advance development. They will simply be left out of whatever growth and development occurs. If the sick and illiterate are a sizable part of the population, as in many sub-Saharan countries, programs that directly address health and education are needed. Aid programs that address these needs effectively remain crucial.

Nevertheless, government-to-government bilateral aid is not the only necessity for alleviating poverty in developing countries, including those in sub-Saharan Africa. The political and economic situations in those countries have aspects that cannot be effectively changed through bilateral aid programs alone. International pressure to confront corruption and move toward good governance has rightly become a central concern of the World Bank and the IMF.[36] Good governance, of course, is not guaranteed by holding multiparty elections. When a large percentage of the population of a developing country is poor and illiterate, the manipulation of elections through patronage and the distortion of information is relatively easy. Under such conditions, free elections do not guarantee accountable government. And such lack of accountability enables a government to use its power to serve the economic interests of its leaders rather than of the poor majority. Thus, development and overcoming poverty requires actions by donor countries and the larger international community that reinforce genuine political accountability. Without such accountability, aid is not likely to benefit the people it aims to help. Private agencies like Oxfam are also concerned that their development initiatives are "owned" and controlled by the people they aim to assist.[37] Involving greater numbers of poor people in the marketplace can be supported through microloans by groups as diverse as the Grameen Bank and Catholic Relief Services.[38]

Aid, both public and private, therefore should aim to increase the participation of the poor in the economic and political life of the society being assisted. In countries where corruption is widespread, this means placing conditions on aid to prevent it from ending up in the pockets of the ruling elite. Through such conditions, donor countries and the larger international community will be able to exert a combination of political and economic pressure to make governments more transparent and more accountable. For example, corruption in Kenya, vividly revealed by what many believe to have been the stealing of the December 2007 elections, continues to impede that country's development. The United States and the World Bank have both been exerting considerable political and economic pressure on the Kenyan government to clean up its act and they should continue to do so.[39]

The Kenyan case also indicates why working to prevent internal conflicts and civil war must become a central goal in any development strategy. Following the 2007 Kenyan elections, violent conflicts along ethnic and class lines broke out in numerous parts of the country. These conflicts were rooted in the strong sense among some ethnic communities, particularly the Luos, that other ethnic groups, particularly the Kikuyus, had been using their control of political power to their own economic advantage. The basis of ethnic tensions in Kenya is far from simple, but the post-2007 election violence in Kenya is a clear indicator of how civil conflict and lack of development can be closely linked in poor nations.[40] Work for development in such contexts can thus require political and diplomatic efforts to address the roots of conflict in order to prevent it.

Private corporations and banks conducting business in developing countries also have a responsibility to take steps to assure that their activities do not deepen corruption or enhance the wealth and power of elites in ways that are harmful and unjust to the poor majority. The UN Global Compact, initiated by Secretary-General Kofi Annan in 2000, affirmed that private corporations, as the primary agents driving globalization, should themselves support human rights and oppose corruption. When corporations do this, they "can help ensure that markets, commerce, technology and finance advance in ways that benefit economies and societies everywhere."[41] Though the implementation of this compact has been far from adequate, it signals that the responsibility to address the economic impact of globalization on the poor falls on both corporations and governments.

Development policy today thus needs to address issues ranging from the strictly economic (such as GNP growth, increased investment, and access to credit) to the political (such as good governance, the prevention of war, and access to health care and education among poor people). Pursuing desired outcomes in these areas will require the engagement of many different actors: governments (through bilateral assistance and governmental funding of private initiatives); intergovernmental organizations (through the activities pursued by agencies such as the World Bank, the UN Development Program, and the Inter-American Development Bank); private commercial and financial corporations; and nongovernmental and faith-based organizations (such as Oxfam and CRS).

The challenge of alleviating poverty in the developing world today can be envisioned as calling a variety of actors, private and public, to make diverse contributions to the overall development project, including governmental grants and loans, investments that avoid exploitation, and projects by both secular and church-based development NGOs. This can lead to envisioning the development challenge as a sort of matrix or grid, where the rows are the health, educational, financial, investment, credit, political, and other needs of particular developing societies, and the columns are the actors that can help respond to these needs. Promoting development that alleviates poverty, therefore, will call for each set of needs to be addressed by one or more of the relevant actors. No one actor can address every need; rather, each actor will have specific responsibilities to contribute in responding to the needs.

In line with what has been suggested here regarding multiple strands of globalization, seeking justice for the poor in our globalizing world raises challenges not only for governments and intergovernmental bodies but also for all actors who benefit from or affect the way global activity impacts the poor. That includes virtually every one of us. The responsibilities we have to help raise up the poor depends on our capacity and power to do so. Acting on such responsibility, we should seek to promote greater equality and reciprocity and reduce conditions of inequality and domination. Since the challenge of alleviating poverty is clearly a complex one, responding to it will call for thoughtful responses from the numerous partnerships that exist among private, governmental, and intergovernmental bodies. It also will call for many individuals who are dedicated to exercising leadership for greater global justice.

PART IV

THE RIGHTS OF REFUGEES AND MIGRANTS

The movement of people across national borders is one of the principal political and moral challenges of our time. The number of people who have been forcibly driven from their homes has reached a record high: over 100 million in 2022. The number who migrate voluntarily is also very high. It is estimated that in 2020 over 280 million people were living outside the country of their birth, a number that is three times higher than the number in 1970. Refugees are fleeing from their home countries because of the dangers of violence, persecution, and war. People officially regarded as voluntary migrants are often driven from their homes due to severe poverty. Environmental degradation and climate change are increasingly found among the major causes of migration. These mass movements have been resisted by many citizens in the receiving countries. Both refugees and migrants are sometimes seen as endangering the cultural values of the people whose homeland they have entered. They can also be regarded as threats to the economic well-being and even of the security of the native-born. The Universal Declaration of Human Rights asserts that refugees fleeing persecution have a right to seek asylum in other countries. The fact that a minimum level of economic well-being is seen as a right suggests that those in extreme poverty should be received by countries that are able to help meet their basic needs. The Catholic Church is a transnational community with a strong official commitment to protecting the rights and well-being of refugees and other migrants. Pope Francis has become perhaps the strongest international voice speaking out on behalf of those on the move. At the same time, the Catholic tradition recognizes the importance of national borders for protecting people against unjust domination by other nations. Thus, securing the rights of refugees and migrants requires first determining when the well-being of those on the move takes priority and when the protection of national borders does so. This part takes stock of such priorities. It sketches how Pope Francis and the US bishops have shown strong leadership in calling for the realization of such priorities, how the US Catholic Church membership has been rather slow to follow this leadership, and what might be done to improve the situation.

10

BORDERS AND THE RIGHTS
OF THE DISPLACED

The international refugee protection system is severely challenged today. In recent decades the forced movement of refugees and internally displaced persons has been rising markedly, reaching an extraordinarily high level today. In mid-2022 the number had reached 100 million, more than at any time since World War II. This equals one in every seventy-eight people on earth.[1] Despite the efforts and achievements of many governments and many humanitarian organizations, the protection of displaced persons from the harms they routinely suffer remains a distant goal. Many analysts believe that the conditions faced by forced migrants today have brought the refugee regime to a turning point. UN Secretary General António Guterres has called the situation a "grim indictment of our times" that calls humanity to "stand together in solidarity."[2] The regime that has been in place since the adoption of the 1951 Convention Relating to the Status of Refugees needs to be reexamined. The challenge in developing more adequate ways of protecting the humanity of those threatened by displacement is in part a moral one. It is a matter of their human rights. These moral and human rights challenges, of course, are deeply embedded in the political, military, economic, environmental, and other conditions that drive people from home. Examining the ethical issues, therefore, requires paying close attention to these social conditions. This chapter focuses on some of the moral duties that are especially important in the effort to change these conditions in ways that lead to a more effective refugee regime.

The first part of the chapter addresses the significance that borders separating national communities and the sovereignty of states present for our moral duties toward displaced people. Do people's rights reach beyond the borders of diverse peoples and sovereign states? If so, do these rights imply that those in other countries have a duty to those who are compelled to flee their homes? How do these duties relate to the responsibilities people have to citizens of their own countries? I argue that there are duties *both* to fellow citizens *and* to displaced persons, especially to those who have no other protection than what is provided by humanitarian assistance, asylum, or both. The second part of the chapter suggests that since we have duties both to fellow citizens and to immigrants from other countries who are facing the crisis of forced displacement, we need to clarify priorities among these types of duty in various circumstances. Such priorities are developed in light of several *negative* duties (e.g., to not treat people in ways that cause displacement in the first place) and several *positive* duties (e.g., to take action when forced migration has already occurred). Acting in accord with both of these priorities helps create a more adequate refugee protection system, a system that enables better fulfillment of our duties to the displaced.

NATION-STATES AND DUTIES BEYOND BORDERS

In the face of the growing number of refugees and other forced migrants and the degree of their suffering in recent years, some analysts have been calling for a radical rethinking of the relevance of national borders for the ethical responsibilities toward displaced persons. Secular political philosophers such as Joseph Carens and refugee scholars like Philip Marfleet argued some years ago that the time may have come to consider making borders fully open to all who are fleeing from persecution, conflict, or disaster.[3] In a similar spirit, philosopher Martha Nussbaum argued that a cosmopolitan community of all human beings has primacy over narrower communities defined in terms of nationality, ethnicity, or religion. Indeed, she called nationality a "morally irrelevant" characteristic of personhood, a position that amounted to an ethical call for open borders.[4]

Such a universalist cosmopolitan ethic echoes the first of the principles that guide the actions of the International Committee of the Red Cross (ICRC) and that is usually taken as a foundation of the humanitarian movement, namely, the principle of "humanity."[5] The chief author of the ICRC's principles, Jean Pictet, notes that in this principle the term "humanity" refers to the whole of humankind and all its members.[6] Concern for humanity, therefore, is concern for *all* members of the human race and the conditions that *all* are facing. To act in accord with humanity is to act with inclusive concern toward all men and women. The principle of humanity thus leads to another of the ICRC's standards: impartiality. To act with humanity is to respond impartially to all members of the human family on the basis of their need, not because of some characteristic that differentiates them from others, such as their citizenship, nationality, race, religion, class, or political opinion.

The universality of the ICRC's principle of humanity is also a characteristic of the normative basis of the modern human rights movement. Human rights are rooted in the universal and equal dignity of all human beings. The preamble of the 1948 Universal Declaration of Human Rights directly links recognition of the "inherent dignity" of all persons with protection of "the equal and inalienable rights of all members of the human family."[7] The commitment of the human rights movement to the dignity of all persons, not just those belonging to particular nations, religions, or ethnicities, is evident from the fact that the UN titled its 1948 statement of human rights a *universal* declaration.

Drawing on the normative standards of both the humanitarian and human rights movements, we can affirm that *all* persons deserve *equal* protection from grave threats to their worth as persons. This is evident in the way terms such as "all," "everyone," and "no one" are used throughout the Universal Declaration of Human Rights. The declaration states that all persons possess human rights without distinction based on "race, color, sex, language, religion, political or other opinion, national or social origin."[8] This relativizes all in-group/out-group boundaries. It challenges understandings of religious, national, and cultural identity that might limit respect only to those people belonging to a particular community. The human rights ethos thus seeks to tear down the walls that divide people into those who count and those who do not count, at least when the most basic requirements of humanity are at stake. No white rule over nonwhite, no Aryan over Jew, no European colonist over non-European colonized, no male over female. Though religious convictions are deeply important to those who hold them, such convictions must never be used to deny the humanity or human rights of others in the name of God. Ethnic and national identities are never legitimate grounds for excluding people from the most basic requirements of their human dignity. Respect for human dignity also requires fulfilling the social and economic rights of all people to adequate food, work, education, and health care, and for the solidarity across economic differences required to fulfill these rights.[9]

This cosmopolitan vision is rooted in a commitment to human dignity that can be supported by secular philosophical argument. Pictet affirmed that the ICRC's principle of humanity requires that "everyone shall be treated as a human being and not as an object, as an end in himself and not as a mere means to an end."[10] This language echoes a major philosophical understanding of human worth or human dignity, namely, that of Immanuel Kant. The core principle of Kant's moral philosophy is that persons are always to be treated as ends in themselves, never simply as means.[11] All persons possess this dignity. Thus, Kant was led to adopt a cosmopolitan morality that sees some important political responsibilities reaching across national borders.

This cosmopolitan orientation can also be supported on religious grounds. Both Judaism and Christianity hold that all persons are brothers and sisters in a single human family no matter what their nationality or ethnicity. Every person has been created in the image and likeness of God.[12] This common creation gives every person a shared dignity and worth that reaches across all boundaries that are humanly constructed, such as the borders between nation-states. These borders are in no way absolute and must be seen as subordinate to the respect due to the shared dignity of every person as an image of God. Pope Francis drew on this biblical vision during his visit to the Greek island of Lesbos, where he assured Syrian refugees seeking entrance into Europe that "God created mankind to be one family"; he called all of Europe to "build bridges" rather than "putting up walls."[13] Such sensitivity to the needs of migrants and refugees is present not only in Christianity but also in Judaism and Islam. Each of the great monotheistic traditions of Judaism, Christianity, and Islam traces its origins back to the Patriarch Abraham, who was himself a migrant from the home of his kinsfolk to the land of Canaan. The identity of Jews is also importantly shaped by the story of the Exodus—a migration from slavery in Egypt to freedom in the land of God's promise. The New Testament portrays Jesus as the leader of a new Israel, who just after His birth had to flee persecution as a refugee to Egypt in the arms of Mary and Joseph. Muslims measure time from the founding event of Muhammad's *hijra,* or migration, from Mecca to Medina.

The founding of each of these major faiths has migration across borders as one of its key elements, which is one of the reasons each of these faith communities sees its religious and ethical commitments as reaching across borders. The great Asian religions also insist that ethical duties do not stop at national or religious boundaries, particularly when refugees and migrants are in danger.[14] A similar sense of universal responsibility can be found in African traditions, where concepts such as *bumuntu* (humanness), *umoja* (unity), and *ujamaa* (solidarity) point to the interconnectedness of all persons.[15] There is little doubt, of course, that religious communities can fall into in-group versus out-group conflicts that are among the causes of forced migration. Nevertheless, most religious traditions possess a strong normative conviction that ethical responsibility reaches across all religious and national boundaries and that moral virtue calls for assistance to people in distress, including strangers, migrants, and refugees.

BORDERS AND THE RIGHTS OF THE DISPLACED 153

Pope John XXIII appealed to this normative universalism in his 1963 encyclical *Pacem in Terris,* which drew on both Christian religious warrants and secular philosophical arguments to affirm that national boundaries do not limit the reach of moral duty. Indeed, John XXIII explicitly argued that citizenship itself is not limited by national boundaries but has an authentically global meaning. In his words, "the fact that one is a citizen of a particular State does not detract in any way from his membership in the human family as a whole, nor from his citizenship in the world community."[16] This affirmation of the reality of global community relativizes the moral significance of national borders and state sovereignty. It means that the duty to protect human rights reaches across borders. Such transborder duties have particular relevance to the plight of refugees and other forced migrants, who by definition lack the protection that would normally be provided by their home state. Since the displaced have lost the protection of their home states, they effectively end up with no rights at all, unless the duty to protect rights is genuinely transnational. The duty to protect the displaced must therefore reach across borders if they are to receive any protection at all. As Pope John stressed, "refugees cannot lose these rights simply because they are deprived of citizenship of their own States."[17]

In international politics, however, states do matter. Even in the midst of today's growing global interdependence, national communities and their borders continue to play a very important role in relation to the rights and needs of displaced people. An authentically cosmopolitan ethos calls for recognition that while all persons share a common humanity, it also requires recognizing that every person has distinctive characteristics, including diverse bonds of kinship, culture, and shared citizenship. Thus, respecting people as they are calls for respect both for their common humanity and also for the ways they differ.[18] One of the key differences between people is their nationality and citizenship. Recognition of this fact has recently led Nussbaum to reverse her earlier position, that national borders are morally irrelevant. She now draws on Grotius and Kant to argue that people exercise their freedom and express their dignity by shaping the institutions of their own nation-states.[19] Seyla Benhabib has developed a similar argument.[20] For these reasons, protecting human dignity will require respect for the self-determination of accountable states. At the same time, both Nussbaum and Benhabib insist that sovereignty must be understood in a way that fully supports the fundamental human rights of all, including migrants and refugees. They seek to protect these rights by calling for porous borders rather than entirely open borders. An adequate assessment of responsibilities toward refugees and other displaced persons thus requires taking into account the importance of states for the protection of dignity and rights. It also must assess the impact of forced migration, both on the dignity of those who have been displaced and on the dignity of those in the communities that receive them.

There are religious warrants for the duty to respect communal differences, just as there are for the duty to respect common humanity. In Judaism, God's covenant with Israel gives the Jewish people a distinctive religious and national identity that must be respected. This stress on religious distinctiveness gives Jews a particularly strong sensitivity to the right of diverse peoples to be different from each other. Of course, this sensitivity to the importance of difference does not eliminate Israel's awareness of the duty to respect the common humanity of all persons affirmed in the creation story and in God's covenant with Noah, which extends beyond Israel to all of creation.[21] Indeed, precisely because of the special covenant that led God to set Israel free from bondage as strangers in Egypt, the Hebrew Bible repeatedly stresses that the Jewish people have strong duties to the strangers they encounter in the land of Israel itself: "You shall not oppress an alien; you well know how it feels to be an alien, since you were once aliens yourselves in the land of Egypt."[22] Thus, Judaism combines universalism and particularism in a way that recognizes both the right to national self-determination and an onerous duty to migrants and refugees that reaches beyond the borders of Israel and the Jewish people.[23]

Catholic social ethics also seeks to combine cosmopolitan universalism with respect for the distinctive identities of peoples. Saints Augustine and Thomas Aquinas surely affirmed a Christian duty to love all humans as our neighbors. At the same time, they recognized that those with whom we have special relationships, such as the members of our family or our political community, deserve special treatment as an expression of our love for them. A key task in Christian ethical reflection is to determine the order of priorities that should exist among these diverse loves (an *ordo amoris*). In some circumstances love for those nearer to us should take priority over concern for those at greater distances. On the other hand, when those farther away have greater needs, they can have priority. Similarly, Catholic social thought also appeals to what has come to be called "the principle of subsidiarity" to determine whether the more local or more global should take priority. This principle affirms that there are special duties within smaller and more proximate communities. In tandem with the principle of solidarity, however, subsidiarity insists that when there is serious need at a greater distance or when local communities cannot or will not respond to this need, larger regional communities or the international community as a whole can have a duty to provide help (*subsidium*) to those in need.[24]

Though the subsidiarity principle was developed within Catholic social thought, it has become a standard point of reference in the European Union (EU) in discussions of the relation between the responsibilities of the larger structures of the union and the responsibilities of each European state. Subsidiarity requires that the union itself should act only when member states cannot achieve required goals or when the union itself is better able to achieve what is needed.[25] In other words, the larger transnational community of the union does not replace the communal bonds that exist in the member states, but rather it supplements the actions of the states when they are unable to take needed action or when the union itself can act more effectively. In an analogous way, subsidiarity implies that the primary responsibility toward internally displaced persons falls on the country of which they are citizens. Their own country has the primary duty to protect them. But if their country of citizenship fails to protect them or acts in a way that compels them to flee, the duty of protection moves to neighboring countries and to larger regional and international actors.

Thus, national borders carry considerable moral weight in determining ethical responsibilities toward displaced persons, but there are also obligations to the displaced that reach across borders. From both a secular philosophical standpoint and in most religious perspectives, there are duties *both* to one's fellow citizens *and* to forced migrants who need protection through asylum or through some other form of emergency assistance. Neither of these types of duty is absolute. Duties to fellow citizens do not always preempt duties to forced migrants, nor do duties to forced migrants always override duties to co-citizens. The key question, therefore, becomes what relative weight should be assigned to each of these duties in diverse circumstances.

THE NEED FOR PRIORITIES

The displacement crises of today call for careful reflection on the relative weights of the rights and duties that arise from our common humanity on the one hand and from our distinctive identities and citizenship in specific states on the other hand. Let me suggest several priorities among these rights and duties, focusing first on action required by *negative* duties not to act in ways that cause displacement and the kinds of mass movements of refugees we are witnessing today, and then on several *positive* duties to take action to alleviate the plight of the displaced and to improve the protection system that is currently in place. These two types of duties can be equally stringent.[26]

Negative Duties

Most of the forced migration in the world today is caused by conflict and war. Many of today's refugees have been driven from homes by the conflicts in Ukraine, Syria, Afghanistan, South Sudan, Myanmar, and Somalia, and many of the internally displaced have been forced to flee by conflict within their own countries.[27] Key negative duties relevant to displacement caused by conflict can be highlighted by drawing on the moral tradition known as the just war ethic. This tradition distinguishes morally legitimate from illegitimate use of force, so it would be helpful to call it the just/unjust war tradition. It has roots in Christian thought, especially Catholicism, but it has analogies in other religious traditions and overlaps in important ways with the tradition of the international law of armed conflict.[28]

In its modern form the just/unjust war tradition draws a sharp line between force used in the defense of human rights and force that violates rights. The *jus ad bellum* norm of just cause requires that force be strictly limited to defending the rights of innocent persons to life, freedom, and security, and the rights of nation-states to self-determination and territorial integrity. Conversely, there is a negative duty *not* to use force aggressively against other peoples to deny them their political freedom, to exploit them economically, or because they are culturally different. Violation of these negative duties is both immoral and criminal.

Such a violation is exactly what happened in perhaps the worst humanitarian crisis of recent times: the Rwanda genocide of 1994, where force was massively used to deny the basic rights of the Tutsi people. It was also appallingly violated in the slaughter at Srebrenica, where thousands of Bosnian Muslims were killed because of their identity in an "ethnic cleansing." Most recently, the invasion of Ukraine by Russia has been a major violation of just war moral norms and of international law. The displacements that resulted from each of these conflicts were massive. This suggests that a central priority in efforts to prevent massive forced migration should be much stronger actions to prevent and halt unjust and illegal use of force.

Just war norms also forbid direct, intentional attacks on civilians as well as collateral harm to civilians that is disproportionate to the good being sought. International law sets forth similar prohibitions in the Geneva Conventions, which insist that civilians be distinguished from soldiers and be protected both from direct attack and from disproportionate collateral harm.[29] Violations of these standards are considered war crimes and can be labeled crimes against humanity if "widespread and systematic."[30] Regrettably, several of the worst recent cases of forced migration have been due to violations of these moral and legal prohibitions of attacks on civilians.

For example, tactics used in the civil war that began in South Sudan in December 2013 have regularly violated the rights of civilians to security. Human Rights Watch and a UN panel of experts concluded that both the government of South Sudan and the opposition forces had "committed extraordinary acts of cruelty that amount to war crimes and in some cases potential crimes against humanity."[31] Because of this mayhem, by 2022 the conflict had displaced over two million South Sudanese refugees and created two million internally displaced people. The strategies and tactics used by both sides in South Sudan have themselves turned South Sudan into a grave humanitarian emergency marked by massive displacement.[32]

The Syrian crisis reinforces the conclusion that armed conflict can lead to mass displacement when adversaries violate their duty not to attack the basic rights of civilians. The UN's Independent Commission of Inquiry on Syria concluded that the war crimes, crimes against humanity, and human rights violations were so severe that the Syrian reality should "shock the conscience of humanity."[33] These violations have led to one of the largest forced migrations in recent history. The flight of refugees from Syria threatened the stability of neighboring countries, including Turkey, which today hosts the largest number of refugees of any country in the world; Lebanon, where more than one in every eight persons within the country's borders is a refugee; and Jordan, which hosts many refugees.

The International Criminal Court (ICC) was established in 1998 to hold people accountable for violations of standards of international law similar to those that occurred in Rwanda and Bosnia and that are continuing in South Sudan, Syria, and Ukraine. The Rome Statute that created the court gave it jurisdiction over genocide, crimes against humanity, war crimes, and the crime of aggression. The Rome Statute arose from the recognition that duties of the international community based on our common humanity can take priority over the sovereignty of independent nation-states when human rights violations rise to the level of atrocity. The ICC has so far not been able to bring to trial some of those it has charged with such atrocities due to its inability to secure cooperation on various fundamental matters. For example, charges against former president Uhuru Kenyatta of Kenya had to be dropped because the ICC prosecutor could not get witnesses to testify, likely because of bribes and threats to their safety. Nevertheless, the court has had success in a number of other cases and it has launched a process that promises to strengthen the accountability faced by those responsible for the atrocities that contribute to some of the worst refugee and migration crises occurring today. The duty to not violate basic rights is surely more likely to be enforced today than in the past, and those who do violate it are less likely to get away with it than used to be the case. People will continue to be forced to flee from their homes as long as they face the danger of being caught up in conflict marked by unjust and indiscriminate violence. Preventing displacement thus requires notably more effective ways to hold the military and political leaders who organize such violence accountable for what they do. Enforcement of the law of war and of the standards of international humanitarian law should thus be a priority in any effort to enhance the effectiveness of the refugee protection system.

Positive Duties

Regrettably, we have learned from history and from insight into human moral weakness that threats to human rights will continue to occur. This raises the question of what *positive* obligations we have to come to the assistance of the displaced when crises in fact occur.

To address this issue we can draw on a mode of moral analysis originally developed in the 1970s in the context of debate about who had the duty to help eliminate the apartheid regime that separated South African people by race and ethnicity. In that debate some maintained that only those who had created the apartheid system had a duty to work to overcome it. But a very different ethical approach was proposed by several scholars at Yale University, who argued that under certain circumstances persons, communities, institutions, and states can have a positive duty to help remedy harms they did not themselves cause. They called their approach the Kew Gardens Principle, for it arose from their reflection on a tragic case that occurred in the Kew Gardens section of New York City in 1964.[34] According to press reports at the time, a young woman named Kitty Genovese was viciously assaulted, stabbed, and died a slow death while thirty-eight people nearby watched and did nothing, failing even to call the police. It has since been learned that the initial reports of what happened were not fully accurate and some calls were in fact made to the police.[35] But the public outrage stimulated by the press reports points to the fact that most people have a conviction that there can be a positive moral duty to aid others in emergency situations. It is not enough to avoid causing harm. In some situations, omission can become as morally objectionable as commission.

Drawing on this conviction, the Kew Gardens principle argues that an agent has a positive responsibility to help when four conditions are present:

(1) there is a critical *need*, (2) the agent has *proximity* to the need, (3) the agent has the *capability* to assist, and (4) the agent is likely the *last resort* from whom help can be expected.[36] Subsequent reflection has added a fifth condition: that the action can be taken *without disproportionate harm* to the one providing assistance. These criteria, of course, cannot be applied mechanically. But they can help us think about the scope of positive responsibilities in the face of the crisis-level suffering that is displacing so many people today.

For example, there can be little doubt that large numbers of people are in grave *need* of protection in Ukraine, Syria, and South Sudan today and that this need is driving many from their homes. Those inside the borders of these crisis-torn countries are vulnerable to harms that could lead to their deaths or to violations of other basic rights, and they are in flight because of this vulnerability. The duty to respond to such need falls first upon those whose *proximity* to the crisis makes them more likely to have knowledge of the need and better understanding of how to respond to it. This means, of course, that the government of the nation where the crisis occurs and local communities within that nation bear the prime responsibility. In South Sudan and Syria, therefore, both the governments and the opposition forces in each country have the negative duty to stop the atrocities that are causing crisis and the positive duty to help lift the burdens of suffering. Duty to take positive action, however, does not end at the national borders of the countries where crisis is present. When people become aware of crisis in a neighboring country or even in a country at a great distance, this awareness leads to what might be called intellectual or psychological proximity. It puts them in *moral* proximity to those who are suffering.

For example, Poland has shown remarkable readiness to receive in a very short time millions of refugees from its neighbor Ukraine. The EU as a whole has received over eight million refugees from Ukraine, often through temporary protection or similar arrangements.[37] There has been a helpful though imperfect response to the duties arising from proximity by the countries neighboring South Sudan as well. Uganda has received numerous South Sudanese refugees and has enabled many of them to become fairly well integrated into the economy of their new home. The regional organization of Sudan's neighboring countries—Djibouti, Ethiopia, Kenya, Somalia, Sudan, Uganda, and Eritrea—is called the Intergovernmental Authority on Development (IGAD). IGAD has played a diplomatic role in seeking to mediate the conflict within South Sudan that began in 2013, as it did in helping secure the Comprehensive Peace Agreement that ended the earlier conflict between the northern and southern regions of the formerly unified country of Sudan before South Sudan became independent in 2011. Regrettably, economic and political self-interest has sometimes distorted the mediation efforts of several countries that are part of IGAD, particularly Uganda and Ethiopia. This has in turn led several countries from outside the region to become involved in an effort known as IGAD Plus, which includes the African Union (AU), the United Nations, China, United States, the United Kingdom, Norway, and the EU. A sense of moral responsibility arose in these more distant countries because of their proximity through awareness. These combined regional and global mediation efforts have certainly been imperfect. Nevertheless, they have made some contribution to the peace that South Sudan desperately needs.[38] Both nearby and distant neighbors can have the knowledge that can help them make at least some difference.

The criterion of *capability* also sheds light on positive duties to respond to crises that displace large numbers of people. In considering this issue it has become common to point out that someone who cannot swim does not have a duty to come to the aid of a child who is drowning if providing the aid requires swimming some distance, while a good swimmer can have a duty to respond. Lebanon, Turkey, and Jordan are today already massively overburdened with Syrian refugees. They do not possess the economic and other resources necessary to take in and support many additional refugees. On the other hand, the resources of the wealthy nations of northern Europe, North America, and the oil-producing Gulf States give them the capability to receive many more refugees and to share the burdens being carried by Syria's already overtaxed proximate neighbors. The assistance being provided to the countries bordering Syria is woefully inadequate. Capability to assist gives many nations in Europe, North America, and the Gulf a duty both to receive many more Syrian refugees than they have and a responsibility to provide more assistance to Syria's nearby neighbors.[39] The duty to share the burden of assistance to displaced people is proportional to the capability of doing so. Countries with greater economic and political capacity to help have proportionally greater responsibilities to do so. These responsibilities may be carried out by granting asylum and refugee status to more of the displaced and, perhaps most urgently, by providing economic and other forms of assistance to countries like Turkey, Lebanon, and Jordan, which are already carrying a disproportionate burden.

The existence of duties such as these is a consequence of the reality that the responsibility to assist displaced people reaches across national borders. The fact that state sovereignty is not a moral or political absolute becomes clear in face of the needs of forcibly displaced persons. In his work on response to the needs of internally displaced people, the Sudanese scholar and diplomat Francis Mading Deng argues that sovereignty is such an important

BORDERS AND THE RIGHTS OF THE DISPLACED   161

value because it secures a country's ability to protect its own people by preventing external powers from taking harmful actions within its national boundaries, for example by invasion or colonial exploitation. Deng calls this sovereignty-as-responsibility.[40] Sovereignty does not mean a government is free to do whatever it will within its own borders, such as taking actions that create large numbers of internally displaced persons or refugees. If a government fails to protect its own people, either because it is unable or unwilling to do so, the duty to assist those who are threatened by this failure can pass to other nations. But the responsibility to assist and to protect the rights of persons threatened with or experiencing displacement falls first on their own government. If their government is unable or unwilling to secure their rights, the responsibility to do so can move to other countries and their people.[41]

Deng's thinking contributed in an important way to the development of the doctrine of the Responsibility to Protect (R2P), initially proposed by the International Commission on Intervention and State Sovereignty (ICISS) and subsequently affirmed at the 2005 UN General Assembly World Summit.[42] R2P states that the international community can have a positive duty "to help protect populations from genocide, war crimes, ethnic cleansing and crimes against humanity." Protective action should come in the first instance from people's own government. Only if that government fails to provide this protection should other countries consider action. When violations of human rights reach the level of atrocity and lead to the displacements that such violations often cause, action by other countries through "diplomatic, humanitarian and other peaceful means" can become appropriate and even required.

The responsibility to protect has been the focus of heated controversy since it was endorsed by heads of state at the UN General Assembly in 2005. Political realists oppose it because they hold that foreign policy should be determined by the interests of one's own people, not by a supposed moral responsibility to other countries. Others see it as a form of neoimperialism. Still others say that the situation in Libya today in the aftermath of the NATO intervention there shows that R2P does not work and that the current massive crisis in Syria and surrounding countries shows that R2P cannot work. Despite these critiques, it is important to note that the responsibility to protect has in fact been invoked on a number of occasions since 2005 and that it has led to effective protection of people from grave rights violations.

For example, when conflict flared in Kenya following the disputed 2007 elections, nonviolent, diplomatic initiatives were taken by numerous international actors to stop the conflict, which took several thousand lives and displaced half a million people. Kofi Annan stated that he saw the crisis in Kenya through "the R2P prism."[43] The response included intense diplomatic initiatives by the UN, the African Union, and a number of other governments from Africa and around the world, including the United States.[44] A power-sharing agreement was reached, and the downward spiral into civil war and what some feared was heading toward genocide was stopped. The Kenyan case illustrates that the responsibility to protect can be successfully carried out through nonviolent political and diplomatic means.

The R2P doctrine has also been invoked on several occasions in the past decade to justify the use of military force to protect people from atrocities, following the General Assembly's affirmation that if diplomatic initiatives do not succeed, the use of armed force can become legitimate as a last resort under chapter VII of the UN Charter. In 2012 France and the Economic Community of West African States took military action with UN approval in the pursuit of peace in Mali, and in 2013 the UN Security Council supported the use of force by French and African Union troops to stop the atrocities that were occurring in the Central African Republic and the displacement of nearly one million refugees and other forced migrants.[45] Though the conflicts in Mali and Central African Republic are certainly not resolved, they indicate that the doctrine of R2P can lead to action that can help prevent grave crisis from becoming much worse and can lead to some improvement in bad situations that force many people from their homes. Two other cases, however, Libya and Syria, raise questions about whether R2P has any relevance to current efforts to respond to the global refugee crisis.

In the Libya case, the UN authorized action to protect civilians when fears arose that Libya's leader, Muammar Gaddafi, was about to commit atrocities. Gaddafi referred to his adversaries in Benghazi as "cockroaches," the very epithet Hutus used for Tutsis during the Rwanda genocide.[46] As a result, the Security Council, with the notable support of the Organization of the Islamic Conference and the League of Arab States, called for the use of "all necessary measures" to protect civilians.[47] NATO intervened with airpower, Gaddafi was killed, and Gaddafi's regime was overthrown. Sadly, Libya has since fallen into political chaos, with armed conflicts among several groups, significant violations of human rights on the basis of religion, the displacement of many, and the unsafe flight of migrants across the Mediterranean.[48]

These consequences confirm for some observers the conviction that pursuing humanitarian goals not required by national self-interest is likely to do more harm than good.[49] I would argue, however, that the intervention in Libya failed not because it was excessive but because it was incomplete. Following the norms that some specialists in the ethics of war are today calling *jus post bellum*, or justice after conflict, NATO and the United States should have followed up their intervention with action to rebuild and to prevent the chaos that developed.[50] What happened in Libya was an incomplete implementation of R2P, not a simple failure. Had the intervention followed through with the peace-building and reconstruction efforts that were clearly required, the situation on the ground in Libya would not have disintegrated and many fewer people would be in flight from the chaos of that tragic situation.

Syria has also been invoked to suggest that R2P is dead. The political complexities and moral ambiguities of the Syrian situation go very deep. But these complexities do not discredit the existence of a duty to protect people facing atrocities when protection is possible. Thomas Weiss has argued that the wisdom of the use of military force to protect people from atrocities is governed by three factors: legality, moral legitimacy, and feasibility.[51] In Syria it is clear that the *legal* prohibitions of war crimes and of other atrocities have been massively violated. The *moral legitimacy* of efforts to stop a conflict that has displaced over half the Syrian population and killed hundreds of thousands of civilians is also evident. The *feasibility* of military intervention to alleviate the crisis, however, remains unclear. This does not undermine the idea that there is a responsibility to protect people from atrocity and from being driven from home by mayhem when it is possible to do so. The apparent lack of presently feasible ways to overcome the crisis in Syria through military action suggests that military intervention is not now called for by R2P. I would argue, however, that the duty to protect the Syrian people does call for continuing political and diplomatic initiatives to find a path toward their protection. Not only Bashar al-Assad and the rebels, but also Russia, Iran, some Gulf States, and others have been keeping the crisis in Syria alive. The global community, therefore, has a duty to continue to engage these powers diplomatically and possibly through other forms of continuing engagement in order to seek a resolution to the conflict.

There is also continuing responsibility to the large number of Syrians who have sought refuge in Europe and other parts of the developed world. At a minimum we need to live up to the 1951 Refugee Convention's call for refugees fleeing persecution to be granted protection. Countries in Europe and North America have the capability and resources to grant asylum or refugee protection to a considerably larger number of Syrians than is happening today. The number of Syrians seeking asylum in Europe is not even close to the number already within the borders of Syria's neighbors.[52] When in fall 2015 Prime Minister David Cameron of the United Kingdom announced that his country would grant refugee protection to twenty thousand Syrian refugees over the next five years, he was appropriately reminded that Lebanon had admitted that many Syrians over the previous two weekends. Indeed, low- and middle-income countries today host 83 percent of the world's refugees, with the very poorest countries hosting 27 percent of the global total.[53] The rich nations of the north have the capability and therefore the responsibility to admit a larger number of refugees and asylum seekers and to assist the poorer countries already hosting most of the world's refugees. A substantial increase in the funds being provided by the north to the poorer countries already hosing most of the world's displaced should be a priority today.

To achieve this, the rich nations of the Northern Hemisphere will have to overcome tendencies to racially or religiously driven xenophobia and the mistaken fear that terrorists are usually hiding among the refugees. In addition, European powers such as France and the United Kingdom, which gained economically from their colonies in Africa and Asia, have a duty to be open to refugees from these regions. A country with a history of military involvement in another nation can also have special obligations to people in flight from that nation. The United States recognized its particular duty to receive refugees from Vietnam after its war in Vietnam. Though the US intervention in Iraq was certainly not the sole cause of the displacement of many Iraqis, it was a significant factor that contributed to the political chaos that led to the huge forced migration of Iraqis that subsequently occurred. Political scientist Stephen Walt recently observed that if the United States and its allies had not invaded Iraq in 2003, the Islamic State would likely not have come into existence.[54] Thus, there would have been fewer people driven from their homes in Iraq and Syria and fewer seeking asylum and refugee protection. For these reasons, the United States and its allies have a particular duty toward these displaced people.

Finally, it is well known that many observers believe there are good reasons to wonder whether national self-interest may not overshadow the duties and actions advocated here. The work of Martha Finnemore and Kathryn Sikkink, however, has shown that advocacy for normative standards in some domains of contemporary international politics has had significant impact.[55] Current standards of the international law related to armed conflict and refugee protection resulted from normative advocacy by groups such as the Red Cross over the past century. More recently, despite the fact that the International Criminal Court is still a developing institution, "normative entrepreneurs" have advanced efforts to hold political leaders accountable. Thus, contrary to the standard realist argument, ethical standards can come to have real impact on the conduct of nations. There is hope, therefore, that the Global Compact on Refugees agreed to at the UN General Assembly in 2018 can lead to genuine innovation in the protection of refugees and other victims of war. Normative pressure from nongovernmental bodies, including religious communities and faith-based agencies, can make important normative contributions to actions more fully in accord with the responsibilities sketched here.

TOWARD A MORE JUST REGIME

The extraordinarily large number of displaced people in the world today means that the nearly absolute value given to national borders and state sovereignty in the modern Westphalian international system must be reassessed. Human rights have been proclaimed as universal norms, and this universality can be supported by secular philosophies such as those developed by Kant and by the major religious traditions of the world, including Judaism, Christianity, and Islam. These rights require that all political actors, both states and nonstate agents, refrain from grave abuses of human rights such as war crimes, crimes against humanity, and other cruelties that effectively treat people as though they are not human at all. Such atrocities are among the major causes of refugee movement and other forms of forced migration today. Acting to prevent such crimes and holding accountable those who nevertheless commit them will be crucial to making the global system of refugee protection more adequate. Similarly, taking positive steps to come to the aid of those who have been driven from home will be essential to a more effective refugee regime. The duty to provide such assistance to those already displaced falls on neighboring countries, on those in the local region, and on the global community as a whole. The responsibility of countries to provide help is proportional both to their proximity to those in need and, more importantly today, to their capacity to provide effective assistance. The rich nations of Europe, North America, and the oil-rich Gulf States thus have an urgent duty to assist poorer countries that are hosting most of the world's refugees today. Developing fair and politically effective ways of assigning the share of the responsibility that different nations carry will be essential to the creation of a more effective refugee system. The leadership of the United Nations and its constituent national governments is essential, but the task is not theirs alone. Many humanitarian NGOs, both secular and faith-based, have broad experience in responding to the needs of the displaced across national borders. These organizations are well positioned to help in the development of a system that is more effective. Hearing their voices will be important as revisions in the refugee regime are being considered. It can be hoped that all available practical wisdom will be drawn upon to create more adequate ways of responding to the present crisis. Many millions of lives are at stake.

11

WELCOMING REFUGEES AND MIGRANTS

The Need for Inclusion

How to help refugees and migrants find new homes in the United States is a hotly debated political and moral issue in American society today. Faith communities are playing important roles in this debate. The Roman Catholic Church is the single largest religious body in the United States. Catholic leaders like Pope Francis and the US bishops are strong advocates on behalf of refugees and migrants. The response of Catholics in the country, however, is rather mixed. This chapter draws on both the norms and the lived experience of the US Catholic community to suggest how faith communities in general and the Catholic community in particular can assist refugees and migrants to become better integrated into the societies that receive them.

The chapter first provides an overview of recent discussions of the role played by religious communities in relation to migration, including forced migration. It outlines the historical story of how the US Catholic community has helped very large numbers of immigrants integrate into US society and culture in the past. It then gives an overview of the norms that should shape the Catholic response to refugees and migrants if and when this response accurately reflects the values held by the Catholic tradition. It highlights several ways that the US Catholic community's adherence to these values is not fully consistent today. The chapter concludes with suggestions about what might be done to improve the Catholic community's observance of the values its leaders propose and to make a more effective contribution to the integration of refugees and migrants into US society and culture.

FAITH COMMUNITIES, REFUGEES, AND MIGRANTS

Religious communities play an important role in assisting migrants, refugees, and other displaced people today, both globally and in the United States. The

WELCOMING REFUGEES AND MIGRANTS   167

narrative of the contributions made by faith communities and their agencies in assisting people on the move has not always received the attention it deserves in policy-oriented and academic studies of migration. In very recent years, however, this appears to be changing. For example, the Annual Dialogue sponsored by the UN High Commissioner for Refugees was devoted in 2012 to faith and the protection of the displaced. This dialogue affirmed the importance of partnerships between the High Commissioner's office and faith-based agencies. It called for the enhancement of what the report called "faith literacy" among UNHCR staff, implying that appreciation of the role of faith-based efforts could be improved.[1] The consultation led to a document titled "Welcoming the Stranger: Affirmations for Faith Leaders." This document declared that "the call to 'welcome the stranger,' through protection and hospitality, and to honor the stranger or those of other faiths with respect and equality, is deeply rooted in all major religions."[2] On the academic side, the Refugee Studies Centre in Oxford, England, organized a workshop on faith-based humanitarianism in contexts of forced migration, leading to a special issue on this theme in the journal published by the center.[3] In addition, several academic studies of the role of faith-based responses to humanitarian crises and refugees have been published recently.[4] This has led refugee specialist Jeff Crisp to ask whether faith-based action is an emerging "hot topic" in the study of refugee response.[5]

Because of the significant role played in the past by faith-based agencies in assisting displaced people, the growing need for recognition of the contribution of these agencies is surprising. The annual budgets of both secular and religiously affiliated humanitarian agencies give a rough indication of the scope of their work. Consider these numbers for recent years: the 2016 operating budget of the secular Oxfam International Confederation was $1.2 billion, while the budget of the religiously linked WorldVision International was nearly twice as large, at $2.2 billion. (These figures are drawn from the publicly available annual reports of the agencies involved.) Similarly, the secular Médecins sans Frontières had a budget of $1.2 billion, while Catholic Relief Services, the US branch of Caritas Internationalis that serves displaced people outside the United States, had a budget of just under $1 billion ($970 million).[6] Were the current figures available for the entire Caritas Internationalis network of 160 members, including Catholic Charities USA, which serves immigrants within the United States, the total Catholic budget would be substantially larger than those of any secular relief or assistance organization.

In the United States, faith-based organizations play an important role in resettling refugees. Six of the nine agencies that the US government relies on to resettle displaced people are faith-based: Church World Service, Episcopal

Migration Ministries, HIAS (formerly the Hebrew Immigrant Aid Society), Lutheran Immigration and Refugee Service, the US Conference of Catholic Bishops/Migration and Refugee Services, and World Relief. From 1987 to 2016 slightly more that one million refugees were resettled. Among these, the Catholic community's Migration and Refugee Services resettled approximately 30 percent of the overall total.[7] This total adds up to more refugees than have been resettled by any nation other than the United States itself.[8] The work of this national Catholic agency is carried out through over one hundred diocesan offices.

In recent decades, Lutheran Immigration and Refugee Services have also welcomed more than 500,000 refugees and migrants; the evangelical organization World Relief has resettled more than 250,000 refugees; and the oldest resettlement organization in the world, HIAS, has helped more than 4.5 million people escape persecution since its founding. HIAS continues its active resettlement work today, including its role in resettling refugees in the United States.[9] The more recently founded Islamic Relief USA has worked to provide humanitarian aid for refugees over its twenty-five-year existence—from Bosnian refugees in Europe, to Kosovars settling in the United States in the late 1990s, to Syrians in numerous countries today.[10] In addition to resettlement work, these agencies also assist people facing the dangers arising from war, disaster, and other serious humanitarian threats. The global and US roles of faith-based agencies support Richard Barnett's observation that "it is impossible to study humanitarianism without being impressed by the importance of religion."[11]

REFUGEE AND IMMIGRANT INTEGRATION IN THE US: THE CATHOLIC STORY

In this section we focus on the response of one religious tradition in the United States: the Catholic community. The Catholic community is but one of the many groups that resettles refugees and helps immigrants integrate into their new country. Both the size of the Catholic population in the US and its distinctive history help us understand the large role of faith-based support for people on the move. The US Catholic community, like all groups of US citizens except Native Americans, has been an immigrant community from the first days of its presence in this country. Africans who arrived in the United States as slaves, for course, came in an especially oppressive way. Many Catholic migrants came to the United States between 1820 and 1920, when over 33 million immigrants arrived on US shores, primarily from

WELCOMING REFUGEES AND MIGRANTS   169

Ireland, Germany, and Italy but other countries as well.[12] When these Catholic immigrants arrived, they were often viewed as threats to the effectively established Protestant presence in US politics and culture. In response to this situation, the US Catholic Church created institutions in many domains of life to provide support for recently arrived Catholic immigrants who faced prejudice and opposition from those who had been longer in the country.

These institutions included parishes, many of which used the home languages of the new arrivals. Parishes were often served by pastors who were themselves immigrants. For example, in 1887 Bishop John Baptist Scalabrini founded the Roman Catholic Scalabrini Congregation to minister to Italian migrants in the Americas. The Catholic community also aided immigrants through its schools, hospitals, migrant service centers, and cultural centers.[13] The Catholic community generated numerous new communities of religious sisters to carry out ministries to recent arrivals who were poor, through parishes, schools, and health care institutions. Many communities of sisters had themselves arrived in the United States as migrants from Europe and they devoted their lives to the spiritual, educational, health, and social needs of their fellow immigrants. Of the 119 communities of religious sisters in the United States in the nineteenth century, 91 originated in Europe or Canada. These women made extraordinary contributions to sustain the faith of the Catholic immigrant community and to enable them to integrate into US society by providing education.[14]

The schools created by the Catholic community made strong a contribution to immigrant integration education by helping recently arrived youth adapt and succeed. What began as a school here and a school there rapidly evolved into a vast educational network that included both elementary and secondary schools and colleges and universities. Although the pressure to create this educational system arose from the Church's desire to educate newly arrived Catholic immigrants in their own faith, pressure also arose from the fact that Catholics were often not welcomed with respect in the US public school system. Today in Catholic primary and secondary schools 150,000 educators serve 1.9 million students.[15] On the level of higher education, the Catholic community's devotion to education generated the creation of what today has become a network of two hundred Catholic colleges and universities serving just under a million students. This educational network arose largely from the effort to respond to the needs of migrants.[16] It played a highly effective role in helping integrate newcomers into US society, both on the level of culture and economically as well.

Similar institutional initiatives to meet the needs of Catholic immigrants also occurred in health care. The founding of hospitals by the Catholic community was a response to the Christian call to provide care for the sick and the dying; this was also the case with the hospitals founded by other faith communities. In the Catholic community, however, the scope of the Church's efforts in health care was mainly due to the recognition that as migrants and refugees who were often not welcomed by other groups, Catholic newcomers needed special assistance if they were to receive the health care they needed. For example, the Sisters of Mercy, the Sisters of Charity, the Sisters of Divine Providence, and a number of other communities of women opened Catholic hospitals in the mid-nineteenth century to serve immigrants who often had little or no access to other health-care facilities because of religious discrimination. Indeed, in the nineteenth century it was sometimes the case that Catholic clergy were prevented from visiting sick members of their faith community in public hospitals.[17] Ministry to the spiritual needs of sick church members thus led to the creation of countless Catholic health-care institutions. The result of this effort was the Catholic community's creation of a health-care network that today includes six hundred hospitals and sixteen hundred long-term care facilities spread across all fifty states, making it the largest group of nonprofit health-care providers in the nation. Today one out of every six hospitalized patients in America is being cared for in a Catholic hospital.[18] The scope and quality of this network is due in part to the Catholic Church's recognition that effective ministry to the needs of its immigrant members required a significant institutional response in the sphere of health care.

Other areas in the life of the Catholic community have also been shaped by this immigrant history. For example, several fraternal societies were established to support the economic and cultural needs of recent arrivals. The Knights of Columbus began in 1882 as an organization whose main purpose was to provide life insurance to its members, but it had considerably broader goals that included the provision of both religious and civic education for newly arrived Catholic migrants. The Knights gave particular attention to Irish immigrants. There were also fraternal societies for other national groups, such as the Central Verein for Germans and the Polish Roman Catholic Union of America for immigrants from Poland.[19] As noted, the migration of Italians stimulated the founding of the Scalabrini religious order, which was and is directly devoted to providing ministry and support to Italian migrants. The Scalabrinians have since expanded their ministry to include all who are on the move, and they support both research on the needs of migrants and refugees and advocacy for policies that will help meet these needs.

The Catholic Church has recognized the needs of migrants directly from its own experience as a community of migrants. Catholics of the past knew well that immigrants were often not well received in the United States. Catholic immigrants faced prejudices that impeded their integration into their new land, and as a result they needed pastoral and institutional support. Thus, both the experience and the self-interest of the Catholic community led to the creation of an institutional structure that supported the integration of new immigrants.

THE CATHOLIC NORMATIVE STANCE

Before turning to some of the reasons why this history is not as well remembered or acted upon today as it might be, it will be useful to sketch some of the normative grounds within Catholic tradition that energized the Church's response to the needs of migrants in the past and the reason it should continue to do so today.

Virtually all religious communities have theological and ethical traditions that call them to assist migrants. Judaism and Christianity hold that all persons are brothers and sisters in a single human family no matter what their nationality or ethnicity. Every person has been created in the image and likeness of God, possessing a dignity and worth that reaches across borders between nation-states.[20] Respect is due not only to co-citizens but also to those who come from elsewhere as migrants and refugees. Indeed, each of the great monotheistic traditions—Judaism, Christianity, and Islam—traces its origins back to the Patriarch Abraham, who was himself a migrant from the home of his kinsfolk to the land of Canaan. The identity of Jews is shaped by the story of the Exodus—a migration from slavery in Egypt to freedom in the land of God's promise. The New Testament portrays Jesus as the leader of a new Israel, who just after His birth had to flee persecution with Mary and Joseph, becoming a refugee in Egypt. Muslims measure time from Muhammad's *hijra*, or migration, from Mecca to Medina, the founding event of the Muslim community. Thus, the founding of these major faiths has flight across borders as one of its key elements. This is one of the reasons each tradition has not only called on the faithful to welcome immigrants but has also established agencies that help resettle those who have been displaced and to assist migrants facing crisis. It is true, of course, that religious communities sometimes sadly contribute to the conflicts that drive people from their homes. Nevertheless, the core normative values of these religious traditions, when properly interpreted, call their followers to work to prevent such conflicts. If conflict occurs, they are called to protect and assist those whom conflict drives from their homes.[21]

In addition to these normative perspectives drawn from the Bible, the Roman Catholic tradition also draws on an ethic based on reason and natural law to provide secular warrants for its approach to refugees and migrants. Catholic social ethics understand justice in a way that can address the plight of the displaced in religiously pluralistic contexts. This understanding of justice is based on the insight that treating people with the dignity they have as members of the human community also requires supporting their active participation as agents in society. Conversely, the injustices that lead to humanitarian emergencies frequently take the form of exclusion—denying people the active engagement in society they need to live with dignity. The US Catholic bishops stress the close link between justice and participation when they insist that "basic justice demands the establishment of minimum levels of participation in the life of the human community for all persons." Put negatively, "the ultimate injustice is for a person or group to be treated actively or abandoned passively as if they were non-members of the human race."[22] Pope Francis calls this exclusion "marginalization"—exclusion from social life and from being able to share in the common good of the human community. He argues forcefully that justice requires that we "say no" to such exclusion.[23]

Exclusion from active participation in social life is central to the harm faced by forcibly displaced people. Forced migrants have been prevented from sharing in the common good of their home societies. Various forms of exclusion have forced them to flee from their homes. In the worst cases, where they are denied asylum or are compelled to live in humanly inadequate camps for years or decades, forced migrants are excluded from the common good of the larger human family. Precisely because they have no community to call home, refugees and displaced people often lack the social and community support needed to attain the minimal requirements of human dignity. To force people to live this way cuts them off from elemental conditions of human well-being. It is one of the most degrading forms of injustice. Being forced to flee and being denied the conditions needed for humane resettlement in effect tells the displaced that they simply do not count as human beings.[24] Forced displacement, therefore, is a denial of human rights by its very nature. Migrants who have moved voluntarily sometimes face similar exclusion in their new lands as well. Xenophobic cultural, ethnic, and religious prejudice can exclude them from participating in social life in ways that threaten their humanity. They will need support and help if they are to attain the social integration required to live in their new society with dignity.

Thus, at the heart of the Catholic community's response to refugees and migrants is a normative vision of active participation in community as a prerequisite of human dignity. The norms of the Catholic tradition call Church members to a receptive stance toward those moving across borders because of threats to their humanity or because of their great need. Beyond such individual response, these norms also call for the creation of institutional agencies that serve people displaced by emergencies, that assist in the resettlement of forced migrants, and that help newly arrived immigrants integrate into their new societies and become at home there.

This normative vision is central in the ministry of Pope Francis, which has made him a leading advocate on behalf of refugees and migrants. Early in his pontificate Francis traveled to the Italian island of Lampedusa, to which many African and Middle Eastern displaced people have fled across the Mediterranean seeking safety from the conflicts in their home countries. Tragically, many have died en route to Lampedusa. The pope challenged Europeans not to allow their consciences to become indifferent to the suffering of these refugees, warning that in the globalized world of today we are in danger of falling into a "globalized indifference."[25] When Francis visited the Greek island of Lesbos, to which many displaced Syrians have fled from the conflict in their country, he called Europe to "build bridges" rather than "putting up walls." In his vision, national borders are in no way absolute and should be seen as subordinate to the respect due to the shared dignity of every person as an image of God. In this normative perspective, welcoming the refugee and the migrant is both a Christian duty and a human obligation.

In his World Day of Peace Message in 2018, Pope Francis affirmed four criteria by which the adequacy of response to refugees and migrants should be judged. They should be received with *welcome*, expanding legal pathways so they can find new homes where their rights will be secure. They should be *protected* in their dignity, especially those who sometimes face particular dangers, such as women and children. Their full development as human persons should be *promoted*, for example, through access to all levels of education. They should be *integrated* into their new community in a way that enables them to be active and respected participants in the life of society.[26] Francis's special concern for the displaced has been evident from the way he has repeatedly addressed these requirements. It is also particularly evident from the fact that when he established a new Vatican office whose responsibilities include overseeing the Church's response to migrants and refugees, the Dicastery for Promoting Integral Human Development, he placed the section dealing with migration under his own personal direction.[27]

Francis stressed his concern for migrants and refugees in the US context in his speech to the joint session of Congress in 2015. He noted that he himself was the son of immigrants and that most members of the US Congress were also descended from immigrants. He called the members of Congress, and all Americans through them, to welcome those seeking asylum and protection. He challenged the United States not to be "taken aback by their numbers," but to remember the Golden Rule: "Do unto others as you would have them do unto you."[28] Pope Francis's speech to the Congress was very well received by members of Congress themselves, by the larger Catholic community, and by the public at large.

Thus, the US Catholic community has a long history of providing concrete forms of assistance to migrants and refugees and helping them integrate into their new society. Catholicism also possesses a strong normative commitment to welcoming immigrants. Contributions by the Church today, therefore, should remember this history and seek to act on the norms of the Catholic tradition.

CHALLENGES FOR THE CATHOLIC COMMUNITY TODAY

Despite this strong history of Church contributions and the normative institutional commitment to the integration of migrants into their new homes, today's Catholic efforts to facilitate the integration of refugees and migrants are mixed. On the positive side, Church leadership continues to call both Church members and the country at large to welcome those who are seeking new homes. Numerous Catholic institutions that shape the day-by-day life of the Church continue to carry out important ministries that aid in the integration of immigrants and refugees. These ministries include religious education, pastoral services, youth ministry, education, English as a Second Language (ESL) classes, naturalization services, health care, legal services, counseling, and interpretation/translation services. A large number of Catholic institutions are also educating their broad constituencies about issues affecting immigrants.[29]

US Catholic agencies also continue to make strong contributions to welcoming and integrating those on the move. For example, the US Catholic bishops' Migration and Refugee Services (MRS) remains one of nine US refugee resettlement organizations. MRS provides direct assistance to the needs of recent arrivals, assisting parishes and other Catholic groups to help migrants integrate. MRS also supports English language instruction, job placement services, and assistance in accessing education and social services, often through local branches of Catholic Charities. In 2018 local Catholic Charities agencies welcomed and helped integrate 300,000 immigrants and refugees.[30] MRS also promotes awareness of the plight of immigrants and refugees both in the Catholic community and in the larger US society through its advocacy work and policy initiatives. Recently, several Catholic agencies increased their direct services to immigrants facing the consequences of the Trump administration's policies. These services included care for children separated from their parents and increased assistance to those facing long stays in detention.

The growing contributions of Catholic agencies is suggested by a study that showed that during the Trump administration, 40 percent of Catholic institutions serving the needs of immigrants reported that the use of their services increased "a lot" and another 20 percent said the use of their services increased "a little."[31] This heightened demand for the services provided by Catholic agencies occurred despite the decline in both the number of refugee admissions and the amount of federal funding for refugee agencies under the Trump administration. Thus, even in the face of reduced federal financial support for resettlement, Catholic institutions continue to play an important role in welcoming refugee and migrant newcomers. This role has continued under the Biden administration.

Nevertheless, institutional resources that have enabled the Catholic community to provide longer-term integration for migrants are less well positioned for this role today than in the past. For example, the number of priests and religious sisters has declined over the past decades. In 1970, Catholic priests in the United States numbered 59,192 and the number of sisters was 160,931. By 2021 the number of priests had declined to 34,923 and the number of sisters to 39,452. Offsetting these declines somewhat, the number of laypersons working full time in Church ministries has increased, but this does not make up for the decreased number of priests and sisters. In addition, during this same period the Catholic population in the US grew through immigration.[32]

The ability of parishes to continue playing their former role in integrating newcomers into US social life has also lessened. The number of US parishes has declined, moving from 18,224 in 1970 to 16,579 in 2021. In the early twentieth century, parishes that focused on serving immigrants helped sustain the distinctive identities of newcomers while also supporting their integration into US society and culture.[33] Today there are fewer parishes that focus their ministry on specific national groups. In addition, in 2021 more than 3,200 Catholic parishes had no full-time pastor.[34] In the southwest region of the country, where the immigrant population is large and growing, the number of parishes is now proportionally fewer in relation to the size of the population than in other parts of the country, where the Catholic population has declined. In addition, a recent study revealed that more than

50 percent of the pastoral leaders in parishes serving Hispanic Catholics felt that their Hispanic members were "minimally" or "not at all" well integrated into the life of the parish.[35] This suggests that despite the report by Catholic agencies that the use of their services by immigrants has grown, the decline in the number of these agencies may mean that the Church is less able to support the integration of migrants and refugees today than in the past.

Catholic schools also have a notably smaller role in the life of the US Catholic community today than in the past. From 1970 to 2021 the number of Catholic elementary schools declined from 9,366 to 4,751, and the number of students in these schools slid from 3.4 million to 1.2 million. During this same period the number of Catholic secondary schools also declined, from 1,986 to 1,174, with the number of students in these schools dropping from 1 million to 530,000.[36] Education, of course, need not be provided by the Church, so these statistics do not indicate that new immigrants are not being educated. They do indicate, however, that today Catholic schools play a less-important role than in the past in helping immigrant children maintain their cultural and religious identities while they integrate into US society. This mixed picture of the capacity of Church institutions suggests that the Catholic community will need to explore new ways to assist migrants if it wants to continue its historically strong contribution to their integration into US society and to live up to the normative standards proposed by Pope Francis and the US bishops.

It is also clear that the attitudes toward immigrants and refugees found among Catholics in the pew raise challenges today. While some US Catholics agree with the pro-refugee and pro-immigrant norms communicated to them in the teaching of the pope and the bishops, others do not. One study based on data from 2012 concluded that Catholics are less likely to follow Church leaders who support a path to citizenship for immigrants than are members of other US Christian churches.[37] Other studies have indicated a notable correlation between the race and ethnicity of US Catholics and their stance on public policies related to migration. For example, survey work by the Public Religion Research Institute (PRRI) in 2019 showed that while 41 percent of all Americans favored building a wall between the US and Mexico, 45 percent of all Catholics and 56 percent of white Catholics did so.[38] This contrasts with the 26 percent of Hispanic Catholics who supported building the wall.[39] Thus, white Catholics appear to have a slightly stronger desire to prevent migration across the southwest border of the country than does the population at large, and a much stronger desire to do so than Hispanic Catholics.

Catholics are also notably divided by race and ethnicity on the issue of granting citizenship to those who have entered the United States without papers. Survey data indicated that in 2016, 55 percent of white Catholics favored opening the way to citizenship for those who have entered the country illegally, compared to 77 percent of Hispanic Catholics.[40] White Catholics also express a comparatively strong desire to prevent Muslims from entering the country. White Catholics say that immigration to the United States from Muslim countries is too high or should be stopped (60 percent). Their objection to Muslim immigration is a bit less strong than the level among white evangelical Protestants (68 percent) and roughly the same as white mainline Protestants (59 percent). On the other hand, just 39 percent of Black Protestants, 37 percent of Hispanic Catholics, 34 percent of religiously unaffiliated Americans, and 23 percent of non-Christians want the number of Muslim immigrants to decline.[41]

These numbers suggest that the Catholic population as a whole holds opinions on migration and refugees that are not very different from the attitudes of the broader US population. White Catholics, however, are less likely to possess a welcoming attitude to migrants and refugees than are Hispanic Catholics or the US population at large.

A recent report by the Center for Migration Studies reinforces the idea that race and ethnicity play significant roles in the readiness of Catholics to welcome and help integrate immigrants and refugees.[42] This study showed that many staff working in Catholic social and charitable agencies (28 percent) believe racism and anti-immigrant sentiment in the receiving communities are obstacles to immigrant integration. These anti-immigrant sentiments are likely observed by the staff of Catholic agencies in the Catholic communities among whom they are working.

Knowing the sources of these attitudes toward immigrant and refugee integration will be important for developing programs to enhance this integration. The data noted here raise the question of whether the stance of white Catholics toward migrants and refugees reflects straightforward racial, ethnic, or religious prejudice. It would be particularly useful to know whether and how attitudes of white Catholics vary according to age, income, and educational levels. Knowing how these attitudes vary by class will be particularly useful since working-class whites are often supporters of Donald Trump and his anti-immigrant rhetoric, while college-educated, upper middle-class Americans have been more pro-immigrant.[43] A 2019 Pew report suggests whites' attitudes on migration vary by class: 35 percent of white college graduates favor expanding a border wall between the United States and Mexico compared to 53 percent of white non–college graduates.[44] Because white Catholics are found in considerable numbers in both the working and middle classes, it would be helpful to know how attitudes toward immigrants and refugees vary among white Catholics by education and income.

Further research on this question will aid the development of Church strategies that seek to advance commitments to normative Catholic teachings by Church members. If class differences among white Catholics help predict their readiness to welcome immigrants, the development of pastoral strategies to encourage such readiness will have to address class differences and develop responses that seek to overcome these class differences.

Future research could also address whether and how recent scandals about sexual abuse by clergy influence the readiness of the Catholic laity to respond positively to the pro-immigrant teachings of Pope Francis and the US bishops. Wallsten and Nteta suggest that the clerical sex abuse crisis may have led many US Catholics to be less responsive to the teachings of Church leaders on immigration.[45] Pew Research has also found a recent rise in the number of US Catholics who believe that Pope Francis is "too liberal," especially among Catholics who are Republicans. From 2015 to 2018 the percent of Republican Catholics who believe Francis is too liberal rose from 23 to 55 percent, while the rise among Catholic Democrats was from 16 to 19 percent.[46] It is possible that the church's handling of the sex abuse crisis is one of the reasons that a number of Catholics hold views on migration different from their leaders' normative positions. Further examination of this issue would therefore be helpful.

TOWARD THE FUTURE

What, then, can be done to strengthen the Catholic community's contribution to the integration of migrants and refugees? Several steps seem possible. First, enabling Catholic parishes, schools, hospitals, and social service agencies to continue doing what they are doing for migrants and refugees but to do it better and more effectively will be important. One way to achieve this will be to call on all Catholic institutions to remember their history and that much of their work arose in response to the needs of earlier refugees and migrants. Calling Catholic laity to remember their history may also be a way to stimulate their commitment to welcoming migrants by refreshing their memory of where they came from and thus who they are.

Improved institutional responses will also require recruiting larger numbers of recent immigrants as well as second- and third-generation immigrants to leadership positions in the Church. Recent data show that 75 percent of those who access Catholic social service agencies are migrants, while only 33 percent of the paid staffs of these agencies and 22 percent of their leaders are immigrants. There is a similar gap in parish life, where 39 percent of those who regularly attend Mass are migrants but only about 20 percent of parish leaders and paid staffs are immigrants.[47] This imbalance does not bode well for the possible influence these Church agencies will have in assisting immigrants to integrate into their new society.

The attention provided by Church agencies to migrant youths also seems to be falling short of what is needed. Roughly two-thirds of younger, millennial generation Catholics who attend Mass regularly are Hispanic.[48] Church programs to meet the distinctive educational and social needs of immigrant youths should be strengthened. As already noted, the schools that have traditionally provided much of the Catholic community's support for immigrant youths are considerably fewer in number today than in the past.[49] Developing alternative parish and educational programs for immigrant Catholic youths will be important and will require both effective leadership and, of course, increased funding.

The Catholic community could also strengthen its educational programs that explicitly address refugee and migration issues among its members in the pew, especially among those in the white community. This, of course, should include highlighting the challenges of the migration issue today and the great need of the 100 million forcibly displaced persons in our world. It is likely, however, that heavy emphasis on the huge number of forcibly displaced could only be more demoralizing and lead to thinking that the problem is simply too large to be dealt with. Developing Church programs that bring white and middle-class Catholics into direct contact with recently arrived immigrants who are Latino, African, or Asian may reduce stereotypes and help replace a desire to exclude with a new openness.

Such openness can also be strengthened by helping Church members understand that in most situations, new migrants contribute to the communities in which they live in important ways. The ancestors of almost all US Catholics came to the country as immigrants and moved on to become successful Americans. The success of so many Catholics today shows that today's migrants and refugees can also succeed. Highlighting the facts about the contributions made by refugees to American society today will also be important. For example, Church educational programs on migration could emphasize that the median income of refugees in the United States is the same as the income of those born in the country, their employment rate is higher than the average citizen, and, on average, they have higher skill levels than do those already living in the United States. Resettled refugees also contribute to the overall common good by paying taxes.[50] Emphasizing such positive achievements by newcomers is more likely to inspire support than is stressing how big the problem is.

The current crisis of leadership in the Catholic community is due in part to the clerical sex abuse catastrophe. The abuse crisis is likely contributing to lay disagreement with normative Church teaching. Thus, the crisis must be dealt with more adequately. The sex abuse crisis is surely not the sole source of the shortfall in Catholic responses to the needs of migrants and refugees today. Lay Catholics are unlikely to take seriously the positions advocated by the bishops and the pope, however, until it is clear that Church leadership has become fully accountable for the abuse that occurred. It is also likely that increased lay participation in Church leadership, especially by persons from immigrant backgrounds, will strengthen the Church's response to the needs of migrants and refugees.

These are but a few suggestions for how faith communities, especially the Catholic community, could respond more adequately to the challenges of welcoming migrants and refugees to the United States today and help them become more integrated into their new society. Communities of faith, including the Catholic community, have a positive history of effective response to the needs of migrants, and they continue to make important contributions. The Catholic community can do much by drawing on its rich history and experience of migration, its vast personal and institutional resources, and its normative religious and ethical underpinnings to respond to the needs of migrants and refugees. The needs are great, and these needs call for a response that is more effective.

PART V

THE RIGHTS OF WOMEN

The Universal Declaration of Human Rights affirms the equal rights of men and women and that everyone is entitled to all the rights set forth without distinction based on sex. Thus, the contemporary human rights movement seeks to promote the same human rights for women as it does for men. Human rights, therefore, are equal for women and men and their protection should not be affected by whether one is female or male. It is clear, however, that many cultures hold that males and females can be and indeed are treated differently. Some of these differences in treatment can be regarded as threats or denials of fundamental human rights. The question thus arises about how to work to secure the equal rights of women while also respecting the cultural rights of communities that wish to treat women differently from men when human rights are at stake. This part seeks to address this issue by distinguishing between efforts to secure the rights of women through persuasive efforts to change traditions that limit women's rights from efforts that use coercion to bring about change. It illustrates the importance of this difference by considering ways to protect women's rights through educational programs that seek to eliminate forms of female initiation through genital cutting and, for example, the military intervention that could have been used to protect women from being killed during the genocide of the Tutsis in Rwanda. Overcoming denial of the rights of women can be compatible with respect for cultural difference if efforts to bring change are pursued through persuasion and education. Through a persuasive approach religious and cultural traditions can be led to stronger commitment to the equal rights of men and women. As earlier chapters of this book have suggested, the Catholic tradition and other religious traditions are living. They can move forward in their support for the equal rights of women. It can be hoped that the arguments here will help advance that movement toward genuinely universal respect for rights.

12

UNIVERSALITY AND WOMEN'S RIGHTS

This chapter explores claims about the universality of human rights in relation to cultural differences. In particular, it considers some ways claims about the universality of human rights relate to issues concerning women and whether protecting women's rights can justify initiatives that seek change across cultural boundaries. It argues that there are indeed human rights that belong universally to all people, including all women. Since these rights are universal, securing them can sometimes justify initiatives that seek cultural change, including change for the benefit of women. In making this argument I distinguish between initiatives that rely on persuasion, education, and moral argument, on the one hand, and interventions that use compulsion and coercion, on the other. Persuasive initiatives to secure women's rights could include, for example, educational programs that aim to gradually change practices linked to culturally defined gender roles. More coercive interventions could include the use of the police power of the state to prevent the rape of women or the use of military power of the nation-state to protect women in war and from the crimes of ethnic cleansing and genocide.

What is argued here builds upon work done by Margaret Farley. Like a number of other feminist thinkers, Farley has been concerned with whether the achievement of a morality that reaches across the boundaries of diverse cultural and religious traditions is a genuine possibility. The issue arises in discussions of the relationship between feminist concerns and the well-being of women in diverse cultures.[1] It is clear that claims about a common human nature shared across cultures have frequently been used in ways oppressive and harmful to women. Nevertheless, appeals to a common humanity are often at the heart of efforts to advance respect for women through critique of social institutions and cultural standards. Such critiques implicitly presuppose that criteria for defining what is truly human can reach across cultural differences, especially as these affect gender roles.

Both the dangers of claims to universal human rights and the ways such claims can serve the well-being of women inform what is said here. This chapter, however, does not address the many issues that arise when feminism and human rights interact. Nor does it deal with many of the tensions between the Christian and Catholic traditions on the one hand and the well-being of women on the other. Addressing these tensions is important, as has been noted in chapter 1 herein. This chapter focuses on the universality of women's rights in a way that is particularly shaped by my experiences working in eastern Africa on a number of occasions in recent years, especially regarding those human rights and women's issues that have recently been particularly acute in the context of Africa.

TWO EXPERIENCES AS BACKGROUND

In light of this African focus, it will be useful to open the argument to be presented here by recounting two different experiences I had while teaching and doing research in Kenya several years ago. The first began with an invitation to give a public lecture in Nairobi on the topic of human rights in contemporary Africa. Four Kenyans were scheduled to respond, so I was concerned about giving adequate attention to the influence of the distinctiveness of African cultures on the understanding of human rights. My lecture considered at some length the thought of several African intellectuals who had been raising objections to the universality of human rights, claiming that human rights are Western constructs and not appropriate standards for social and political life in Africa. These thinkers noted that when the standards set forth in the UN's Universal Declaration of Human Rights were codified in the aftermath of World War II, nearly all peoples on the African continent were under European colonial rule. Africans and their cultures had virtually no voice in the drafting of the Universal Declaration. Some African thinkers argue that the prevailing conception of human rights expresses the more individualistic understanding of the person held by most contemporary Europeans and North Americans, and that this conception of human rights conflicts with the stronger sense of solidarity common in African cultures. For example, the Nigerian C. C. Mojekwu has advocated this view. In Mojekwu's words,

African concepts of human rights are very different from those of Western Europe. Communalism and communal right concepts are fundamental to understanding African culture, politics and society. One should not make the mistake of thinking that the colonial interlude washed away these fundamental cultures in society.[2]

The perceived link between human rights and the individualistic bias of Western liberalism has led a number of Africans to express their suspicions of "rights talk" in recent discussions.

Mojekwu's stress on communal rights concepts rather than individual self-determination is also prominent in the African Charter on Human and Peoples' Rights adopted in 1981 by the Organization of African Unity. The African Charter differs from the Universal Declaration of Human Rights by calling itself a charter of human and *peoples'* rights. It declares not only that all human beings are equal but that all *peoples* are as well. This difference is explained in the preamble to the charter, which states that "historical tradition and the values of African civilization . . . should inspire and characterize . . . reflection on the concept of human and peoples' rights."[3] Thus, the charter affirms that *peoples* have the right to self-determination, *peoples* have the right to pursue economic and social development according to the policy they have freely chosen, *peoples* have the right to freely dispose of their wealth and natural resources, and *peoples* have the right to economic, social, and cultural development. Accompanying this list of peoples' rights is a list of duties. These include the duty of the individual to contribute to the national community by placing his or her physical and intellectual abilities at its service as well as the duty not to compromise the security of the state of which one is a national or a resident.[4]

Though my lecture in Nairobi did not accept the claim of some African intellectuals and politicians that the solidaristic orientation of African cultures invalidates the universality of human rights, it did take their concerns seriously. Thus, I was surprised that one of my respondents, Gibson Kamau Kuria, objected to the attention I had given to their views. As a lawyer active in the political struggles of the Kenyan opposition against the authoritarian government then in power, Kuria strongly rejected hesitations about the appropriateness of human rights standards in the Kenyan context. He saw no conflict between respect for the cultures of the people of Africa and support for human rights. Indeed, he argued that the African intellectuals I had discussed, as well as those Western postcolonial theorists holding similar views, were making a fundamental mistake about the key issues facing the people of Africa in the contemporary situation. He acknowledged that their challenge to the appropriateness of human rights standards was motivated by a desire to protect the people of Africa from colonial control and domination by Western powers, but he also maintained that it would be anachronistic to see this as the central challenge facing Africa today.

Kuria argued that a considerably more urgent issue is the protection of African people against the oppression being visited upon them by indigenous African politicians, such as Daniel arap Moi, who had been ruling Kenya for several decades. The predominance of one-party states, the desire of the few for unrestrained power over the many, the use of politics to advance the narrow interests of particular ethnic groups, and straightforward corruption driven by greed are serious threats to the well-being of many African people today.[5] The defense of human rights is a key element in a strategy that aims at resisting these threats. A critique of human rights norms, therefore, plays into the hands of those who would use political power to advance their own narrowly defined interests. Kuria clearly had in mind the fact that Moi had regularly defended one-party rule as necessary in light of the cultural traditions of Kenya.[6] Kuria rejected this position forcefully: "The people in power try to say we [Africans] are different from other communities in the world. This is wrong. Human rights are for all."[7] In other words, Kuria shared the moral objective of protecting the well-being of African people against domination and control by elites with the African thinkers who were suspicious of human rights standards as excessively Western, but he saw the threats coming from a different quarter than they did. This suggests that any assessment of claims about the universality of human rights norms should be based not only on how the values that human rights seek to defend relate to diverse cultural traditions but also on which threats to these values are most salient.

A second experience I had in Kenya cast a somewhat different light on the question of the universality of human rights than did Kuria's strong defense of transcultural norms. About half the students in a course I was teaching in Nairobi on Christian social ethics were seminarians studying for the Catholic priesthood in the Jesuit order. A recent Jesuit General Congregation had taken a strong position in calling Jesuits to greater awareness of the injustices faced by women. Among the injustices mentioned by the congregation is female circumcision, which it described as a form of violence against women, along with dowry deaths and the murder of unwanted infant girls.[8] Since the practice of female circumcision is practiced in Kenya, I decided to raise this issue as a case in point in discussing the rights of women. I assigned a chapter that defends female initiation and circumcision in Jomo Kenyatta's anthropological study of Kikuyu cultural practices, *Facing Mount Kenya*.[9] This text was accompanied by another, an article from a recent issue of *The Hastings Center Report* that gave an overview of the ethical issues and argued that it should be

eliminated gradually through efforts that work respectfully with cultural traditions.[10] To my considerable surprise, the students divided about evenly on
whether the practice should be supported as essential to the initiation into
adult womanhood in the African cultures where it is practiced or opposed as
a violation of women's rights to bodily integrity and to self-determination in
their sexual lives. Those supporting the practice viewed others' opposition
as an indication of their weakened African authenticity, due to regrettable
Europeanization. This opposition to them was a sign that one had begun to
"think like a *mzungu*" ("white man" in Kiswahili).

Further, following the discussion of this topic, I expressed my surprise
at the number of students supporting the traditional practice to one Kikuyu
woman working in a secretarial position in a Nairobi university. When I did
so, she laughed, shook her head in a genial way, and said that I just didn't
understand the people I was trying to teach. In a matter-of-fact way she
commented that she herself had undergone the ritual as a teenage girl, that
her daughters had also, and that she hoped this practice would continue for
generations to come. She was a fairly well-educated urban woman, not a girl
from the "bush."

AN ARGUMENT ON UNIVERSALITY
AND DIFFERENCE

The arguments I encountered in Nairobi regarding female circumcision,
genital surgery, or female genital mutilation (the terminology is evaluatively
loaded) as a part of female initiation are echoed in the literature that continues to address the question. Amnesty International frames the question
as a human rights issue. It sees female genital mutilation (FGM) as a form
of violence against women. The practice is viewed as closely linked with the
enforcement of the inequality of women in political, social, and economic
life and as reinforcing the submissiveness of women. Thus, it is a fundamental issue of universal human rights and it should be abolished. In the words
of an Amnesty International report,

> FGM is a practice that compounds unspeakable violence against
> women and young girls with discrimination, repression, and inequal-
> ity. As the issue becomes more visible in the public sphere, states that
> allow FGM to be perpetuated face increasing criticism and scrutiny
> by the international community. It must be made clear that no form
> of violence against women can be justified by any cultural claim.[11]

In other words: FGM is a straightforward human rights issue; human rights are universal; cultures can and should be challenged in the name of these universal norms.

American philosopher Martha Nussbaum, who has strongly defended respect for cross-cultural moral standards, sees the practice as a violation of just such standards. Nussbaum acknowledges that women in developing countries face other forms of deprivation and oppression that are more serious than those connected with traditional genital surgeries. Among these she includes inadequate and unequal nutrition, health care, and education, inequality before the law, domestic violence, and rape.[12] Nevertheless, these traditional surgeries are serious violations of the physical integrity of women, denials of women's opportunity to experience some forms of sexual pleasure, and enforcement mechanisms for female inequality.

There are women in African cultures who are in fact already challenging these practices. Such internal criticism from within the cultures in which they occur is beginning to change these practices. And there is little doubt that some women within these cultures "wish outside aid" to help them in their efforts to work for change.[13] Opponents of the practices in developed countries, therefore, should not fear the charge of being "Westernizers" or colonialists when they take initiatives to help African women eliminate these practices. Rather, they should work for cultural transformation alongside the women who are seeking change in African societies. Nussbaum concludes that, in the face of the harm done to women by genital mutilation, we in the developed world "should be ashamed of ourselves if we do not use whatever privilege and power has come our way to make it disappear forever."

On the opposite side of the academic argument are two anthropologists— one African and one American, one female and one male. In a provocative reflection on rites of genital cutting among her own Kono people in Sierra Leone, Fuambai Ahmadu notes that she has herself undergone an initiation rite involving excision of the clitoris. She considers herself "neutral" about the continuation of the practice but objects to the view that being an educated woman should be identified with being opposed to the traditional practice. In her experience the rite had some negative aspects, to be sure, chiefly excruciating pain. But both to her and among the women she studies as a professional anthropologist, it also has notably positive dimensions. In effect Ahmadu turns on its head the feminist argument against the practice. In the Kono culture the positive dimensions include "the 'acting out' and celebration of women's preeminent roles in history and society." The rite is an initiation into a "fear-inspiring world, controlled and dominated by women," and the scar left by the surgery is a symbol of common female identity and power.[14]

UNIVERSALITY AND WOMEN'S RIGHTS 189

Thus, Ahmadu argues strongly against the idea that progress for women and the eradication of the traditional practice are identical. She favors developing practices that reduce the medical risks while retaining the cultural significance of the traditional rites for women's identity. And she supports allowing young women to make up their own minds about whether to undergo the surgery.

American anthropologist Richard Shweder cites Ahmadu with strong approval. He also appeals to a recent study that maintains that the medical effects of the traditional practice are much less harmful than opponents often maintain.[15] In addition, he argues that if we consider the practice from the viewpoint of those who actually undergo it, we will learn that it has genuine value in their eyes. They see it as making them "more beautiful, more feminine, more civilized, and more honorable." "The weight of the evidence suggests that the overwhelming majority of youthful female initiates believe that they have been improved (physically, socially, and spiritually) by the ceremonial ordeal and symbolic process (including the pain) associated with initiation."[16]

Shweder does not advocate a cultural relativism that declares that anything goes. He holds that universal values do exist. These values can be realized in multiple ways, however, in different forms of life realized in different cultures. Appreciation of diverse cultures from the inside reveals that they are imaginative ways of being human. It is not possible to realize all of these imagined ways of being human in the same lives at the same time. Thus, pluralism is inevitable, and having true respect for human beings calls for having genuine respect for the way they have come to imagine human flourishing. When Westerners consider the traditional practices of female genital surgery, therefore, they are challenged to move beyond an initial impulse of rejection and even revulsion to at least consider the value the practice has in the lives of those who perform it. Respect for their worth as persons as well as the value of tolerance demand nothing less. Like Ahmadu, Shweder leaves open the possibility that the practice might be gradually replaced by other modes of initiation, and he holds that no young women should be forced to undergo it involuntarily. His appeal for greater openness to the practice is thus based on arguments that have a lot in common with the discourse of both human rights and women's rights.

KANTIAN AND ARISTOTELIAN
MOMENTS IN RIGHTS DISCOURSE

What do these competing responses to the practices associated with female initiation in some African cultures imply about human rights and women's rights? Some light can be shed on the issue by distinguishing two aspects of the arguments about human and women's rights. These can be called the Kantian and Aristotelian moments in the development of an understanding of rights. The Kantian moment concerns the question of who is the *subject* of rights or to whom the requirements of the human rights ethos are owed. The Aristotelian moment, on the other hand, addresses the *content* of the human rights ethos. It deals with the question of what specific goods people have a legitimate claim to—the goods others are responsible to provide for them. This question can also be put in negatively: What are the harms that people have a legitimate claim not to have inflicted on them and that others are responsible to avoid inflicting?

Each of these questions highlights a different aspect of the issue of whether it is reasonable to assert that there are universal human rights that apply in the diverse cultures of the world today. The Kantian question concerns the beneficiaries of such a purported universal human rights morality. It concerns the scope of the community that a common morality aims to govern. In other words, it asks about the "we" that is constituted as a moral community by holding the same moral standards in common. The Aristotelian question, on the other hand, concerns the content of such a common morality. What kinds of treatment are people entitled to receive from others and what forms of treatment should they always be immune from? Let us consider these questions in turn.

The Universal Declaration of Human Rights is based on the conviction that there is a worldwide community of which all human beings are members and within which human rights are secured. The terms "all," "everyone," and "no one" are used repeatedly as the first words in the articles of the Universal Declaration that specify the various human rights. The "everyone" who are the subjects of human rights are to be understood without distinctions based on "race, color, sex, language, religion, political or other opinion, national or social origin."[17] Thus, to the question of who possesses human rights, the declaration's answer is unambiguous: *all* human beings do. The universality of human rights, therefore, aims to relativize all in-group/out-group boundaries when it comes to the protection of the rights it affirms. This is a challenge to all definitions of religious and cultural identity that suggests rights are owed only to the people who possess that identity. Though discrimination on the basis of membership in an identity group may be legitimate regarding some goods, it is not legitimate when those goods are a matter of human rights.

This stress on universality in human rights discourse follows Kant's lead, not only in affirming the existence of universal moral obligations but also in closely linking the reality of moral obligation with the requirement of respect for humanity as such. Kant simultaneously affirms both the universal reach of moral obligation and the duty to treat every human being as an end and never a means only. Human rights discourse has analogies with Kant's moral philosophy to the extent that it associates the universal reach of moral obligation with the intrinsic dignity of persons. There are, of course, well-known problems with Kant's philosophical arguments for this ethical stance. There are ways to reach Kant's conclusions, however, that may have fewer problems than ones associated with Kant's systematic moral philosophy. Let me suggest the very general outlines of one such approach.

The reality of human persons—the kind of beings that humans in fact are—is at the root of many important moral claims that persons make upon one another.[18] Human beings are not things; they possess both self-consciousness and a self-transcendent capacity to reach beyond themselves in knowledge, freedom, and love. A person's capacity for self-transcendence gives rise to a moral claim that she be treated in ways that sustain or at least do not destroy that capacity. To respect a person's ability to know, to make choices, and to form bonds of love is to respect the claim of what she is and to acknowledge what she can become. Similarly, a second person is capable of experiencing that claim precisely because the second person also possesses the capacity for self-transcendence. This other person is not confined within the limits of his self-consciousness but can genuinely encounter the other as a fellow human being. Thus, one human being *is* a kind of *ought* in the face of another. Each person's capacity for self-transcendence makes a claim on another's capacity for self-transcendence. One's ability to know and understand calls out for acknowledgment in the understanding and concern by others. One person's freedom places requirements on the freedom of others. One person's capacity to form bonds of relationship with others calls for acknowledgment and support through the concern of others.[19] These affirmations lead to a vision of the human race as a genuine moral community with reciprocal obligations among all its members. This vision of a universal human community is the basis of the cosmopolitan aspects of Kant's political thought. It sets Kant, and the Kantian aspects of a human rights ethic, at odds with approaches that see cultural differences as so basic that it becomes impossible to affirm that there are any universal moral obligations or rights common to human beings.[20]

To assert this is to make a claim about what is practically reasonable—about what "makes sense" with regard to the way we treat each other and about how moral obligation should be understood.[21] It is a practically reasonable principle of morality that arises from the human condition itself. Indeed, one could argue that all persons who wish to act reasonably should act in accord with the basic requirements of these claims of personhood. Such practical reasonableness takes priority over the simple acceptance of the traditions of one's own culture or of the cultures of the other peoples with whom one interacts.[22] Further, it means that if those traditions contain elements that appear to deny some human beings the respect that their capacity for self-transcendence requires, then those traditions should be critically challenged and, if necessary, changed. In other words, the *ought* that arises in the encounter among persons makes demands both upon all persons and also upon their cultural traditions. The rights that give expression to the claims that arise from the condition shared by all human beings are thus universal. Insistence that they be respected is not a form of imperialism or colonialism. It serves the same goal as what those calling for respect for diverse cultures see at the heart of their commitment, namely, genuine liberation from any form of domination or oppression.

The demand that the self-transcendence of human beings receive respect, however, remains a very general expression of what is required by a universal or common morality. This Kantian moment in rights discourse does not of itself adequately specify what these culture-transcending moral rights or obligations might actually be. It needs to be made more specific and concrete. In fact, the question of whether there are such universal standards will remain largely speculative until more concrete proposals are made concerning what rights or duties are taken to be universal. The effort to spell out the meaning of respect for human dignity in greater detail can be called the Aristotelian moment in the discussion of the relation between cultural differences and the universality claimed for human rights. Aristotle developed his ethics by seeking to identify what the good life is for human beings. A good life has more than one dimension or characteristic. Aristotle suggested that a good life involves a number of diverse kinds of activity, including both intellectual and practical pursuits.[23] In an analogous way, there will be multiple preconditions for the realization of dignity in people's lives. Answering the question of whether there are universal human rights will depend on determining whether some of these activities are conditions for human well-being in all cultures.

Answering this question calls for reflection on historical and social experience. Such reflection can begin from the insight, articulated by Aristotle but surely intelligible in all cultures, that human beings are really different from both beasts and from gods and should be treated differently from both beasts and gods.[24] Not being a beast is having the capacity to move beyond self-enclosed materiality. This capacity for self-transcendence, which was stressed in Kant's ethics, is unique to beings with consciousness or spirit. It

UNIVERSALITY AND WOMEN'S RIGHTS 193

is a key index of the distinctive worth of human personhood and it points to a central aspect of how humans can reasonably expect to be treated by each other. We should support one another in undertaking activities of the spirit, such as growing in knowledge, exercising freedom, or forming and sustaining personal relationships such as friendship. At a minimum we should refrain from preventing one another from engaging in these activities of the spirit. At the same time, human beings are not gods, and human self-transcendence is that of a bodily being; it has material conditions. Human dignity can only be realized if these material conditions are present and it cannot be realized if they are lacking. Human well-being thus requires not only that one's freedom be secured and protected; it also requires food, shelter, bodily integrity, medical care in sickness, and a number of other material supports. Therefore, it can be reasonably affirmed that we have some responsibilities to enable one another to share in the material goods and physical, bodily activities that are among the conditions required for living with dignity. Again, at the minimum we have a duty not to deprive other persons of these material basics.

Practical reflections on the actual experience of what it is to be human such as these shaped the thinking of those who developed the list of human rights contained in the UN's Universal Declaration. Such reflection has minimal metaphysical presuppositions, and a plausible case can be made that they are compatible with the imaginative visions of human well-being found in most cultures of the world. Of course, such practical reflection on human experience may not lead to full agreement on the total set of activities that are prerequisites for living well or even living with basic human dignity. It is also true that people from different cultural and religious traditions will explain the origins and full significance of human dignity and what it requires through different narratives, metaphysical theories, or theologies. Despite these differences in interpretation, however, it does not seem impossible that all practically reasonable people can agree that human dignity means not being enslaved, not being politically oppressed, or not starving when alternative conditions are genuine possibilities. The quest for standards of a common morality and for a universal human rights ethic is the effort to identify prerequisites of human dignity such as these. The drafters of the Universal Declaration believed they had at least made a good start in such an effort. The challenge today, in light of the debates about the influence of cultural pluralism, is to determine whether we can affirm a set of human and women's rights as practically reasonable for all. To dismiss the idea that there are such rights simply *because* it claims to reach across the boundaries dividing cultural traditions would be to decide the matter without giving it the practical reflection it deserves.

Lisa Cahill has observed that the most basic standards of a universal or global common morality may be somewhat less difficult to identify than the highly disputed hard cases might lead one to suspect. Cahill points out that across considerable cultural and religious differences there are certain basic needs and goods that virtually all people today agree are due to everyone. The UN Millennium Declaration, for example, has set development goals that very few people, including those who stress the significance of cultural differences, would be willing to challenge. These include eradicating extreme poverty and hunger, achieving universal primary education, reducing child mortality, improving maternal health, and combating AIDS, malaria, and other infectious diseases.[25]

These goals, like many of those set forth in other consensus documents, indicate that there is agreement on at least some basic values across cultures and religious traditions. In Cahill's words these documents "demonstrate that there are certain basic human needs and goods that are not that difficult to recognize globally."[26] One could add a number of negative proscriptions to the positive prescriptions on which most traditions can readily achieve consensus. These might include the moral prohibition of murder, genocide, torture, enslavement, and less extreme abuses, such as political oppression and the theft of what rightly belongs to another. Agreement on these matters carries us well along the way toward affirming that many of the human rights affirmed in the Universal Declaration are truly becoming part of a universal ethic or common morality.

RELEVANCE TO WOMEN'S RIGHTS: BACK TO CASES

Where does this leave us regarding the claim that there are rights particularly applicable to women that transcend cultures and are thus universal? Before turning again to a disputed issue such as the relation between human rights and female genital surgeries in African cultures, it may be useful to consider another rights issue with special relevance to women on which there appears to be considerably more consensus.

The sexual violation of women has long been a commonplace in the midst of warfare. In fact, through most of human history the rape of women seems to have been taken for granted as an expected aspect of war. In very recent decades, however, the sexual abuse of women by men in the midst of war has come to the fore as a central human rights issue. The contemporary human rights ethos emerged in response to the atrocities of the Holocaust and the Nazi genocide of the Jewish people. Women suffered these abominations just as men did. But it has taken the vivid awareness of very recent atrocities to bring to the fore certain rights that are especially relevant to women during war. For example, feminist legal scholar Catharine MacKinnon illustrates such atrocities by citing a personal communication to her by an American researcher investigating the abuse of women in Croatia and Bosnia during the war unleashed as the former Yugoslavia disintegrated:

> Serbian forces have exterminated over 200,000 Croatians and Muslims thus far in an operation they've coined "ethnic cleansing." In this genocide, in Bosnia-Herzegovina alone over 30,000 Muslim and Croatian girls and women are pregnant from mass rape. Of the 100 Serbian-run concentration camps, about 20 are solely rape/death camps for Muslim and Croatian women and children.[27]

MacKinnon argues that such violations have rarely or never been seen as violations of the human rights of women as such. If the women undergoing systematic rape survive, the abuse has traditionally been discounted as an inevitable consequence of war. If the women perish, their deaths are seen as the deaths of Muslims or Bosnians, not women. So these gross violations of the rights of women during war have long been masked.[28]

The passionate protests of MacKinnon and many others against this obscuring of the sexual and gendered aspects of these abuses have begun to bear some fruit. There has been a growing consensus that those who harm women this way should be held fully accountable for violating fundamental human rights. The strongest evidence for this has arisen in an African context. In 1998 the International Criminal Tribunal for Rwanda convicted Jean-Paul Akayesu of genocide, incitement to genocide, and crimes against humanity for his participation in the events in the Gitarama District of Rwanda during the massacres that occurred there in 1994. This verdict was a landmark in international and humanitarian law, for it was the first conviction ever handed down for the crime of genocide. In the context under discussion here it was also significant for its findings that the sexual violence committed against women in the midst of the Rwanda conflict was itself both a crime against humanity and part of the crime of genocide. The tribunal found that Akayesu, the Hutu *bourgmestre* (mayor) of Taba commune, knew of, encouraged, and failed to prevent sexual violence and rape against a number of Tutsi women. The court found that his action of encouraging the rape of these women was directed at systematically degrading them in their own right (a crime against humanity). He also sought to sexually degrade Tutsi women precisely as members of the Tutsi ethnic group, and this was as part of his participation in an effort to eliminate the Tutsi ethnic group overall. Thus, the rapes Akayesu encouraged fall under the legal definition of genocide. In the words of the international tribunal, these women "were subjected to sexual violence because they were Tutsi. Sexual violence was a step in the process of destruction of the Tutsi group—destruction of the spirit, of the will to live, and of life itself."[29]

The tribunal's decisions, therefore, concluded that the rape of the Tutsi women in Taba was an assault on their very humanity and was part of an attempt to deny their dignity and worth as persons, as beings who should be treated with respect for their capacity for self-transcendence. It was a direct violation of the requirement that these women should be treated with the respect due to persons who are ends in themselves. The rapes that took place in the midst of the Rwanda genocide were certainly not due simply to Hutus imagining that sexual or gender roles might be organized differently from the way Europeans or Americans organize them. These rapes were intended, the tribunal held, quite literally to dehumanize Tutsi women. And this effort to dehumanize Tutsi women was a part of the broader effort to destroy the humanity of all Tutsi persons by killing them. Jean-Paul Akayesu is not simply a person from another culture, engaging in a way of living out his sexual life that Europeans and Americans find strange or even disturbing but should nonetheless tolerate. Rather, in the Francophone expression that is tragically often heard in Rwanda today, Jean-Paul Akayesu is a *genocidaire*. His behavior was not simply culturally different variation; it was a violation of minimal requirements of humanity and basic human rights that all people in all cultures can be morally required to respect. For these violations, the international tribunal sentenced him to spend the rest of his life in prison.[30]

PERSUASIVE INITIATIVES AND COERCIVE INTERVENTIONS

The differences between the human rights aspects of female genital surgeries and of the rape of Tutsi women in the midst of the Rwandan genocide highlights several important aspects of the debate about the universality of human rights in general and of women's rights in particular. Sometimes assertions about human rights and women's rights seek to persuade others to abolish practices one sees as harmful to the realization of human dignity. Amnesty International and Martha Nussbaum both believe that genital surgery as part of the initiation of girls into adult womanhood is a serious violation of their dignity. They call for vigorous efforts to eliminate this practice. The means they envision using to bring about change are persuasion and education. They propose moral arguments and make appeals to moral imagination to persuade the members of the cultures that practice these forms of initiation to abandon them. Even as they envision passing laws in African countries that would make these practices illegal, they advocate such legislation by the route of persuasion and reasoned argument. In other words, they do not envision using coercion to change the cultures where these rites are practiced. Their approach to cultural change in the name of the rights of women is nonviolent. The force of Ahmadu's and Shweder's arguments on the other side of this debate hinges in part on their suggestion that approaches like those of Amnesty International and Nussbaum are in fact coercive manipulations of cultures. But the suggestion that Amnesty and Nussbaum want to "coerce" cultural change seems misdirected. Further, both Ahmadu and Shweder themselves suggest that it would be better to replace genital surgery with other practices that could play a similar role in the initiation of girls into adulthood. It appears that if the suggestion that cultural change requires coercion is dropped, Ahmadu and Shweder might be able to reach consensus with Amnesty International and Nussbaum on the implications of women's rights in this domain.

The difference between seeking to secure women's rights through persuasion versus doing so by coercion becomes clearer if we contrast possible responses to female genital surgery with the response to the rape of Tutsi women in Rwanda. Many human rights advocates have argued that the larger world should have intervened with the use of force to stop the Rwandan genocide, a view I share. The human rights violations in Rwanda were of such a serious nature that the use of coercion—indeed, military coercion—was not only justified but morally required. Roméo Dallaire, the Canadian general who had been in command of the UN peacekeeping forces in Rwanda at the time of the genocide, has described the inaction of the international community as a "loss of innocence" that "disgusted" him as a human being.[31] Indeed, Dallaire suffered a serious psychological breakdown in the aftermath of the genocide because of his sense that he had not done enough to persuade international agencies to take more concerted military action.[32]

J. Bryan Hehir, a highly regarded specialist in ethics and international politics, has referred to the world's inaction in Rwanda as an "abject international failure."[33] Hehir argues that avoidance of the use of force should be the starting point for all efforts to secure human rights but that truly massive human rights violations such as genocide and ethnic cleansing call for departing from the norm of nonintervention. The classic just war criterion of just cause can be understood and developed in a way that can legitimate and sometimes require overriding the presupposition against the use of force. Hehir suggests this should have occurred in the face of the Rwandan genocide and the ethnic cleansing campaign in Bosnia. In both Rwanda and Bosnia, systematic sexual abuse of women was an integral part of actions that later were judged as crimes against humanity and genocide. Preventing and stopping such grave and systematic rights violations when they are occurring can be just cause for the coercive use of force.

Thus, action to protect the rights of women does not come in only one form. It can take the form of initiatives that seek to persuade people to change their values and behavior. Such persuasive initiative appeals to the practical reason and moral imagination of those one seeks to persuade. It respects the capacity for self-transcendence through practical reason and moral imagination in those being addressed. It shows respect for members of the cultures that practice these rites, both by seeking to advance the dignity of their members and in the way cultural changes are advocated. The ability to imagine that life can be different is a key element of the human capacity for self-transcendence and rationality. To maintain that African peoples who practice genital surgery on girls should not even be exposed to alternatives to these practices is really, though perhaps unwittingly, to suggest that they lack the capacity to make judgments about their own human good. On the other hand, working for women's rights through persuasion that avoids manipulation and subtle forms of coercion across cultural differences expresses commitment to human dignity understood in its "Kantian" dimensions.

Such persuasion begins with the presupposition that members of African peoples deserve the respect of being treated as persons who are fully capable of evaluating their existing cultural practices and determining whether they should be continued or not. Of course, those who undertake such efforts at persuasion must be similarly ready to revise their understanding of the effects of the initiation rites through intellectual and imaginative engagement with worldviews that initially seem strange or even abhorrent. Such willingness to revise one's views, or at least to tolerate the behavior that is judged unacceptable until those who practice it conclude that change is called for, is essential if change is to be brought about by persuasion rather than coercion. It requires a mutual exchange among the partners in the cultural interchange, and this mutuality itself requires commitment to the fundamental human equality of those involved. I have elsewhere called such reciprocal engagement with those who are different "intellectual solidarity."[34] This kind of respect for the dignity and capacity for self-transcendence of those who are different is a most basic requirement of a Kantian understanding of human rights. At the same time, in calling those who practice genital surgeries to consider altering their understanding of what their human dignity really requires it proposes a revision of what we have called the "Aristotelian" aspects of their understanding of the requirements of human dignity. Thus, the Kantian requirement of respect of persons as ends in themselves and the Aristotelian concern to discover the genuine human good in an inductive way can meet in a persuasive dialogue about the practice of female circumcision. Pursuing human and women's rights this way can be compatible with a commitment that advances the rights of women and at the same time shows real respect for peoples from the diverse cultures of the world.

But there are limits to this persuasive approach to both human and women's rights, as the rapes committed during the Rwanda genocide suggest. Some practices are direct attacks on the human person as such. Hutu behavior in Rwanda was not simply the result of a conception of the human good that the Hutu people and their leaders believed they should seek to realize in their life together. Rather, it was based in a conviction, sometimes explicit, sometimes implicit, that Tutsi persons do not count as human beings at all. The genocide that took place in Rwanda, including the rape of women that was part of it, sought to deny the fundamental dignity of Tutsi people, both by degrading them to a subhuman level and by killing them outright. In the terms we have been using here, it was an effort to deny the Kantian dimension of the dignity of all Tutsi people. In this broad sense it was a crime against the very humanity of the Tutsi people, both collectively and individually.

Protection against this sort of violation is the precondition for securing all other human rights—both the rights of individual persons and the rights of cultural groups of persons. It is for this reason that Henry Shue has called the rights that protect one against violations of this kind "basic rights." In Shue's words, "basic rights are the morality of the depths. They specify the line beneath which no one is to be allowed to sink."[35] Basic rights are the prerequisites for the enjoyment of all other rights and goods. Thus, basic rights may never be consistently traded off to obtain less basic goods, for the less basic goods cannot themselves be enjoyed when basic rights are being denied. For example, education is a very great good and one can argue that all persons have a right to at least the rudiments of an adequate education. One could also argue that education is a higher or more fully human good than the minimum condition of not being assaulted or killed. Shue argues persuasively that prevention of assault or murder is more basic than the provision of education, since assault and murder surely prevent education from happening.

Thus, the right to security from assault or murder is more basic than the right to public provision of education.[36] In a similar way, the human right not to be subjected to genocide or ethnic cleansing and women's rights not to be raped as a military strategy intended to demoralize and ultimately to eliminate an ethnic group are truly basic rights. They are more basic than the cultural rights that ensure that diverse cultural groups interact in a way marked by mutuality, equality, and reciprocity. Without protection against genocide, ethnic cleansing, and other crimes against humanity that are directed at the very personhood of group members, no humane interaction of cultures will be possible at all. It is for this reason that the use of coercion may sometimes be justifiable to prevent the systematic violation of basic rights, while persuasion will be the appropriate means to the promotion of rights that are less basic. This, I take it, is why it makes sense to conclude that preventing what happened to women in Rwanda and Bosnia may be grounds for military intervention, while changing the practice of female circumcision should be pursued through educational and persuasive means.

A distinction drawn by John Rawls can help illuminate what is at stake here. Rawls distinguishes between liberal peoples and those he calls "decent peoples." Liberal peoples, as Rawls describes them, support the full range of rights we associate with liberal and, perhaps, social democracy in the West. These include the rights embodied in constitutional democracy, such as institutional protections of full political equality, the rights to vote and hold office independent of religion or cultural background, and the right to full freedom to exercise religious beliefs in public. Decent peoples have a less inclusive understanding of rights. As Rawls describes them, such people will grant all members of their society the right to be consulted and heard in the political process. They may not, however, understand the right to be heard as requiring a universal right to suffrage or to hold office. Rawls can envision what he calls a "decent consultation hierarchy" that sets some restrictions on suffrage or on holding office, perhaps based on religion or culture.[37] The primary case Rawls has in mind here is clearly some form of Islamic republic that seeks to combine both Muslim and democratic values.[38]

It is important to note that Rawls thinks that being a "consultation hierarchy" of this sort is compatible with respect for the most basic human rights as Shue describes them. In fact, for such a society to be considered "decent," in Rawls's terms, it must respect a class of human rights that are particularly urgent. These include freedom from slavery, liberty of conscience, and security of ethnic groups from mass murder and genocide.[39] These rights are taken to be at the very core of a common morality on which all reasonable people can agree in practice, both reasonable Western liberals and reasonable people living in decent hierarchical traditions. In relation to the argument advanced here, the right of women not to be abused as they were in Rwanda and Bosnia can be affirmed as an essential expression of respect for the humanity of women, everywhere and independent of the importance of respect for cultural differences. It can be appealed to as a basis for intervention to stop such abuse of women, even military intervention. On the other hand, the Western understanding of what the dignity of women requires is grounds for seeking to persuade some eastern African cultures to replace the use of circumcision in the initiation of girls. This Western understanding of women's dignity, however, is not an adequate ground for resorting to coercion to bring about cultural change.

The distinction between basic rights and the fuller list of rights associated with Western liberalism thus has significant practical relevance, both for human rights in general and for women's rights in particular. This distinction is related to the difference between moral norms that we judge should be enforced by law and backed by the police or military power versus those we think should be secured through persuasion, education, and moral argument. It is notable that Rawls draws the distinction between liberal societies and decent societies in a book on the *law* of peoples. The urgent rights that he associates with decency are those that must be respected by peoples who want to avoid the status of outlaw. Peoples who do not respect these truly basic rights are subject to international condemnation and sanctions. If the violations of these rights are grave, peoples who commit the violations may become subject to intervention by the use of force.[40]

Respect for the religious and cultural beliefs of the diverse communities in our world is surely a crucial requirement of our time. It is also an essential element of an ethic committed to human rights and women's rights. This chapter has shown that commitment to respect for cultural diversity does not settle all the issues that arise in the present-day pursuit of human rights and women's rights. Distinctions need to be drawn between more and less basic rights and between the means that are proposed to secure them. If a community appeals to its religious or cultural traditions to justify racism (as did some Afrikaner Christians in South Africa during the apartheid era), or to legitimate denying education to girls (as do the Taliban in their interpretation of Islam), or to support the practice of female circumcision (as do some African cultures), practical reason justifies raising serious objections. These objections should be raised first of all in the mode of persuasion and moral argument. In some circumstances, however, it may be appropriate as a last resort to go beyond persuasion to some form of coercive sanction. Such coercion could be exercised by international courts with genuine enforcement powers, by the use of economic pressure such as the sanctions that were directed against the apartheid regime in South Africa, or, in the extreme, by military intervention to prevent crimes such as ethnic cleansing or genocide. There are limits to what can be done in the name of culture and religion, even in an ethic that strongly supports the right to cultural and religious freedom. These limits are set by what we can reasonably conclude are the most fundamental prerequisites of human dignity.

Thus, discerning the appropriate ways to secure the rights of women in our time challenges us with a twofold task. First, we need to pay careful attention to the fundamental dignity of women as ends in themselves and beings who possess the capacity for self-transcendence. This is the most basic requirement of any human rights ethic and also of any ethic that promotes the rights of women. Second, we need to engage in the cross-cultural dialogue that is required to bring us a more adequate understanding of what this dignity concretely requires in our multicultural, multireligious world. Neither of these tasks can be pursued alone; each will help clarify the understanding of rights and duties discovered in the other. The pursuit of both tasks is essential to discerning when change should be proposed through argument, education, or persuasion or if grave abuses are occurring that require more forceful intervention. The promotion of human rights and women's rights requires practical wisdom based on experience and on prudential choices guided by a spirit of solidarity. It is a task worthy of all the intellectual and practical endeavor it will require.

NOTES

CHAPTER 1

1. Jaroslav Pelikan, *The Vindication of Tradition: The 1983 Jefferson Lecture in the Humanities* (New Haven, CT: Yale University Press, 1984), 65.
2. Stephen Hopgood, *The Endtimes of Human Rights* (Ithaca, NY: Cornell University Press, 2013); Yascha Mounk, *The People vs. Democracy: Why Our Freedom Is in Danger and How to Save It* (Cambridge, MA: Harvard University Press, 2018); Samuel Moyn, *Not Enough: Human Rights in an Unequal World* (Cambridge, MA: Belknap, 2018).
3. Pelikan, *The Vindication of Tradition*, 58.
4. Pope Gregory XVI, Mirari Vos Arbitramur, August 15, 1832, excerpt in *Enchridion Symbolorum Definitionem et Declarationem de Rebus Fidei et Morum* 32, ed. Henricus Denzinger and Adolphus Schönmetzer (Rome: Herder, 1963), no. 2730, 549.
5. Preamble to Universal Declaration of Human Rights, http://www.un.org/en/universal-declaration-human-rights.
6. Pope Leo XIII, *Rerum Novarum*, 1891, nos. 40, 43–53, and 49–51, http://w2.vatican.va/content/leo-xiii/en/encyclicals/documents/hf_l-xiii_enc_15051891_rerum-novarum.html.
7. For a sketch of the development of this tradition from Leo XIII to Paul VI, see my *Claims in Conflict: Retrieving and Renewing the Catholic Human Rights Tradition* (Ramsey, NJ: Paulist, 1979), 41–106. Subsequent developments are treated in Meghan Clark, *The Vision of Catholic Social Thought: The Virtue of Solidarity and the Praxis of Human Rights*, (Minneapolis, MN: Fortress, 2014).
8. Samuel Huntington, "Religion and the Third Wave," *National Interest* 24 (Summer 1991): 29–42. This article is based on Huntington's *The Third Wave: Democratization in the Late Twentieth Century* (Norman: University of Oklahoma Press, 1991).
9. Monica Duffy Toft, Daniel Philpott, and Timothy Shah, *God's Century: Resurgent Religion and Global Politics* (New York: W. W. Norton, 2011), chap. 4, esp. tables 4.1, 4.2, 4.3, and 4.4. On Islam and democracy, see Daniel Philpott, *Religious Freedom in Islam? Intervening in a Public Debate* (Oxford: Oxford University Press, 2019); and Daniel Philpott, "Religious Freedom in Islam: A Global Landscape," *Journal of Law, Religion & State* 2 (2013): 3–21.

204 NOTES

10. Brian J. Grim and Roger Finke, *The Price of Freedom Denied: Religious Persecution and Conflict in the Twenty-First Century* (Cambridge: Cambridge University Press, 2011), 19.
11. UN High Commissioner for Refugees (UNHCR), "Global Trends Forced Displacement in 2022," https://www.unhcr.org/globaltrends.
12. "Pope Francis's Visit to Refugees at Mòria Refugee Camp and Meeting with the People of Lesvos and with the Catholic Community, Lesvos, Greece, April 16, 2016," on the website of the Holy See, http://w2.vatican.va/content/francesco/en/speeches/2016/april/documents/papa-francesco_20160416_lesvos-rifugiati.html. See also "Pope Francis Takes 12 Refugees Back to Vatican After Trip to Greece," *New York Times*, April 16, 2016, https://www.nytimes.com/2016/04/17/world/europe/pope-francis-visits-lesbos-heart-of-europes-refugee-crisis.html.
13. UNHCR, "Global Trends," https://www.unhcr.org/globaltrends. The full *Global Trends 2021* report is linked on this same page.
14. Donald Kerwin, "The US Refugee Resettlement Program—A Return to First Principles: How Refugees Help to Define, Strengthen, and Revitalize the United States," Center for Migration Studies Report, June 2018, http://cmsny.org/wp-content/uploads/2018/06/CCUSA-CRS-USCCB-US-Refugee-Resettlement-Report.pdf.
15. See Anne Case and Angus Deaton, "Mortality and Morbidity in the 21st Century," paper prepared for the Brookings Panel on Economic Activity, March 23–24, 2017, https://www.brookings.edu/wp-content/uploads/2017/03/6_casedeaton.pdf. See also Case and Deaton's earlier study, "Rising Morbidity and Mortality in Midlife among White Non-Hispanic Americans in the 21st Century," *Proceedings of the National Academy of Sciences* 112, no. 49 (December 8, 2015): 15078–83.
16. For an overview of some significant changes in Church moral teaching, see John T. Noonan, *A Church That Can and Cannot Change: The Development of Catholic Moral Teaching* (Notre Dame, IN: University of Notre Dame Press, 2005). Noonan shows that not long ago popes and bishops were condemning the rights to religious freedom, free speech, and democratic self-governance; were supporting the legitimacy of slavery; and were defending and practicing the use of coercion and even torture in support of religious truth.
17. *Compendium of the Social Doctrine of the Church*, no. 144, http://www.vatican.va/roman_curia/pontifical_councils/justpeace/documents/rc_pc_justpeace_doc_20060526_compendio-dott-soc_en.html.
18. See *Compendium of the Social Doctrine of the Church*, no. 244. Popes Francis, Benedict XVI, and John Paul II have often affirmed such complementarity as well.
19. Pope Francis, Apostolic Exhortation Amoris Laetitia, March 19, 2016, no. 56, http://w2.vatican.va/content/francesco/en/apost_exhortations/documents/papa-francesco_esortazione-ap_20160319_amoris-laetitia.html.

CHAPTER 2

1. For an overview of and response to some of these objections, see Mary Ann Glendon, "The Bearable Lightness of Dignity," *First Things* 213 (May 2011): 41–45.
2. Ruth Macklin, "Dignity Is a Useless Concept," *BMJ* 327 (December 20–27, 2003): 1419–20.
3. Steven Pinker, "The Stupidity of Dignity," *New Republic*, May 28, 2008, 28.

NOTES 205

4. Pinker, "The Stupidity of Dignity," 31.

5. Michael Ignatieff, *Human Rights as Politics and Idolatry* (Princeton, NJ: Princeton University Press, 2001), 53–55.

6. For Lee Kuan Yew's "Asian values" argument, see Fareed Zakaria, "Culture Is Destiny: A Conversation with Lee Kwan Yew," *Foreign Affairs* 73, no. 2 (March–April, 1994): 109–26. The African postcolonialist stand is developed in a practical way in Mahmood Mamdani, *Saviors and Survivors: Darfur, Politics, and the War on Terror* (New York: Pantheon, 2009).

7. Preamble to the Universal Declaration of Human Rights, http://www.un.org/en /documents/udhr (accessed May 8, 2012).

8. Samuel Moyn has argued that the Holocaust was at best tangential and perhaps even irrelevant to the drafting of the Universal Declaration. See Moyn, *The Last Utopia: Human Rights in History* (Cambridge, MA: Belknap, 2010), chap. 2. Moyn has quite effectively shown that the close linkage of human rights discourse and the Holocaust became much more explicit several decades after the declaration was drafted than at the time of the drafting. However, the appeal to deeds that "outraged the conscience of mankind" and the proclamation of the Universal Declaration just one day after the Genocide Convention suggests that that the two are not as unrelated as Moyn maintains. Indeed, later appeals to the Universal Declaration to resist genocide would not be possible without the link between the two that is at least incipient in the human rights discourse from the time of the drafting of the Universal Declaration. I diverge from Moyn in holding that changes in emphasis and even in the understanding of the content of human dignity do not necessarily imply radical discontinuity. "Development of doctrine," as the term is used is Catholic theology, sees historical change, even dramatic change, as at least sometimes compatible with continuity in tradition. Moyn, on the other hand, sees change as most often suggesting discontinuity.

9. Moyn also rejects this linkage of the Universal Declaration to subsequent anticolonial movements. See Moyn, *The Last Utopia*, chap. 3. My divergence from Moyn again rests on noting that subsequent appeals to the Universal Declaration by anticolonialists would not be possible without this incipient anticolonial affirmation in the declaration itself.

10. Immanuel Kant, *Grounding for the Metaphysics of Morals*, trans. James W. Ellington, 3rd ed. (Indianapolis, IN: Hackett, 1993), 40–41.

11. Though Moyn is right that anticolonial movements of the 1950s and 1960s sought national self-determination by states, the Universal Declaration affirms human rights in a way that goes beyond such a state-centered understanding of self-determination. Jacques Maritain, who contributed to the philosophical underpinnings of the Universal Declaration, makes a forceful argument that rights must reach beyond state sovereignty. See Maritain, *Man and the State* (Chicago: University of Chicago Press, 1951), chap. 2 and 194–201.

12. Universal Declaration of Human Rights, article 2.

13. See especially Aristotle, *Nicomachean Ethics*, book X, chaps. 4–6.

14. This phrase, and some of the analysis that follows, is drawn from Margaret A. Farley, "A Feminist Version of Respect for Persons," *Journal of Feminist Studies in Religion* 9, no. 1–2 (Spring–Fall 1993): 183–98.

15. Farley, 187, 189.

16. That human beings are neither beasts nor gods and should be treated accordingly is a presupposition of ethical politics. See Aristotle, *Politics*, book I, chap. 3, 1253a. Martha Nussbaum takes this as a fundamental presupposition of her "capabilities approach" to ethics

206 NOTES

in social and economic life. See, for example, Nussbaum, "Human Capabilities, Female Human Beings," in *Women, Culture, and Development: A Study of Human Capabilities*, ed. Martha Nussbaum and Jonathan Glover (Oxford: Oxford University Press, 1995), 73.

17. See William Luijpen, *Phenomenology of Natural Law* (Pittsburgh, PA: Duquesne University Press, 1967), chap. 6, "Justice as an Anthropological Form of Co-Existence," especially 180. For approaches that are both similar and interestingly different from this, see also Jean-François Lyotard, "The Other's Rights," in *On Human Rights: The Oxford Amnesty Lectures 1993*, ed. Stephen Shute and Susan Hurley (New York: Basic, 1993), 135–47; and Jacques Derrida, *Of Hospitality* (Stanford, CA: Stanford University Press, 2000).

18. Jacques Maritain, introduction to *Human Rights: Comments and Interpretations*, symposium edited by UNESCO (New York: Columbia University Press, 1949), 9.

19. Maritain, 10 (emphasis added).

20. Thomas Aquinas, *Summa Contra Gentiles* I, chaps. 112 and 113, trans. Anton C. Pegis, in *Basic Writings of Saint Thomas Aquinas* 2, ed. Anton C. Pegis (New York: Random House, 1945), 220, 223.

21. Pope John XXIII, *Pacem in Terris*, no. 10; and Vatican Council II, Gaudium et Spes, no. 22. Both in *Catholic Social Thought: The Documentary Heritage*, expanded edition, ed. David J. O'Brien and Thomas A. Shannon (Maryknoll, NY: Orbis, 2010).

22. Vatican II, Gaudium et Spes, no. 41.

23. Vatican II, Gaudium et Spes, nos. 15–17.

24. For the way John Courtney Murray's argument for religious freedom drew on practical reflection on historical experience, see Murray, *The Problem of Religious Freedom* (Westminster, MD: Newman, 1965), esp. 17.

25. Vatican II, Dignitatis Humanae (Declaration of Religious Freedom), no. 2, in *The Documents of Vatican II*, ed. Walter M. Abbott and Joseph Gallagher (New York: America Press, 1966). Michael Rosen perceptively discusses the importance of this development of Catholic thought on human dignity and rights in his *Dignity: Its History and Meaning* (Cambridge, MA: Harvard University Press, 2012), 47–54, 90–100. For my own treatment of the historical development of Catholic thought on dignity and rights, see my *Claims in Conflict: Retrieving and Renewing the Catholic Human Rights Tradition* (New York: Paulist, 1979).

26. Vatican II, Gaudium et Spes, no. 12. On this theme, see International Theological Commission, *Communion and Stewardship: Human Persons Created in the Image of God* (2004), esp. chap. 2, www.vatican.va/roman_curia/congregations/cfaith/cti_documents/rc_con_cfaith_doc_20040723_communion-stewardship_en.html (accessed May 10, 2012); and the more recent Jack Mahoney, *Christianity in Evolution: An Exploration* (Washington, DC : Georgetown University Press, 2011), chap. 2.

27. Vatican II, Gaudium et Spes, no. 25.

28. Pope Benedict XVI, Address to the Pontifical Academy of Social Sciences, April 30, 2010, http://www.vatican.va/holy_father/benedict_xvi/speeches/2010/april/documents/hf_ben-xvi_spe_20100430_scienze-sociali_en.html (accessed May 25, 2010).

29. International Theological Commission, *Communion and Stewardship*, nos. 81–94.

30. Pope Benedict XVI, "Faith, Reason and the University: Memories and Reflections," address at meeting with representatives of science, University of Regensburg, September 12, 2006, http://www.vatican.va/holy_father/benedict_xvi/speeches/2006/september/documents/hf_ben-xvi_spe_20060912_university-regensburg_en.html.

CHAPTER 3

1. Zeid Ra'ad Al Hussein, "The Impossible Diplomacy of Human Rights," lecture given on the occasion of receiving the 2017 Raymond "Jit" Trainor Award for Excellence in the Conduct of Diplomacy, Georgetown University and US Institute of Peace, February 16, 2017, video and text versions available at https://isd.georgetown.edu/2017/02/16/2017-trainor-award/.
2. UNHCR, "Global Trends 2022," https://www.unhcr.org/global-trends-report-2022.
3. See Stephen Hopgood, *The Endtimes of Human* Rights (Ithaca, NY: Cornell University Press, 2013); and Eric A. Posner, *The Twilight of Human Rights Law* (Oxford: Oxford University Press, 2014).
4. See Johannes Morsink, *The Universal Declaration of Human Rights and the Holocaust: An Endangered Connection* (Washington, DC: Georgetown University Press, 2019).
5. Samuel Moyn, *The Last Utopia: Human Rights in History* (Cambridge, MA: Belknap, 2010); and *Not Enough: Human Rights in an Unequal World* (Cambridge, MA: Belknap, 2018).
6. See Peter Uvin, *Aiding Violence: The Development Enterprise in Rwanda* (West Hartford, CT: Kumarian, 1998); and Peter Uvin, "Development Aid and Structural Violence: The Case of Rwanda," *Development* 42, no. 3 (1999): 49–56.
7. See Carol Rittner, John Roth, and Wendy Whitworth, eds., *Genocide in Rwanda: Complicity of the Churches?* (St. Paul, MN: Paragon, 2004); and Timothy Longman, *Christianity and Genocide in Rwanda* (New York: Cambridge University Press, 2010).
8. Pope Francis's apology is quoted in Holy See Press Office, "Press Communiqué: Audience with the President of the Republic of Rwanda," March 20, 2017, http://press.vatican.va/content/salastampa/en/bollettino/pubblico/2017/03/20/170320c.html. The Rwandan bishops expressed their regret this way: "We apologize for all the wrongs the church committed. We apologize on behalf of all Christians for all forms of wrongs we committed. We regret that church members violated (their) oath of allegiance to God's commandments." See Ignatius Ssuuna, "Rwanda: Catholic Bishops Apologize for Role in Genocide," Associated Press, November 21, 2016, https://apnews.com/842d2a4f306c43f096a57039c2071fbe.
9. Pope Gregory XVI, *Mirari vos arbitramur*, August 15, 1832, excerpt in Henricus Denzinger and Adolphus Schönmetzer, *Enchridion Symbolorum Definitionem et Declarationem de Rebus Fidei et Morum*, 32nd ed. (Rome: Herder, 1963), no. 2730, p. 549.
10. Vatican Council II, Gaudium et Spes, no. 41, http://www.vatican.va/archive/hist_councils/ii_vatican_council/documents/vat-ii_const_19651207_gaudium-et-spes_en.html.
11. Samuel Huntington, "Religion and the Third Wave," *The National Interest* 24 (Summer 1991): 29–42. This article is based on Huntington, *The Third Wave: Democratization in the Late Twentieth Century* (Norman: University of Oklahoma Press, 1991).
12. Preamble to the Universal Declaration of Human Rights, http://www.un.org/en/universal-declaration-human-rights. For a recent study of the importance of the Holocaust as a stimulus to the writing of the Universal Declaration, which refutes Samuel Moyn's rejection of this linkage, see Johannes Morsink, *The Universal Declaration of Human Rights and the Holocaust* (Washington, DC: Georgetown University Press, 2019). For a sketch of the shifts in Catholic attitudes toward the Jewish people at Vatican II, see John W. O'Malley,

208   NOTES

What Happened at Vatican II? (Cambridge, MA: Harvard University Press, 2008), 218–224, 275–277.

13. Pope John XXIII, *Pacem in terris*, nos. 8–9, http://w2.vatican.va/content/john-xxiii/en/encyclicals/documents/hf_j-xxiii_enc_11041963_pacem.html.

14. Vatican II, Dignitatis Humanae (Declaration on Religious Freedom), no. 1, http://www.vatican.va/archive/hist_councils/ii_vatican_council/documents/vat-ii_decl_1965 1207_dignitatis-humanae_en.html.

15. Pope John XXIII, *Pacem in terris*, no. 10; Vatican II, Gaudium et Spes, no. 22.

16. See Steven Pinker, *The Better Angels of Our Nature: Why Violence Has Declined* (New York: Penguin, 2011), 42–56.

17. For a discussion of these two revolutions, see Pinker, chaps. 4 and 7.

18. Jonathan Glover presents a stark picture of the continuing reality of the suffering of war, oppression, and genocide in the twentieth century in his *Humanity: A Moral History of the 20th Century*, 2nd ed. (New Haven, CT: Yale University Press, 2012).

19. Peter Stamatov, *The Origins of Global Humanitarianism: Religion, Empire, and Advocacy* (New York: Cambridge University Press, 2013), esp. chaps 1 and 2; and Roger Ruston, *Human Rights and the Image of God* (London: SCM, 2004).

20. Montesinos's sermon as recorded by Bartolomé de las Casas, *Historia de Las Indias*, in *Obras escogidas*, studio critico y edición por Juan Perez de Tudela Buesco, 5 vols. (Madrid: Atlas, 1957–58), vol. 2, col. 176, cited in Roger Ruston, *Human Rights and the Image of God* (London: SCM, 2004), 67.

21. Francisco Vitoria, "On the American Indians," in *Vitoria: Political Writings*, ed. Anthony Pagden and Jeremy Lawrance (Cambridge: Cambridge University Press, 1991), 231–92; and Bartolomé de Las Casas, *In Defense of the Indians*, trans. and ed. Stafford Poole (DeKalb: Northern Illinois University Press, 1992).

22. See Vitoria, "Lectures on Thomas Aquinas," which treats a classic articulation of natural law, Aquinas's Treatise on Law in *Summa Theologiae* I–II, q. 90–105, in Francisco Vitoria, *Vitoria: Political Writings*, ed. Anthony Pagden and Jeremy Lawrance (Cambridge: Cambridge University Press, 1991), 155–204.

23. For a persuasive argument that the sixteenth-century writings of Vitoria, with their appeal to natural law, anticipates modern, universalist ideas of human rights, see Roger Ruston, *Human Rights and the Image of God* (London: SCM, 2004), esp. parts 2 and 3, 76–77.

24. International Commission on Intervention and State Sovereignty, "The Responsibility to Protect" (Ottawa, Canada: International Development Research Center, 2001), https://www.idrc.ca/en/book/responsibility-protect-report-international-commission-intervention-and-state-sovereignty.

25. UN General Assembly, *2005 World Summit Outcome Document*, September 16, 2005, nos. 138–39, http://www.un.org/en/preventgenocide/adviser/pdf/World%20Summit%20Outcome%20Document.pdf.

26. Mahmood Mamdani, *Saviors and Survivors: Darfur, Politics, and the War on Terror* (New York: Pantheon, 2009), 300.

27. Alan J. Kuperman. "Obama's Libya Debacle: How a Well-Meaning Intervention Ended in Failure," *Foreign Affairs* 94, no. 2 (March–April 2015): 66–77. See also Derek Chollet and Ben Fishman, "Who Lost Libya: Obama's Intervention in Retrospect, a Close Call," *Foreign Affairs* 94, no. 3 (May–June, 2015): 154–57.

28. "Libya Protests: Defiant Gaddafi Refuses to Quit," *BBC News*, February 22, 2011, http://www.bbc.com/news/world-middle-east-12544624.

NOTES   209

29. UN Security Council, Resolution 1973 (2011), nos. 4 and 6, http://www.un.org/en/ga/search/view_doc.asp?symbol=S/RES/1973%282011%29.

30. Amnesty International, *Libya Is Full of Cruelty' Stories of Abductions, Sexual Violence and Abuse from Migrants and Refugees* (London: Amnesty International, 2015), 5–6, http://www.amnestyusa.org/research/reports/libya-is-full-of-cruelty-stories-of-abduction-sexual-violence-and-abuse-from-migrants-and-refugees.

31. See Kuperman. "Obama's Libya Debacle."

32. See Chollet and Fishman, "Who Lost Libya."

33. Thomas G. Weiss, "Military Humanitarianism: Syria Hasn't Killed It," *Washington Quarterly* 37, no. 1 (Spring 2014): 7–20.

34. International Coalition for the Responsibility to Protect, *The Crisis in Kenya 2; International Response to Halt the Spread of Violence*, http://www.responsibilitytoprotect.org/index.php/crises/crisis-in-kenya.

35. Roger Cohen, "How Kofi Annan Rescued Kenya," *New York Review of Books* 55, no. 13 (August 14, 2008).

36. On Mali, see UN Security Council Resolution 2085 (2012), http://www.globalr2p.org/media/files/sres2085-on-mali.pdf; on Central African Republic, see also UN Security Council Resolution 2127 (2013), http://www.un.org/en/ga/search/view_doc.asp?symbol=S/RES/2127(2013)&referer=http://www.un.org/en/sc/documents/resolutions/2013.shtml&Lang=E.

37. For divergent views on the difference application of R2P could have made in Rwanda, see Alan J. Kuperman, "Rwanda in Retrospect," *Foreign Affairs* 79, no. 1 (January–February, 2000): 94–118; and Alison L. Des Forges and Alan J. Kuperman, "Alas, We Knew," *Foreign Affairs* 79, no. 3 (May–June 2000): 141–44. Des Forges's extensive experience in Rwanda makes her side of this argument much more persuasive.

38. See Francis Mading Deng, ed., *Sovereignty as Responsibility: Conflict Management in Africa* (Washington, DC: Brookings Institution, 1996).

39. Pope Benedict XVI, Address to the General Assembly of the United Nations Organization, April 18, 2008, http://w2.vatican.va/content/benedict-xvi/en/speeches/2008/april/documents/hf_ben-xvi_spe_20080418_un-visit.html; and Pope Benedict XVI, *Caritas in veritate*, no. 67, http://w2.vatican.va/content/benedict-xvi/en/encyclicals/documents/hf_ben-xvi_enc_20090629_caritas-in-veritate.html.

40. Archbishop Bernardito Auza, "The Responsibility to Protect and Accountability for Prevention," Statement at the Informal Interactive Dialogue on the Report of the Secretary-General on the Responsibility to Protect and Accountability for Prevention, New York, September 6, 2017, https://holyseemission.org/contents/statements/59b07e40cc3c3.php.

41. Francisco Suárez, *On Laws and God the Lawgiver (De Legibus)*, II.ixx.9, in *Selections from Three Works of Francisco Suárez, SJ*, vol. 2, trans. and ed. Gwladys L. Williams et al. (Oxford: Clarendon, 1944), 348.

42. Suárez, 348–49.

43. See Pinker, *The Better Angels of Our Nature*; Pinker, "A History of Violence," Edge Master Class, 2011, available online at https://www.edge.org/conversation/steven_pinker-a-history-of-violence-edge-master-class-2011.

44. Kathryn Sikkink, *Evidence for Hope: Making Human Rights Work in the 21st Century* (Princeton, NJ: Princeton University Press, 2017).

45. See Sikkink, 143–46, esp. figs. 5.2 and 5.3.

210 NOTES

46. Bruce M. Russett and John R. Oneal, *Democracy, Interdependence, and International Organizations* (New York: Norton, 2001). See also Russett's earlier book, *Grasping the Democratic Peace: Principles for a Post–Cold War World* (Princeton, NJ: Princeton University Press, 1994).

47. Henry Shue, *Basic Rights: Subsistence, Affluence, and U.S. Foreign Policy*, 2nd ed. (Princeton, NJ: Princeton University Press, 1996), 18.

CHAPTER 4

1. UN, Universal Declaration of Human Rights, arts. 27–28.

2. See Fareed Zakaria, "Culture Is Destiny: A Conversation with Lee Kuan Yew," *Foreign Affairs* 73, no. 2 (March–April 1994): 112. For a later statement that suggests Lee came to hold that East Asian societies may be evolving in ways that will make them more culturally and social receptive to human rights and democracy, see Lee Kuan Yew, *From Third World to First: The Singapore Story: 1965–2000* (New York: HarperCollins, 2000), 487–500.

3. Chris C. Mojekwu, "International Human Rights: The African Perspective," in *International Human Rights: Contemporary Issues*, ed. Jack L. Nelson and Vera M. Green (Stanfordville, NY: Human Rights Publishing Group, 1980), 92–93.

4. African Charter on Human and People's Rights, arts. 19–22, in *The International Law of Human Rights in Africa: Basic Documents and Annotated Bibliography*, ed. M. Hamalengwa, C. Flinterman, and E. V. O. Dankwa (Dordrecht: Martinus Nijhoff, 1988).

5. African Charter on Human and People's Rights, art. 29.

6. For a Western critique of human rights as excessively Western, see Michael Ignatieff, *Human Rights as Politics and Idolatry* (Princeton, NJ: Princeton University Press, 2001), 58–77. Other aspects of my response to these Confucian, African, and postmodern critiques are in *The Global Face of Public Faith: Politics, Human Rights, and Christian Ethics* (Washington, DC: Georgetown University Press, 2003), chap. 11, "Human Rights and Development: The African Challenge," and chap. 12, "Faiths, Cultures, and Global Development."

7. Karl Marx, "On the Jewish Question," in *Writings of the Young Marx on Philosophy and Society*, ed. Loyd D. Easton and Kurt H. Guddat (Garden City, NY: Doubleday Anchor, 1967), 236–37.

8. Karl Marx, "Critique of the Gotha Program," in *Writings of the Young Marx on Philosophy and Society*, ed. Loyd D. Easton and Kurt H. Guddat (Garden City, NY: Doubleday Anchor, 1967), 119.

9. Samuel Moyn, *Not Enough: Human Rights in an Unequal World* (Cambridge, MA: Harvard University Press, 2018), 220.

10. See Human Rights Watch, "About Us," https://www.hrw.org/about/about-us.

11. Samuel Moyn, *The Last Utopia: Human Rights in History* (Cambridge, MA: Harvard University Press, 2010), 222.

12. Moyn, *Not Enough*, 216.

13. Kim Dae-jung, "Is Culture Destiny? The Myth of Asia's Anti-Democratic Values," *Foreign Affairs* 73, no. 6 (November–December 1994): 189–94.

14. Amartya Sen, "Asian Values and Human Rights," *New Republic*, July 14, 1997, 33–40; and Amartya Sen, *Development as Freedom* (New York: Knopf, 1999), chap. 10.

NOTES 211

15. Paulin J. Hountondji, "The Master's Voice: Remarks on the Problem of Human Rights in Africa," in *Philosophical Foundations of Human Rights*, ed. Alwin Diemer et al. (Paris: UNESCO, 1986), 328–29.

16. Wole Soyinka, "Best Idea: Every Dictator's Nightmare," *New York Times Magazine*, April 18, 1999, 90ff., https://archive.nytimes.com/www.nytimes.com/library/magazine/millennium/m1/soyinka.html.

17. See Johannes Morsink, *The Universal Declaration of Human Rights: Origins, Drafting, and Intent* (Philadelphia: University of Pennsylvania Press, 1999), 222–32; and Johannes Morsink, *Inherent Human Rights: Philosophical Roots of the Universal Declaration* (Philadelphia: University of Pennsylvania Press, 2009), chap. 5, esp. 235–52.

18. Samuel Moyn maintains that the historical account that posits the atrocities of the Holocaust as the stimulus for moving human rights to the forefront of recent moral awareness "might be the most universally repeated myth about their origins." See Moyn, *The Last Utopia*, 6 and passim. This is far from a myth, as has been shown by the careful historical studies of Johannes Morsink. See especially Morsink's book-length refutation of Moyn on this point: *The Universal Declaration of Human Rights and the Holocaust: An Endangered Connection* (Washington, DC: Georgetown University Press, 2019).

19. See Maurice Cranston, *What Are Human Rights?* (New York: Taplinger, 1973), 66–68; and Maurice Cranston, "Human Rights: Real and Supposed," in *Political Theory and the Rights of Man*, ed. D. D. Raphael (Bloomington: Indiana University Press, 1967), 43–51.

20. Henry Shue, *Basic Rights: Subsistence, Affluence, and U.S. Foreign Policy*, 2nd ed. (Princeton, NJ: Princeton University Press, 1996), 39.

21. See "brotherhood, n." *OED Online*, accessed March 2021, https://www.oed.com/view/Entry/23803?redirectedFrom=brotherhood.

22. René Cassin, "Historique de la Déclaration Universelle de 1948," in *La Pensée et l'action*, 108, trans. and qtd. in Morsink, *The Universal Declaration of Human Rights*, 287.

23. Jacques Maritain, "Introduction," in *Human Rights: Comments and Interpretations*, record of symposium, edited by UNESCO (New York: Columbia University Press, 1949), 9.

24. Morsink attributes this phrase to the "snappy title" of Alan Dershowitz's recent book, *Rights from Wrongs: A Secular Theory of the Origins of Rights* (New York: Basic, 2004), in which Dershowitz argues that we can learn what rights are from the wrongs we encounter. See Morsink, *Inherent Human Rights: Philosophical Roots of the Universal Declaration* (Philadelphia: University of Pennsylvania Press, 2009), 58. The phrase "rights from wrongs" is also the title of a chapter in Cass R. Sunstein's study of a "second bill of rights" proposed by US president Franklin Roosevelt in 1944, proclaiming what are now known as social and economic rights. See Sunstein, *The Second Bill of Rights* (New York: Basic, 2004), chap. 3.

25. See Morsink, *Inherent Human Rights*, esp. 32, 58, and passim.

26. Vienna Declaration and Programme of Action, Adopted by the World Conference on Human Rights in Vienna on June 25, 1993, 1, https://www.ohchr.org/EN/Professional Interest/Pages/Vienna.aspx.

27. Richard McKeon, "The Philosophic Bases and Material Circumstances of the Rights of Man," in *Human Rights: Comments and Interpretations*, Record of Symposium, edited by UNESCO (New York: Columbia University Press, 1949), 35.

28. Immanuel Kant, *Grounding for the Metaphysics of Morals*, trans. James W. Ellington, 3rd ed. (Indianapolis, IN: Hackett, 1993), 36.

29. Kant, 40–41.

212 NOTES

30. Kant, 41.
31. See Kant, 42–43.
32. The claim that recent Western thinking has adopted an understanding of the free, autonomous person as "unencumbered" by social relationships is argued by Michael Sandel in his *Liberalism and the Limits of Justice*, 2nd ed. (New York: Cambridge University Press, 1998).
33. Alan Wolfe, *Moral Freedom: The Search for Virtue in a World of Choice* (New York: W. W. Norton, 2001), 195.
34. Wolfe, 202, 222.
35. For a helpful discussion of the need for both autonomy and relationship in respect for persons, see Margaret A. Farley, "A Feminist Version of Respect for Persons," *Journal of Feminist Studies in Religion* 9, no. 1–2 (Spring–Fall 1993): 183–98.
36. Aristotle, *Politics*, book I, chap. 2, 1253a2. For the English translation of the texts of Aristotle cited here, see *The Basic Works of Aristotle*, ed. Benjamin Jowett in Richard McKeon (New York: Random House, 1941).
37. Aristotle, *Politics*, book I, chap. 2, 1253a10–19.
38. Aristotle, 1253a26. Martha Nussbaum takes this statement as a fundamental presupposition of her "capabilities approach" to ethics in social and economic life. See, for example, Nussbaum, "Human Capabilities, Female Human Beings," in *Women, Culture, and Development: A Study of Human Capabilities*, ed. Martha Nussbaum and Jonathan Glover (Oxford: Oxford University Press, 1995), 73. There are significant overlaps of the capabilities approach with an ethic of human rights.
39. See William Luijpen, *Phenomenology of Natural Law* (Pittsburgh, PA: Duquesne University Press, 1967), chap. 6, "Justice as an Anthropological Form of Co-Existence," esp. 180.
40. USCCB, "Economic Justice for All: Pastoral Letter on Catholic Social Teaching and the U.S. Economy," 1986, no. 77, https://www.usccb.org/upload/economic_justice_for_all.pdf.
41. The use of these phrases to suggest that human rights are no longer relevant or adequate follows Stephen Hopgood, *The Endtimes of Human Rights* (Ithaca, NY: Cornell University Press, 2013); and Eric A. Posner, *The Twilight of Human Rights Law* (Oxford: Oxford University Press, 2014).

CHAPTER 5

1. Vatican Council II, Dignitatis Humanae (Declaration on Religious Freedom), no. 2, in *The Documents of Vatican II*, ed. Walter M. Abbott (New York: Guild Press/America Press/ Association Press, 1966).
2. Pope Gregory XVI, *Mirari Vos Arbitramur*, encyclical of August 15, 1832, excerpt in *Enchridion Symbolorum Definitionem et Declarationem de Rebus Fidei et Morum*, 32, ed. Henricus Denzinger and Adolphus Schönmetzer (Rome: Herder, 1963), no. 2730, p. 549.
3. Murray appeared on the cover of *Time* on December 12, 1960; Reinhold Niebuhr on March 8, 1948; and Karl Barth on April 20, 1962.
4. See Murray's five articles on Leo XIII, the first four published in *Theological Studies* in 1953 and 1954, the fifth (dealing with both Leo XIII and Pius XII) not published in Murray's lifetime but now available in John Courtney Murray, SJ, *Religious Liberty: Catholic Struggles with Pluralism*, ed J. Leon Hooper (Louisville, KY: Westminster/John Knox, 1993), 49–125.

NOTES 213

5. Francis J. Connell, memorandum found in Connell Papers, Redemptorist Archives, Baltimore Province, cited in Joseph A. Komonchak, "Catholic Principle and the American Experiment: The Silencing of John Courtney Murray," *U.S. Catholic Historian* 17, no. 1 (Winter 1999): 31.
6. Vatican II, Dignitatis Humanae.
7. Pope John Paul II, "Respect for Human Rights: The Secret of True Peace," World Day of Peace Message, January 1, 1999, no. 5, http://www.vatican.va/holy_father/john_paul_ii/messages/peace/documents/hf_jp-ii_mes_14121998_xxxii-world-day-for-peace_en.html.
8. Samuel P. Huntington, "Religion and the Third Wave," *National Interest* 24 (Summer 1991): 30. Huntington's argument about the sources of democratization is more fully developed in his *The Third Wave: Democratization in the Late Twentieth Century* (Norman: University of Oklahoma Press, 1991).
9. Pope Benedict XVI, World Day of Peace Message, January 1, 2011, no. 1, http://www.vatican.va/holy_father/benedict_xvi/messages/peace/documents/hf_ben-xvi_mes_20101208_xliv-world-day-peace_en.html.
10. Pope Benedict XVI, Address to Members of the Diplomatic Corps, January 10, 2011, http://www.vatican.va/holy_father/benedict_xvi/speeches/2011/january/documents/hf_ben-xvi_spe_20110110_diplomatic-corps_en.html.
11. Pope Benedict XVI, World Day of Peace Message 2011, no. 2.
12. Pope Benedict XVI, no. 5.
13. Pope Benedict XVI, nos. 6 and 8.
14. Vatican II, Dignitatis Humanae, no. 4.
15. Murray, comment on Dignitatis Humanae, no. 4, in Abbott, *The Documents of Vatican II*, 683n11.
16. See Pope Benedict XVI, Address to Members of the Diplomatic Corps, 2011; and Pope Benedict XVI, World Day of Peace Message, 2011, no. 4.
17. USCCB, *Forming Consciences for Faithful Citizenship* (2007), no. 22, http://www.usccb.org/faithfulcitizenship/FCStatement.pdf (accessed June 30, 2011).
18. USCCB, *Forming Consciences for Faithful Citizenship: A Call to Political Responsibility from the Catholic Bishops of the United States with New Introductory Letter* (2019), https://www.usccb.org/issues-and-action/faithful-citizenship/upload/forming-consciences-for-faithful-citizenship.pdf. The citation here is to the introductory letter.
19. USCCB, 2009 Pastoral Letter, "Marriage: Love and Life in the Divine Plan," 22, http://www.usccb.org/laity/loveandlife/MarriageFINAL.pdf (accessed June 30, 2011). The reference to the *Catechism of the Catholic Church* is to no. 2357.
20. USCCB, *Forming Consciences for Faithful Citizenship, 2019*, no. 70.
21. USCCB, *Marriage*, 26.
22. The Manhattan Declaration was issued on November 20, 2009, and is available online at http://www.manhattandeclaration.org/home.aspx.
23. Cardinal Francis George, OMI, president on the National Conference of Catholic Bishops, Statement on Universal Health Care, March 23, 2010, http://www.usccb.org/healthcare/cardinal-george-healthcare-statement.pdf.
24. Nevertheless, official representatives of the bishops have held that the bishops rightly make such detailed judgment on policy, maintaining that "providing guidance to Catholics on whether an action by government is moral or immoral, is first of all the task of the bishops, not of any other group or individual." See Cardinal Daniel DiNardo, chairman

of the USCCB Committee on Pro-Life Activities; Bishop William Murphy of Rockville Centre, New York, chairman of the USCCB Committee on Domestic Justice, Peace and Human Development; and Bishop John Wester of Salt Lake City, chairman of the USCCB Committee on Immigration, "Setting the Record Straight," May 21, 2010, http://www.usccb.org/comm/archives/2010/10–104.shtml.

25. USCCB, *The Challenge of Peace: God's Promise and Our Response* (Washington, DC: USCCB, 1983). Murray's influence on this pastoral letter was mediated by the work of J. Bryan Hehir, a devoted follower of Murray who served as principal consultant to the bishops in the drafting of the letter.

26. David Kinnemann and Gabe Lyons, *Unchristian: What a New Generation Really Thinks about Christianity—and Why It Matters* (Grand Rapids, MI: Baker, 2007), cited in Robert D. Putnam and David E. Campbell, *American Grace: How Religion Divides and Unites Us* (New York: Simon and Schuster, 2010), 121.

27. Putnam and Campbell, *American Grace*, 130. See pp. 123–32 for their fuller discussion of this shift.

28. Pew Forum on Religion and Public Life, *U.S. Religious Landscape Survey* (2008), "Summary of Key Findings."

29. Putnam and Campbell, *American Grace*, 140–41.

30. Putnam and Campbell, 384–88.

31. Putnam and Campbell, 384.

32. These and other issues are discussed as matters that should be of moral and religious concern to Catholics in USCCB, *Forming Consciences for Faithful Citizenship* (Washington, DC: USCCB, 2007).

33. Mary Jo Bane, "God and Country," *Democracy: A Journal of Ideas* 19 (Winter 2011): 91. This essay by Bane is a review of Putnam and Campbell, *American Grace*.

34. See Thomas Aquinas, *Summa Theologiae*, Ia–IIae, q. 90, art. 2.

35. Bane, "God and Country," 92.

36. Murray, *We Hold These Truths*, chap. 7; see Aquinas, *Summa Theologiae*, Ia–IIae, q. 96, arts. 2 and 3.

37. Murray, *We Hold These Truths*, 163. Saint Augustine discusses the issue of tolerating prostitution in his *De ordine*, book II, 4, 12; and the limits of the moral reach of civil law in *De libero arbitrio*, book I, 5, 1. Murray refers these passages from Augustine, and also to Aquinas.

38. Aquinas, *Summa Theologiae*, Ia–IIae, q. 96, art. 3.

39. John Courtney Murray, SJ, "Memo to Cardinal Cushing on Contraception Legislation," in *Bridging the Sacred and the Secular*, ed. J. Leon Hooper (Washington, DC: Georgetown University Press, 1994), 83.

40. Toward the very end of his life, however, Murray seems to have held that the traditional teaching could no longer be theologically sustained. I say "seems to" because the text of the talk in which he was reported to have argued this, given in Toledo, Ohio, on May 5, 1967, is not found in the Murray archives. However, J. Leon Hooper has studied with care the press reports on this talk and presented his best effort to reconstruct what Murray said. See John Courtney Murray, SJ, "Appendix: Toledo Talk," in *Bridging the Sacred and the Secular*, 336–37.

41. Murray, "Memo to Cardinal Cushing," 83.

42. Murray, 83.

NOTES 215

43. Vatican II, Dignitatis Humanae, no. 7.
44. Murray, "Arguments for the Human Right to Religious Freedom," in Murray, *Religious Liberty*, 239. It is noteworthy that Thomas Aquinas uses the same standard: civil law should intervene coercively only in moral matters "without the prohibition of which human society could not be maintained" (*Summa Theologiae*, Ia–IIae, q. 96, art. 2).
45. Vatican II, Dignitatis Humanae, no. 7.
46. Murray, comment on Dignitatis Humanae, no. 7, in Abbott, *Documents of Vatican II*, 686n20.
47. See Mary Ann Glendon, *Abortion and Divorce in Western Law: American Failures, European Challenges* (Cambridge, MA: Harvard University Press, 1987).
48. For Murray's own exposition of the view of those who opposed him on this question, see Murray, "The Problem of Religious Freedom," in Murray, *Religious Liberty*, 130–37.
49. Murray, *We Hold These Truths*, 66. The council affirms this in Dignitatis Humanae, no. 3
50. Murray, "Leo XIII and Pius XII: Government and the Order of Religion," in Murray, *Religious Liberty*, 106.
51. The sentence is from Murray, "Arguments for the Human Right to Religious Freedom," in Murray, *Religious Liberty*, 239. The parallel sentence from the council is from Dignitatis Humanae, no. 7.
52. See my "Catholicism and American Political Culture: Confrontation, Accommodation, or Transformation," in *Inculturation of the Church in North America*, ed. T. Frank Kennedy (New York: Crossroad, 2006), 17–22.

CHAPTER 6

1. See, for example, José Casanova, *Public Religions in the Modern World* (Chicago: University of Chicago Press, 1994).
2. Vatican Council II, Gaudium et Spes (Pastoral Constitution on the Church in the Modern World), no. 41, http://www.vatican.va/archive/hist_councils/ii_vatican_council /documents/vat-ii_const_19651207_gaudium-et-spes_en.html.
3. Since 1991 there has been a significant increase in the percentage of Americans who hold that religious leaders should not seek to influence government decisions or the way people vote. The belief that religion is "too political" is particularly strong among young Americans. See Robert D. Putnam and David E. Campbell, *American Grace: How Religion Divides and Unites Us* (New York: Simon and Schuster, 2010), 121.
4. Vatican II, Gaudium et Spes, no. 43.
5. Vatican II, Dignitatis Humanae (Declaration on Religious Liberty), in *Vatican Council II: Constitutions, Decrees, Declarations*, rev. trans., ed. Austin Flannery (Northport, NY: Costello, 1996), no. 3.
6. Vatican II, Gaudium et Spes, no. 16.
7. See Joseph A. Komonchak, "The Silencing of John Courtney Murray," in *Cristianesimo nella storia: Saggi in onore di Giuseppe Alberigo* (Bologna: Il Mulino, 1996), 657–702; and Joseph A. Komonchak, "Catholic Principle and American Experiment: The Silencing of John Courtney Murray," *U.S. Catholic Historian* 17, no. 1 (1999): 28–44.
8. Vatican II, Dignitatis Humanae, no. 2.
9. Vatican II, no. 10.

10. John Courtney Murray, SJ, "The Arguments for the Human Right to Religious Freedom," in *Religious Liberty: Catholic Struggles with Pluralism*, ed. J. Leon Hooper (Louisville, KY: Westminster/John Knox, 1993), 238.
11. Vatican II, Dignitatis Humanae, no. 2.
12. Vatican II, no. 2.
13. Vatican II, no. 2.
14. Vatican II, no. 4.
15. See R. Scott Appleby, *The Ambivalence of the Sacred: Religion, Violence, and Reconciliation* (Lanham, MD: Rowman and Littlefield, 2000).
16. See Brian J. Grim and Roger Finke, *The Price of Freedom Denied: Religious Persecution and Conflict in the Twenty-First Century* (Cambridge: Cambridge University Press, 2011), xi–xii.
17. Grim and Finke, 19.
18. Martha Nussbaum, *The New Religious Intolerance: Overcoming the Politics of Fear in an Anxious Age* (Cambridge: Belknap, 2012), esp. chaps. 1 and 6.
19. "Macron Wins French Presidential Election," *Le Monde*, April 24, 2022, https://www .lemonde.fr/en/politics/article/2022/04/24/macron-wins-french-presidential-election _5981506_5.html.
20. Monica Duffy Toft, Daniel Philpott, and Timothy Samuel Shah, *God's Century: Resurgent Religion and Global Politics* (New York: W. W. Norton, 2011), 152.
21. Vatican II, Gaudium et Spes, no. 19.
22. For a valuable set of studies of such nonviolent movements in recent politics, see Adam Roberts and Timothy Garton Ash, eds., *Civil Resistance and Power Politics: The Experience of Non-violent Action from Gandhi to the Present* (New York: Oxford University Press, 2009).
23. See Samuel Huntington, "Religion and the Third Wave," *National Interest* 24 (Summer 1991): 29–42.
24. Toft, Philpott, and Shah, *God's Century,* chap. 4, esp. tables 4.1, 4.2, 4.3, and 4.4.
25. See John Courtney Murray, SJ, *The Problem of Religious Freedom* (Westminster, MD: Newman, 1965), chap. 2, "The Tradition," especially its treatment of the "freedom of the Church" at 47–64.
26. Pope John XXIII, *Pacem in Terris*, nos. 8–27. Pope John affirms most of the human rights set forth in the Universal Declaration on Human Rights. *Pacem in Terris* is available on the Holy See's website, http://www.vatican.va/holy_father/john_xxiii/encyclicals /documents/hf_j-xxiii_enc_11041963_pacem_en.html.
27. See the preamble to the UN Universal Declaration of Human Rights, http://www.un.org /en/documents/udhr; and John XXIII, *Pacem in Terris*, nos. 1 and 8–9.
28. John Courtney Murray, SJ, "The Declaration on Religious Freedom: A Moment in Its Legislative History," in Murray, *Religious Liberty*, 25.
29. For a discussion of this debate between Murray and progressive, largely Francophone, theologians who wanted to affirm religious freedom, see Richard J. Regan, *Conflict and Consensus: Religious Freedom and the Second Vatican Council* (New York: Macmillan, 1967).
30. Murray, "The Declaration on Religious Freedom," 31–32.
31. See Jacques Maritain, *Primauté du spiritual* (Paris: Plon, 1927).
32. Murray, "The Declaration on Religious Freedom," in *War, Poverty, Freedom: The Christian Response*, ed. Concilium, no. 15 (New York: Paulist, 1966), 13.

NOTES   217

33. Vatican II, Dignitatis Humanae, in *The Documents of Vatican II*, Walter M. Abbott and Joseph Gallagher, eds. (New York: America Press, 1966), no. 7. See Murray's comment on this passage at 686n20.
34. Vatican II, Dignitatis Humanae, no. 2.
35. Murray's statement of the "free society" principle is in his "The Arguments for the Human Right to Religious Freedom," 239. The parallel sentence from the council is in Dignitatis Humanae, no. 7, translated in Abbott and Gallagher, *The Documents of Vatican II*.
36. Dignitatis Humanae, no.7, translated in Abbott and Gallagher, *The Documents of Vatican II*.
37. For an argument that advancement of religious freedom is today very often linked with similar advancement of other freedoms, rights, and peace, see Grim and Finke, *The Price of Freedom Denied*, chap. 7, "Do Religious Freedoms Really Matter?" For a particularly strong case on the link between religious freedom and peace, see Task Force on International Religious Freedom of the Witherspoon Institute, Timothy Shah, principal author, *Religious Freedom: Why Now? Defending an Embattled Human Right* (Princeton, NJ: Witherspoon Institute, 2012), esp. part 2.
38. Vatican II, Gaudium et Spes, no. 80.

CHAPTER 7

1. See Elizabeth Shakman Hurd, *Beyond Religious Freedom: The New Global Politics of Religion* (Princeton, NJ: Princeton University Press, 2015).
2. USCCB Ad Hoc Committee for Religious Liberty, "Our First, Most Cherished Liberty: A Statement on Religious Liberty," 2012, http://www.usccb.org/_cs_upload/issues-and -action/religious-liberty/61515_1.pdf.
3. Michael W. McConnell, "Why Is Religious Liberty the 'First Freedom'?" *Cardozo Law Review* 21, no. 4 (February 2000): 1243–44.
4. John T. Noonan Jr., *The Lustre of Our Country: The American Experience of Religious Freedom* (Berkeley: University of California Press, 1998), 2.
5. Noonan, 7–8.
6. I am in debt to Cathleen Kaveny, professor of theological ethics and law at Boston College, for helping me interpret several recent decisions of the US Supreme Court on cases involving religious freedom. I also want to recognize that she may have hesitations about some of the ways I have used her help.
7. See, for example, USCCB, Committee for Pro-Life Activities, "Twelve Things Everyone Should Know about the 'Contraceptive Mandate,'" January 6, 2014, http://www.usccb .org/issues-and-action/religious-liberty/fortnight-for-freedom/upload/Twelve-Things -Everyone-Should-Know-About-the-Contraceptive-Mandate.pdf.
8. *Burwell v. Hobby Lobby Stores, Inc.*, 573 US 682 (2014).
9. *Little Sisters of the Poor v. Pennsylvania*, 591 US ___, WL 3808424 (2020).
10. *Masterpiece Cakeshop v. Colorado Civil Rights Commission.* 584 US ___, 138 S.Ct. 1719 (2018).
11. *Bostock v. Clayton County, Georgia*, 590 US ___, 140 S.Ct. 1731 (2020).
12. *Hosanna-Tabor Evangelical Lutheran Church and School v. Equal Opportunity Commission*, 565 US 171 (2012); *Our Lady of Guadalupe School v. Morrissey-Berru*, 591 US ___, 140 S.Ct. 2049 (2020).

218 NOTES

13. See USCCB, "President of U.S. Bishops' Conference Issues Statement on Supreme Court Decision on Legal Definition of 'Sex' in Civil Rights Law," June 15, 2020, http://www.usccb.org/news/2020/20-93.cfm.

14. Dreher is quoted in Jane Coaston, "Social Conservatives Feel Betrayed by the Supreme Court—and the GOP That Appointed It," *Vox*, July 1, 2020, https://www.vox.com/2020/7/1/21293370/supreme-court-conservatism-bostock-lgbtq-republicans.

15. See *June Medical Services LLC v. Russo*, 591 US ___, 140 S.Ct. 2103 (2020). Battles over the relation between religious freedom and US law certainly go beyond the subjects of contraception or the rights of homosexual and transgender persons. The Supreme Court recently pleased those on the more progressive side of the culture wars by striking down a Louisiana law that would effectively have limited the number of abortions in that state. See *June Medical Services LLC v. Russo*, 591 US ___, 140 S.Ct. 2103 (2020). Just a day later, however, the court pleased those on the conservative side by ruling that Montana's exclusion of students in faith-based schools from a state-funded program providing scholarships to students in private schools illegitimately limits the free exercise of religion (*Espinoza v. Montana Department of Revenue*, 591 US ___, 140 S.Ct. 2246 [2020]. A fuller consideration of the current legal issues would have to consider these cases, but that is not needed here.

16. Doug Saunders, "'Religious Freedom' Sends the Wrong Message to the Wrong People," *Globe and Mail* (Toronto), November 23, 2012, cited in Douglas Laycock, "Religious Liberty and the Culture Wars," *University of Illinois Law Review* 3 (2014): 870.

17. For an account of O'Rourke's stance, see Patrick Svitek, "Beto O'Rourke Says Religious Institutions Should Lose Tax-Exempt Status If They Oppose Gay Marriage," *Texas Tribune*, October 11, 2019, https://www.texastribune.org/2019/10/11/beto-orourke-religious-institutions-gay-marriage/. For a critique of O'Rourke on this issue, see John Inazu, "Democrats Are Going to Regret Beto's Stance on Conservative Churches," *The Atlantic*, October 12, 2019, https://www.theatlantic.com/ideas/archive/2019/10/beto-orourkes-pluralism-failure/599953/.

18. Public Religion Research Institute, "Americans Show Broad Support for LGBT Nondiscrimination Protections," March 12, 2019, https://www.prri.org/research/americans-support-protections-lgbt-people/.

19. Laycock, "Religious Liberty and the Culture Wars," 865.

20. Laycock, 869.

21. See Douglas Laycock, "The Only Way Forward: Religious Liberty and the Respect for Marriage Act," *Commonweal* 150, no. 1 (January 2023): 11–13.

22. Cardinal Timothy Dolan, "The 'Respect for Marriage Act' Stacks the Deck against Religious Freedom," November 15, 2022, available at the USCCB website, https://www.usccb.org/Dolan-Respect-for-Marriage-Act-Stacks-Deck-against-Religious-Freedom.

23. Brian J. Grim and Roger Finke, *The Price of Freedom Denied: Religious Persecution and Conflict in the Twenty-First Century* (Cambridge: Cambridge University Press, 2011), 19.

24. UNHCR, "Rohingya Emergency," https://www.unhcr.org/en-us/rohingya-emergency.html; and International Crisis Group, "Building a Better Future for Rohingya Refugees in Bangladesh," Briefing 155/Asia 25, April 2019, https://www.crisisgroup.org/asia/south-east-asia/myanmar/b155-building-better-future-rohingya-refugees-bangladesh.

25. Matthew J. Walton, "Religion and Violence in Myanmar: Sitagu Sayadaw's Case for Mass Killing," Snapshot, *Foreign Affairs*, November 6, 2017.

26. International Court of Justice, Application of the Convention on the Prevention and Punishment of the Crime of Genocide (The Gambia v. Myanmar), Order on Provisional

NOTES 219

Measures, January 23, 2020, esp. no. 86, https://www.icj-cij.org/files/case-related/178/178-20200123-ORD-01-00-EN.pdf.

27. Lindsay Maizland, "China's Repression of Uighurs in Xinjiang," Council on Foreign Relations, updated November 25, 2019, https://www.cfr.org/backgrounder/chinas-repression-uighurs-xinjiang.

28. Austin Ramzy and Chris Buckley, "'Absolutely No Mercy': Leaked Files Expose How China Organized Mass Detentions of Muslims," *New York Times*, November 16, 2019, https://www.nytimes.com/interactive/2019/11/16/world/asia/china-xinjiang-documents.html.

29. Steven Lee Myers, "China Defends Crackdown on Muslims, and Criticizes Times Article," *New York Times*, November 18, 2019, https://www.nytimes.com/2019/11/18/world/asia/china-xinjiang-muslims-leak.html.

30. Amy Qin, "In China's Crackdown on Muslims, Children Have Not Been Spared," *New York Times*, December 28, 2019, https://www.nytimes.com/2019/12/28/world/asia/china-xinjiang-children-boarding-schools.html?action=click&module=Top%20Stories&pgtype=Homepage.

31. Adrien Zenz, "Sterilizations, IUDs, and Mandatory Birth Control: The CCP's Campaign to Suppress Uyghur Birthrates in Xinjiang" (Washington, DC: Jamestown Foundation, 2020); Associated Press, "China Cuts Uighur Births with IUDs, Abortion, and Sterilization," June 29, 2020, https://apnews.com/269b3de1af34e17c1941a514f78d764c.

32. Freedom House, "The Battle for China's Spirit: Religious Revival, Repression, and Resistance under Xi Jinping," Special Report, February 2017, 1, https://freedomhouse.org/sites/default/files/FH_ChinasSprit2017_Abridged_FINAL_compressed.pdf.

33. Cited in John L. Allen, *The Global War on Christians: Dispatches from the Frontlines of Anti-Christian Persecution* (New York: Image, 2016), 33.

34. Pew Research Center, "Trends in Global Restrictions on Religion," complete report, June 23, 2016, 20, available at https://www.pewforum.org/2016/06/23/trends-in-global-restrictions-on-religion/.

35. These reports are available on the website of the US branch of Aid to the Church in Need, at https://www.churchinneed.org/.

36. Open Doors, "World Watch List," available at https://www.opendoorsusa.org/.

37. Allen, *The Global War on Christians*; Paul Marshall, Lela Gilbert, and Nina Shea, *Persecuted: The Global Assault on Christians* (Nashville, TN: Thomas Nelson, 2013); and especially Daniel Philpott and Timothy Samuel Shah, eds., *Under Caesar's Sword: How Christians Respond to Persecution* (Cambridge: Cambridge University Press, 2018).

38. Matthew Barber, "They That Remain: Syrian and Iraqi Christian Communities amid the Syria Conflict and the Rise of the Islamic State," in *Christianity and Freedom, Vol. 2, Contemporary Perspectives*, ed. Allen D. Hertzke and Timothy Daniel Shah (New York: Cambridge University Press, 2016), 455.

39. For the data on displacement cited here, see Kent R. Hill, "On the Brink of Extinction: Christians in Iraq and Syria," in *Under Caesar's Sword: How Christians Respond to Persecution*, ed. Daniel Philpott and Timothy Samuel Shah (Cambridge: Cambridge University Press, 2018), esp. 46–47.

40. See Francis M. Deng, "Sudan—Civil War and Genocide," *Middle East Quarterly* 8, no. 1 (Winter 2001): 13–21.

41. See Fredrick Nzwili, "Christians in Sudan Face Increased Hostility," from Religion News Service, July 16, 2013, available at the *Washington Post*'s On Faith site, http://www

220 NOTES

.washingtonpost.com/national/on-faith/christians-in-sudan-face-increased-hostility/2013/07/16/7c9ad0a4-ee4b-11e2-bb32-725c8351a69e_story.html.

42. Institute for Economics & Peace, *Global Terrorism Index 2019: Measuring the Impact of Terrorism* (Sydney, November 2019), 16, http://visionofhumanity.org/reports.

43. Robert A. Dowd, "To Whom Do We Turn: How Christians Respond to Religious Persecution. Lessons from Kenya, Nigeria, and Sudan," in *Under Caesar's Sword: How Christians Respond to Persecution,* ed. Daniel Philpott and Timothy Samuel Shah (Cambridge: Cambridge University Press, 2018), 77.

44. Kevin Clarke, "Are Nigeria's Christians the Target of Genocide?" *America,* July 2, 2020, https://www.americamagazine.org/politics-society/2020/07/02/are-nigerias-christians-target-genocide; and Aid to the Church in Need, "Persecuted and Forgotten? A Report on Christians Oppressed for Their Faith, 2017–2019," 30, https://www.churchinneed.org/wp-content/uploads/2019/12/Persecuted-Forgotten_digital.pdf.

45. Paul Marshall, "Patterns and Purposes of Contemporary Anti-Christian Persecution," in *Christianity and Freedom, Vol. 2, Contemporary Perspectives,* ed. Allen D. Hertzke and Timothy Daniel Shah (New York: Cambridge University Press, 2016), 59.

46. *Zubik v. Burwell,* 578 US ___, 136 S.Ct. 1557 (2016).

47. Douglas Laycock, "How the Little Sisters of the Poor Case Puts Religious Liberty at Risk," in *Religious Liberty and the Culture Wars,* ed. Douglas Laycock (Grand Rapids, MI: Eerdmans, 2018), vol. 3, 469–71.

48. See Justice Ginsburg's dissent in *Little Sisters of the Poor Saints Peter and Paul Home v. Pennsylvania,* 591 US ___, 140 S.Ct. 2367 (2020).

49. Vatican Council II, Dignitatis Humanae (Declaration on Religious Freedom), no. 6, http://www.vatican.va/archive/hist_councils/ii_vatican_council/documents/vat-ii_decl_19651207_dignitatis-humanae_en.html. See also John Courtney Murray, "The Declaration on Religious Freedom: A Moment in Its Legislative History," in *Religious Liberty: An End and a Beginning,* ed. John Courtney Murray (New York: Macmillan, 1966), 31–32.

50. See Thomas Aquinas, *Summa Theologiae* I–II, q. 90, art. 2.

51. Aquinas, *Summa Theologiae* I–II, q. 96, arts. 3 and 4. For excellent discussions of the scope and limits of the moral role of civil law heavily influenced by these articles of the *Summa Theologiae,* see chap. 7, "Should There Be a Law?" in John Courtney Murray, SJ, *We Hold These Truths: Catholic Reflections on the American Proposition* (Lanham, MD: Rowman and Littlefield, 2005); and Cathleen Kaveny, *Law's Virtues: Fostering Autonomy and Solidarity in American Society* (Washington, DC: Georgetown University Press, 2012), chap. 1, "Autonomy, Solidarity, and Law's Pedagogy."

52. Vatican II, Dignitatis Humanae (Declaration on Religious Freedom), no. 7. See Murray's comment on this passage in footnote 20 of the Declaration in *The Documents of Vatican II,* ed. Walter M. Abbott and Joseph Gallagher (New York: America Press, 1966), 686. This concept of public order is similar to what John Rawls has called a political conception of justice, which he distinguishes from a comprehensive conception of the full human good. See John Rawls, *Political Liberalism* (New York: Columbia University Press, 1993), 13–14, 174–76, and elsewhere.

53. Vatican II, Dignitatis Humanae (Declaration on Religious Freedom), no. 2.

54. Pope John XXIII, *Pacem in Terris,* April 11, 1963, nos. 11–27, http://www.vatican.va/content/john-xxiii/en/encyclicals/documents/hf_j-xxiii_enc_11041963_pacem.html.

NOTES 221

55. For accounts of post–Vatican II Catholic struggles for the full range of human rights, both political and economic, see Samuel Huntington, "Religion and the Third Wave," *National Interest* 24 (Summer 1991): 29–42; and Monica Duffy Toft, Daniel Philpott, and Timothy Samuel Shah, *God's Century: Resurgent Religion and Global Politics* (New York: W. W. Norton, 2011), chap. 4.
56. Aquinas, *Summa Theologiae* I–II, q. 96, art. 3.
57. John Courtney Murray, "Memo to Cardinal Cushing on Contraception Legislation," in *Bridging the Sacred and the Secular: Selected Writings of John Courtney Murray, SJ*, ed. J. Leon Hooper (Washington, DC: Georgetown University Press, 1994), 83.
58. Murray, "Memo to Cardinal Cushing," 83.
59. John Courtney Murray, "Arguments for the Human Right to Religious Freedom," in Murray, *Religious Liberty: Catholic Struggles with Pluralism*, ed. J. Leon Hooper (Louisville, KY: Westminster/John Knox, 1993), 239.
60. Vatican II, Dignitatis Humanae (Declaration on Religious Freedom), no. 7.
61. International Theological Commission, *Religious Freedom for the Good of All: Theological Approach to Contemporary Challenges* (2019), no. 8, http://www.vatican.va/roman_curia /congregations/cfaith/cti_documents/rc_cti_20190426_liberta-religiosa_it.html. The text quoted here is the English translation of the Italian version available on the commission's website.
62. See my "Catholicism and American Political Culture: Confrontation, Accommodation, or Transformation," in *Inculturation of the Church in North America*, ed. T. Frank Kennedy (New York: Crossroad, 2006), 17–22.
63. On the possibility of finding common ground among those holding differing religious and moral convictions, see Melissa Rogers's helpful book, *Faith in American Public Life* (Waco, TX: Baylor University Press, 2019), 227–29 and passim. See also Laycock, "Religious Liberty and the Culture Wars," 877.
64. Cathleen Kaveny, "The Ironies of the New Religious Liberty Litigation," *Daedalus* 149, no. 3 (Summer 2020): 84.

CHAPTER 8

1. World Bank, Poverty and Equity Data portal, http://povertydata.worldbank.org/poverty /home/. For encouraging studies of the reductions in global poverty, see Angus Deaton, *The Great Escape: Health, Wealth, and the Origins of Inequality* (Princeton, NJ: Princeton University Press, 2013); and Steven Radelet, *The Great Surge: The Ascent of the Developing World* (New York: Simon and Schuster, 2015).
2. World Bank, *Poverty and Shared Prosperity 2022: Correcting Course*, main messages, xiii, at https://openknowledge.worldbank.org/bitstream/handle/10986/37739/978146481 8936ov.pdf.
3. World Bank, *Taking on Inequality: Poverty and Shared Prosperity 2016*, 4, https://open knowledge.worldbank.org/bitstream/handle/10986/25078/9781464809583.pdf.
4. See the "Global Inequality" page on the website that accompanies Martin Ravaillion's book *The Economics of Poverty: History, Measurement, and Policy* (Oxford: Oxford University Press, 2016), at https://economicsandpoverty.com/read/global-inequality/. Ravaillion is professor of economics at Georgetown University and the former director of research at the World Bank.

222 NOTES

5. See Facundo Alvaredo, Lucas Chancel, Thomas Piketty, Emmanuel Saez, and Gabriel Zucman, *World Inequality Report 2018: Executive Summary* (World Inequality Lab), 5–6, at http://wir2018.wid.world/files/download/wir2018-summary-english.pdf.

6. Angus Deaton, "The U.S. Can No Longer Hide from Its Deep Poverty Problem," *New York Times*, January 24, 2018, https://www.nytimes.com/2018/01/24/opinion/poverty-united-states.html.

7. Amartya Sen, *Development as Freedom* (New York: Alfred A. Knopf, 1999), 22–23.

8. Anne Case and Angus Deaton, "Mortality and Morbidity in the 21st Century," *Brookings Papers on Economic Activity*, Spring 2017, https://www.brookings.edu/wp-content/uploads/2017/08/casetextsp17bpea.pdf. See also their book development of this matter, *Deaths of Despair and the Future of Capitalism* (Princeton, NJ: Princeton University Press, 2020).

9. Sen, *Development as Freedom*, 104–7. For Sen's update on his approach to the "missing women," see his "Many Faces of Gender Inequality," *Frontline: India's National Magazine* 18, no. 22 (October 27–November 9, 2001).

10. For a libertarian, free market–oriented critique of Pope Paul VI's argument that inequality has contributed to the lack of development of poorer countries, see P. T. Bauer, *Reality and Rhetoric: Studies in the Economics of Development* (Cambridge, MA: Harvard University Press, 1986), chap. 5, "Ecclesiastical Economics: Envy Legitimized."

11. See the page "How Might We Reach a Broad Political Consensus against Inequality," on the website that accompanies Martin Ravaillion's *Economics of Poverty*, at https://economicsandpoverty.com/2017/12/15/how-might-we-reach-a-broad-political-consensus-against-inequality/.

12. Thomas Aquinas, *Summa Contra Gentiles*, part I, chaps. 112 and 113, in *Basic Writings of Saint Thomas Aquinas*, vol. 2, trans. and ed. Anton C. Pegis (New York: Random House, 1945), 220, 223.

13. For a discussion of basic equality, see Jeremy Waldron, *One Another's Equals: The Basis of Human Equality* (Cambridge, MA: Harvard University Press, 2017), 2–4 and passim.

14. Pope John XXIII, *Pacem in Terris*, no. 10; and Vatican Council II, Gaudium et Spes, no. 22, both in *Catholic Social Thought: The Documentary Heritage*, expanded ed., ed. David J. O'Brien and Thomas A. Shannon (Maryknoll, NY: Orbis, 2010).

15. Vatican II, Gaudium et Spes, no. 41.

16. Vatican II, nos. 15–17.

17. On the relation between Christian love as equal regard and equal forms of love that call for different treatment, see Gene Outka, *Agape: An Ethical Analysis* (New Haven, CT: Yale University Press, 1972), esp. chaps. 1 and 8.

18. Thomas Aquinas, *Summa Theologiae* II–II, q. 57, art 1., in *St. Thomas Aquinas: Summa Theologica*, vol. 3, trans. Fathers of the English Dominican Province (Allen, TX: Christian Classics, 1981), 1425.

19. Aquinas, *Summa Theologiae* II–II, q. 61, arts. 1 and 2.

20. Aquinas, q. 58, art. 10.

21. Aristotle, *Nicomachean Ethics*, book V, 1131a, 22–25, trans. Martin Ostwald (Indianapolis, IN: Bobbs-Merrill, 1962).

22. Michael Walzer, *Spheres of Justice: A Defense of Pluralism and Equality* (New York: Basic, 1983), 6.

23. Walzer, 100ff. The same position is affirmed in the tradition of Catholic social thought. See Pope Leo XIII's 1891 encyclical, *Rerum Novarum*, no. 34, in *Catholic Social Thought:*

NOTES   223

The Documentary Heritage, expanded ed., ed. David J. O'Brien and Thomas A. Shannon (Maryknoll, NY: Orbis, 2010), 31–32.

24. For a classic argument that not all goods ought to be for sale on the market, see Arthur M. Okun, *Equality and Efficiency: The Big Tradeoff* (Washington, DC: Brookings Institution, 1975). Drawing on Okun, Michael Walzer develops this in greater depth in *Spheres of Justice*.

25. John T. Noonan Jr., "Development in Moral Doctrine," *Theological Studies* 54 (1993): 662–77. See also John T. Noonan Jr., *The Church Can and Cannot Change: The Development of Catholic Moral Teaching* (Notre Dame, IN: University of Notre Dame Press, 2005).

26. Noonan, "Development in Moral Doctrine," 664–67.

27. Noonan, 667.

28. Pope Gregory XVI, *Mirari vos arbitramur* 1832, in *The Christian Faith in the Doctrinal Documents of the Catholic Church*, rev. ed., ed. and trans. J. Neuner and J. Dupuis (Staten Island, NY: Alba House, 1982), no. 10007.

29. Vatican II, Dignitatis Humanae (Declaration on Religious Freedom), no. 2, at http://www.vatican.va/archive/hist_councils/ii_vatican_council/documents/vat-ii_decl_196 51207_dignitatis-humanae_en.html.

30. Vatican II Gaudium et Spes, no. 41.

31. Pope John Paul II, *Veritatis splendor*, August 6, 1993, no. 31, at http://w2.vatican.va /content/john-paul-ii/en/encyclicals/documents/hf_jp-ii_enc_06081993_veritatis -splendor.html. There is, unfortunately, an ambiguity in John Paul II's discussion of religious freedom. Most of the time it is interpreted in a way that is compatible with Vatican II's statement that this right "continues to exist even in those who do not live up to their obligation of seeking the truth and adhering to it," i.e., the right exists for believers and unbelievers alike. See Second Vatican Council, Dignitatis Humanae, no. 2. At other times John Paul suggests that religious freedom means the right to hold the truth, as when the he says, "In a certain sense, the source and synthesis of these rights [all human rights] is religious freedom, understood as the right to live in the truth of one's faith and in conformity with one's transcendent dignity as a person." See Pope John Paul II, *Centesimus Annus*, 1991, no. 47. I think the ambiguity here is a studied one. I have discussed it in relation to the clear positions of Vatican II and of John Courtney Murray in "Freedom and Truth: Religious Liberty as Immunity and Empowerment," in *John Courtney Murray and the Growth of Tradition*, ed. J. Leon Hooper and Todd Whitmore (Kansas City, MO: Sheed and Ward, 1996), 129–48.

32. John Henry Newman, *An Essay on the Development of Christian Doctrine* (Garden City, NY: Doubleday, 1960), 200–204.

33. Newman, 189.

34. Second Vatican Council, Gaudium et Spes, no. 19.

35. For evidence of the strong alliance between Catholicism and democracy that has developed since the Vatican II, see José Casanova, "Civil Society and Religion: Retrospective Reflections on Catholicism and Prospective Reflections on Islam," *Social Research* 68, no. 4 (Winter 2001): 1041–81; Daniel Philpott, "The Catholic Wave," *Journal of Democracy* 15, no. 2 (April 2004): 32–46; and Samuel Huntington, "Religion and the Third Wave," *The National Interest* 24 (Summer 1991): 29–42.

36. Monica Duffy Toft, Daniel Philpott, and Timothy Shah, *God's Century: Resurgent Religion and Global Politics* (New York: W. W. Norton, 2011), chap. 4, esp. tables 4.1, 4.2, 4.3, and

224 NOTES

4.4. On Islam and democracy, see Philpott, *Religious Freedom in Islam* (Oxford: Oxford University Press, 2019); and Daniel Philpott, "Religious Freedom in Islam: A Global Landscape," *Journal of Law, Religion & State* 2 (2013): 3–21.

37. See John Courtney Murray, *The Problem of Religious Freedom* (Westminster, MD: Newman, 1965), chap. 2, "The Tradition," especially its treatment of the "freedom of the church" at 47–64.

38. Pope John XXIII, *Pacem in Terris*, 1963, nos. 8–27, affirms most of the human rights set forth in the Universal Declaration on Human Rights, at http://w2.vatican.va/content /john-xxiii/en/encyclicals/documents/hf_j-xxiii_enc_11041963_pacem.html.

39. Vatican II, Gaudium et Spes, no. 24.

40. Pope Francis, Evangelii Gaudium, Apostolic exhortation issued November 24, 2013, no. 202, http://w2.vatican.va/content/francesco/en/apost_exhortations/documents /papa-francesco_esortazione-ap_20131124_evangelii-gaudium.html.

41. Pope Francis, Evangelii Gaudium, no. 53.

42. See USCCB, "Economic Justice for All: Pastoral Letter on Catholic Social Thought and the U.S. Economy," 1986, no. 77, in *Catholic Social Thought: The Documentary Heritage*, ed. David O'Brien and Thomas Shannon (Maryknoll, NY: Orbis, 1992), 576–77 (italics in the original).

CHAPTER 9

1. The "preferential option for the poor" is a theme that appears repeatedly in "Economic Justice for All." See nos. 16, 52, 87, 88, 170, 186, 252, 260, 267, 274, 291, 336, and 362. The references in nos. 252, 260, 267, 274, and 291 all speak to international economic issues. The letter clearly drew upon Latin American liberation theology. See the treatment by Gustavo Gutiérrez, "Option for the Poor," in *Mysterium Liberationis: Fundamental Concepts of Liberation Theology*, ed. Ignacio Ellacuría and Jon Sobrino (Maryknoll, NY: Orbis, 1993), 235–50.

2. Rembert G. Weakland, OSB, *A Pilgrim in a Pilgrim Church: Memoirs of a Catholic Archbishop* (Grand Rapids, MI: Eerdmans, 2009), 286.

3. See "The Destructive New Logic That Threatens Globalization," *The Economist*, January 12, 2023, https://www.economist.com/leaders/2023/01/12/the-destructive-new -logic-that-threatens-globalisation; "Has Covid-19 Killed Globalisation?" *The Economist*, May 14, 2020, https://www.economist.com/leaders/2020/05/14/has-covid-19-killed -globalisation; and Angie Basiouny, "Is This the End of Globalization?" *Knowledge at Wharton*, April 18, 2022, https://knowledge.wharton.upenn.edu/article/is-this-the-end -of-globalization/.

4. Robert O. Keohane and Joseph S. Nye, "Globalization: What's New? What's Not? (And So What?)," *Foreign Policy* (Spring 2000): 105.

5. For an in-depth analysis of the diverse dimensions of globalization, see David Held, Anthony McGrew, David Goldblatt, and Jonathan Perraton, *Global Transformations: Politics, Economics, and Culture* (Stanford, CA: Stanford University Press, 1999). Similar though not identical dimensions of globalization are distinguished and analyzed in Joseph S. Nye and John D. Donahue, eds., *Governance in a Globalizing World* (Washington, DC: Brookings Institution Press, 2000), pt. 1, "Trends in Globalization."

NOTES 225

6. See Divyanshi Wadhwa, "The Number of Extremely Poor People Continues to Rise in Sub-Saharan Africa," World Bank data-blog, accessed September 19, 2018, https://blogs .worldbank.org/opendata/number-extremely-poor-people-continues-rise-sub-saharan -africa; and World Bank, "Understanding Poverty," https://www.worldbank.org/en /understanding-poverty.

7. Wadhwa, "The Number of Extremely Poor People."

8. Pope John Paul II, *Centesimus Annus* (*On the Hundredth Anniversary of Rerum Novarum*), no. 33.

9. See Joseph E. Stiglitz, *Globalization and Its Discontents* (New York: W. W. Norton, 2002); and William Easterly, *The Elusive Quest for Growth: Economists' Adventures and Misadventures in the Tropics* (Cambridge, MA: MIT Press, 2001).

10. Daniel Gerszon Mahler et al., "Pandemic, Prices, and Poverty," World Bank data-blog, accessed April 13, 2022, https://blogs.worldbank.org/opendata/pandemic-prices-and -poverty.

11. See UN Sustainable Development Goals at https://www.un.org/sustainable development/.

12. Pope John Paul II, "Address to the Pontifical Academy of Social Sciences," April 27, 2001, no. 2, http://www.vatican.va/holy_father/john_paul_ii/speeches/2001/documents/hf _jp-ii_spe_20010427_pc-social-sciences_en.html.

13. Pope John Paul II, "Address to the Pontifical Academy of Social Sciences."

14. Catholic social thought thus overlaps with the normative standpoint of the recent "Manifesto for a Global Economic Ethic: Consequences for Global Businesses," issued June 6, 2009, by the UN under the auspices of the Global Ethics Foundation led by Hans Küng. The manifesto stresses "humanity" and "reciprocity" as its central ethical norms. Available at http://www.unglobalcompact.org/docs/news_events/9.1_news_archives/2009_10 _06/Global_Economic_Ethic_Manifesto.pdf.

15. John Paul II, *Sollicitudo Rei Socialis* (*On Social Concern*), no. 26, in *Catholic Social Thought: The Documentary Heritage*, ed. David J. O'Brien and Thomas A. Shannon (Maryknoll, NY: Orbis, 1992).

16. Pope Benedict XVI, *Caritas in veritate* (*Charity in Truth*), no. 42, https://www.vatican.va /content/benedict-xvi/en/encyclicals/documents/hf_ben-xvi_enc_20090629_caritas -in-veritate.html.

17. NCCB, "Economic Justice for All," no. 77, in *The Documentary Heritage*, ed. David J. O'Brien and Thomas A. Shannon (Maryknoll, NY: Orbis, 1992), 576–77 (italics in the original).

18. Joseph S. Nye Jr., "Globalization's Democratic Deficit: How to Make International Institutions More Accountable," *Foreign Affairs* 80, no. 4 (July–August 2001): 2–6; and, on recent adjustments, the World Bank press release, "World Bank Reforms Voting Power, Gets $86 Billion Boost," at http://web.worldbank.org/WBSITE/EXTERNAL/NEWS /0,,contentMDK:22556045~pagePK:34370~piPK:34424~theSitePK:4607,00.html (accessed May 28, 2010).

19. Pope Benedict XVI, Address to the Pontifical Academy of Social Sciences, April 30, 2010, http://www.vatican.va/holy_father/benedict_xvi/speeches/2010/april/documents/hf _ben-xvi_spe_20100430_scienze-sociali_en.html.

20. Pope Benedict XVI, Address to the Pontifical Academy of Social Sciences.

21. Pope John XXIII, *Pacem in Terris* (*Peace on Earth*), no. 135.

226 NOTES

22. Pope John XXIII, *Pacem in Terris*, nos. 135–8.
23. Pope Benedict XVI, *Caritas in veritate*, no. 67 (italics in the original).
24. Anne Marie Slaughter, *A New World Order* (Princeton, NJ: Princeton University Press, 2005), 10. For a study of the emerging role of NGOs, see Margaret E. Keck and Kathryn Sikkink, *Activists beyond Borders: Advocacy Networks in International Politics* (Ithaca, NY: Cornell University Press, 1998).
25. David Hollenbach, *The Common Good and Christian Ethics* (Cambridge: Cambridge University Press, 2002), 229.
26. NCCB, "Economic Justice for All," no. 260.
27. NCCB, no. 266.
28. See Jeffrey Sachs, *The End of Poverty: Economic Possibilities for Our Time* (New York: Penguin, 2005). See also Sachs, "Hold the Rich Nations to Their Word," *Financial Times*, December 16, 2009, http://www.ft.com/cms/s/0/e361fa90-e9e2-11de-ae43-00144 feab49a.html.
29. UN, Monterrey Consensus, no. 42, in *Financing Development: Building on Monterrey* (New York: United Nations, 2002), 8, http://www.un.org/esa/ffd/documents/Building %20on%20Monterrey.pdf.
30. See William Easterly, *The White Man's Burden: Why the West's Efforts to Aid the Rest Have Done So Much Ill and So Little Good* (New York: Penguin, 2006).
31. Dambisa Moyo, *Dead Aid: Why Aid Is Not Working and How There Is a Better Way for Africa* (New York: Farrar, Strauss, and Giroux, 2009), 47 (italics in the original).
32. See Moyo, 145.
33. See the powerful narrative of Githongo's struggle against corruption in Kenya in Michaela Wrong, *It's Our Turn to Eat: The Story of a Kenyan Whistle Blower* (London: Fourth Estate, 2009).
34. Paul Collier, "Time to Turn Off the Aid Tap? Review of *Dead Aid* by Dambisa Moyo," *The Independent*, January 30, 2009, http://www.independent.co.uk/arts-entertainment /books/reviews/dead-aid-by-dambisa-moyo-1519875.html (accessed May 28, 2010). For a fuller development of Collier's views, see his two recent books, *The Bottom Billion: Why the Poorest Countries Are Failing and What Can Be Done about It* (New York: Oxford University Press, 2007) and *Wars, Guns, and Votes: Democracy in Dangerous Places* (New York: Harper Perennial, 2009).
35. See Michael Gerson's critique of Moyo's book, "'Dead Aid,' Dead Wrong," *Washington Post*, April 3, 2009, http://www.washingtonpost.com/wp-dyn/content/article/2009 /04/02/AR2009040203285.html. Gerson worked in the White House under George W. Bush as chief speechwriter and senior policy adviser.
36. See World Bank, *Global Monitoring Report: Millennium Development Goals, Strengthening Mutual Accountability, Aid, Trade, and Governance* (2006), http://siteresources.worldbank .org/INTGLOBALMONITORING2006/Resources/2186625-1145565069381/GMR 06Complete.pdf.
37. See Oxfam America, *Ownership in Practice: The Key to Smart Development*, Research Report, September 21, 2009, http://www.oxfamamerica.org/publications/ownership-in -practice-the-key-to-smart-development.
38. See the CRS microloan webpage at http://crs.org/microfinance.
39. See US Secretary of State Hilary Rodham Clinton, "Remarks with Kenyan Foreign Minister Moses Wetangula, Nairobi, Kenya," August 5, 2009, http://www.state.gov/secretary /rm/2009a/08/126890.htm.

NOTES 227

40. See Collier, *Wars, Guns, and Votes*, esp. chap. 5, "Wars: The Political Economy of Destruction."
41. Overview of the UN Global Compact, http://www.unglobalcompact.org/aboutthegc/index.html (accessed May 31, 2010).

CHAPTER 10

1. See UNHCR, Global Trends webpage for 2022, https://www.unhcr.org/en-us/globaltrends.html?query=Global%20Trends.
2. UN Secretary General António Guterres, World Refugee Day Statement, 2022, https://www.un.org/en/observances/refugee-day/messages.
3. Joseph Carens, "Aliens and Citizens: The Case for Open Borders," *Review of Politics* 49, no. 2 (Spring 1987): 251–73; and Philip Marfleet, *Refugees in a Global Era* (New York: Palgrave Macmillan, 2006), 288–90.
4. Martha C. Nussbaum, "Patriotism and Cosmopolitanism," in *For Love of Country* (Boston: Beacon Press, 2002), 5. Nussbaum subsequently changed her view on the importance of nation-states.
5. ICRC, "The Fundamental Principles of the International Red Cross and Red Crescent Movement," International Committee of the Red Cross, https://www.icrc.org/en/document/fundamental-principles-red-cross-and-red-crescent.
6. J. Pictet, "The Fundamental Principles of the Red Cross: Commentary," United Nations, January 1, 1979, https://www.icrc.org/en/doc/resources/documents/misc/fundamental-principles-commentary-010179.htm.
7. UN General Assembly, "The Universal Declaration of Human Rights," United Nations, 1948, https://www.ohchr.org/en/human-rights/universal-declaration/translations/english.
8. UN General Assembly, "The Universal Declaration of Human Rights," art. 2, United Nations, 1948.
9. UN General Assembly, "International Covenant on Economic, Social, and Cultural Rights," United Nations, 1966, https://www.ohchr.org/en/instruments-mechanisms/instruments/international-covenant-economic-social-and-cultural-rights.
10. Pictet, "The Fundamental Principles."
11. Immanuel Kant, *Grounding for the Metaphysics of Morals*, trans. James W. Ellington (Indianapolis, IN: Hackett, 1993), 36.
12. Genesis 1:27.
13. Pope Francis, "Visit to Refugees, Mòria Refugee Camp, Lesvos, Greece," 2016a, http://w2.vatican.va/content/francesco/en/speeches/2016/april/documents/papa-francesco_20160416_lesvos-rifugiati.html; Pope Francis, "Meeting with the People of Lesvos and with the Catholic Community. A Remembering of the Victims of Migration, Lesvos, Greece," 2016b, http://w2.vatican.va/content/francesco/en/speeches/2016/april/documents/papa-francesco_20160416_lesvos-cittadinanza.html.
14. For a fuller development of this idea, see David Hollenbach, "Religion and Forced Migration," in *The Oxford Handbook of Refugee and Forced Migration Studies*, ed. Elena Fiddian-Qasmiyeh et al. (Oxford: Oxford University Press, 2014), 447–59.
15. Muombo Nkulu-N'Sengha, "Religion, Spirituality, and R2P in a Global Village," in *Responsibility to Protect: Cultural Perspectives in the Global South*, ed. Rama Mani and Thomas G. Weiss (New York: Routledge, 2011), 38–40.

228 NOTES

16. Pope John XXIII, *Pacem in Terris*, no. 25, https://www.vatican.va/content/john-xxiii/en/encyclicals/documents/hf_j-xxiii_enc_11041963_pacem.html.
17. Pope John XXIII, no. 105.
18. Kwame A. Appiah, *Cosmopolitanism: Ethics in a World of Strangers* (New York: W. W. Norton, 2006), xiv–xviii.
19. Martha C. Nussbaum, *Frontiers of Justice: Disability, Nationality, Species Membership* (Cambridge: Belknap, 2006), 255–62.
20. Seyla Benhabib, *The Rights of Others: Aliens, Residents and Citizens* (Cambridge: Cambridge University Press, 2004).
21. Genesis 9:1–17.
22. Exodus 23:9. See also Leviticus 19:33–34 and many other places.
23. Jonathan Sacks, *The Dignity of Difference: How to Avoid a Clash of* Civilizations, rev. ed. (New York: Continuum, 2003), chap. 3.
24. Pope Pius XI, *Quadragesimo Anno*, 1931, nos. 79–80, https://www.vatican.va/content/pius-xi/en/encyclicals/documents/hf_p-xi_enc_19310515_quadragesimo-anno.html.
25. EU, Treaty on European Union, Consolidated Version, title 1, art. 5, no. 3, 2012, http://eur-lex.europa.eu/legal-content/EN/TXT/HTML/?uri=CELEX:12012M/TXT&from=EN.
26. Henry Shue, *Basic Rights: Subsistence, Affluence, and U.S. Foreign Policy* (Princeton, NJ: Princeton University Press, 1980), 51–60.
27. See Jean-Marie Guéhenno, "Conflict Is Key to Understanding Migration," *Carnegie Europe* (2016), http://www.crisisgroup.org/en/regions/op-eds/2016/guehenno-conflict-is-key-to-understanding-migration.aspx.
28. LeRoy Walters, "Five Classic Just War Theories: A Study of the Thought of Thomas Aquinas, Vitoria, Suárez, Gentili, and Grotius," PhD diss., Yale University, 1971; J. Bryan Hehir, "The Just War Ethic and Catholic Theology: Dynamics of Change and Continuity," in *War or Peace? The Search for New Answers*, ed. Thomas A. Shannon ed. (Maryknoll, NY: Orbis, 1980), 15–39; Michael Walzer, *Just and Unjust Wars: A Moral Argument with Historical Illustrations* (New York: Basic, 1977); Sohail Hashmi, *Islamic Political Ethics: Civil Society, Pluralism, and Conflict* (Princeton, NJ: Princeton University Press, 2002).
29. Geneva Conventions, Additional Protocol 1, Relating to the Protection of Victims of International Armed Conflicts (1949), art. 48, https://www.icrc.org/eng/assets/files/other/icrc_002_0321.pdf.
30. Geoffrey Robertson, *Crimes against Humanity: The Struggle for Global Justice*, 3rd ed. (New York: New Press: 2006), 430–39.
31. Human Rights Watch, *South Sudan's New War: Abuses by Government and Opposition Forces*, 2014, https://www.hrw.org/report/2014/08/07/south-sudans-new-war/abuses-government-and-opposition-forces; Panel of Experts on South Sudan, "Interim Report of the Panel of Experts on South Sudan established pursuant to Security Council Resolution 2206," South Sudan Humanitarian Project, 2015, http://www.southsudanhumanitarian project.com/reports/docr-532/.
32. See UNHCR, Sudan Emergency, updated November 2022, https://www.unhcr.org/en-us/south-sudan-emergency.html.
33. UN Human Rights Council, "Report of the Independent International Commission of Inquiry on the Syrian Arab Republic," 2014, no. 138, http://www.abc.net.au/mediawatch/transcripts/1408_un.pdf.
34. John Simon, Charles W. Powers, and Jon P. Gunnemann, *The Ethical Investor: Universities and Corporate Responsibility* (New Haven, CT: Yale University Press, 1972).

NOTES 229

35. Nicolas Lemann, "A Call for Help: What the Kitty Genovese Story Really Means," *New Yorker*, March 2, 2014, https://www.newyorker.com/magazine/2014/03/10/a-call-for-help.

36. Simon, Powers, and Gunnemann, *The Ethical Investor*, 23–25.

37. UNHCR, Ukraine Emergency, February 2023, https://www.unhcr.org/en-us/ukraine-emergency.html.

38. International Crisis Group, "South Sudan: Keeping Faith with the IGAD Peace Process," 2015, http://www.crisisgroup.org/en/regions/africa/horn-of-africa/south-sudan/228-south-sudan-keeping-faith-with-the-igad-peace-process.aspx.

39. Ariane Rummery and Jonathan Clayton, "Greater Support in Countries of First Asylum Needed to Stem Refugee Outflows" (New York: UNHCR, 2015), http://www.unhcr.org/55ddd2c86.html.

40. Francis Mading Deng, *Sovereignty as Responsibility: Conflict Management in Africa* (Washington, DC: Brookings Institution, 1996).

41. Susan F. Martin, "Rethinking the International Refugee Regime in Light of Human Rights and the Global Common Good," in *Driven from Home: Protecting the Rights of Forced Migrants*, ed. David Hollenbach (Washington, DC: Georgetown University Press, 2010), 15–33.

42. ICISS, *The Responsibility to Protect* (Ottawa, Canada: International Development Research Center, 2001); UN General Assembly, "World Summit Outcome Document," nos. 138–39 2005, http://www.globalr2p.org/media/files/wsod_2005.pdf.

43. Roger Cohen, "How Kofi Annan Rescued Kenya," *New York Review of Books*, August 14, 2008, https://www.nybooks.com/articles/2008/08/14/how-kofi-annan-rescued-kenya/.

44. International Coalition for the Responsibility to Protect, "The Crisis in Kenya," n.d., http://www.responsibilitytoprotect.org/index.php/crises/crisis-in-kenya.

45. UN Security Council, "Resolution 2085 (Authorizing Intervention in Mali)" (New York: United Nations, 2012), http://www.securitycouncilreport.org/atf/cf/%7B65BFCF9B-6D27-4E9C-8CD3-CF6E4FF96FF9%7D/s_res_2085.pdf; UN Security Council, "Resolution 2127 (Authorizing Intervention in Central African Republic)," 2013, http://www.un.org/en/ga/search/view_doc.asp?symbol=S/RES/2127(2013)&referer=http://www.un.org/en/sc/documents/resolutions/2013.shtml&Lang=E.

46. "Libya Protests: Defiant Gaddafi Refuses to Quit," *BBC News*, 2011, online http://www.bbc.com/news/world-middle-east-12544624.

47. UN Security Council, "Resolution 1973 (Authorizing Action in Libya), 2011, nos. 4 and 6, http://www.nato.int/nato_static/assets/pdf/pdf_2011_03/20110927_110311-UNSCR-1973.pdf.

48. Amnesty International, "'Libya Is Full of Cruelty': Stories of Abduction, Sexual Violence, and Abuse from Migrants and Refugees," Amnesty International, 2015, 5–6, https://www.amnesty.org/en/documents/mde19/1578/2015/en.

49. Alan J. Kuperman, "Obama's Libya Debacle: How a Well-Meaning Intervention Ended in Failure," *Foreign Affairs* 94, no. 2 (2015): 66–77.

50. Derek Chollet and Ben Fishman, "Who Lost Libya: Obama's Intervention in Retrospect, a Close Call," *Foreign Affairs* 94, no. 3 (2015): 154–57.

51. Thomas G. Weiss, "Military Humanitarianism: Syria Hasn't Killed It," *Washington Quarterly* 37, no. 1 (2014): 7–20.

52. International Crisis Group, "The Global Refugee Crisis: Statement by the Board of Trustees of the International Crisis Group," 2016, http://www.crisisgroup.org/en/publication-type/statements/the-global-refugee-crisis-statement-by-the-board-of-trustees-of-the-international-crisis-group.aspx.

230 NOTES

53. UNHCR, "Global Trends: Forced Displacement in 2021," 2, https://www.unhcr.org/62a9d1494/global-trends-report-2021.
54. Stephen M. Walt, "Don't Give ISIS What It Wants," *Foreign Policy* 16 (November 2015), http://foreignpolicy.com/2015/11/16/dont-give-isis-what-it-wants-united-%09states-reaction/.
55. Martha Finnemore and Kathryn Sikkink, "International Norm Dynamics and Political Change," *International Organization* 52, no. 4 (1998): 887–917.

CHAPTER 11

1. UNHCR, "On Faith-Based Organizations, Local Faith Communities, and Faith Leaders: Partnership Note," 2014, http://www.unhcr.org/en-us/protection/hcdialogue%20/539ef28b9/partnership-note-faith-based-organizations-local-faith-communities-faith.html?query=Affirmations%20for%20Faith%20Leaders, nos. 1.1–1.3.
2. UNHCR, "Welcoming the Stranger: Affirmations for Faith Leaders," http://www.unhcr.org/enus/protection/hcdialogue%20/51b6de419/welcoming-stranger-affirmations-faith-leaders.html?query=Affirmations%20for%20Faith%20Leaders.
3. Refugee Studies Centre, *Journal of Refugee Studies* 24, no. 3 (September 2011), special issue: Faith-Based Humanitarianism in Contexts of Forced Displacement.
4. Michael Barnett and Janice Gross Stein, eds., *Sacred Aid: Faith and Humanitarianism* (Oxford: Oxford University Press, 2012); Peter Stamatov, *The Origins of Global Humanitarianism: Religion, Empires, and Advocacy* (New York: Cambridge University Press, 2013); Jennifer B. Saunders, Elena Fiddian-Qasmiyeh, and Susanna Snyder, eds., *Intersections of Religion and Migration: Issues at the Global Crossroads* (New York: Palgrave Macmillan, 2016).
5. Jeff Crisp, "25 Years of Forced Migration," *Forced Migration Review*, November 2012, 4–8, https://www.fmreview.org/25th-anniversary/crisp.
6. The figures cited here have been assembled by the author from the annual reports of the agencies involved.
7. USCCB Resettlement Services, http://www.usccb.org/about/resettlement-services/index.cfm. See also Donald Kerwin, "The US Refugee Resettlement Program—A Return to First Principles: How Refugees Help to Define, Strengthen, and Revitalize the United States," Center for Migration Studies, New York, June 2018, http://cmsny.org/publications/us-refugee-resettlement-program/.
8. Kerwin, "The US Refugee Resettlement Program."
9. Pricilla Alvarez, "The Conservative Churches Resettling Refugees," *The Atlantic*, September 11, 2016, https://www.theatlantic.com/politics/archive/2016/09/the-conservative-churches-resettling-refugees/499421/; Hebrew Immigrant Aid Society, "History" and "What We Do," n.d., https://www.hias.org/.
10. Islamic Relief USA, "What We Do, Aid to Refugees," http://irusa.org/refugee-crisis/.
11. Michael Barnett, *Empire of Humanity* (Ithaca, NY: Cornell University Press, 2011), 17. For helpful studies of some practical ways religion influences engagement in humanitarian action today, see Barnett and Stein, *Sacred Aid*.
12. Jay P. Dolan, *The American Catholic Experience: A History from Colonial Times to the Present* (Garden City, NY: Doubleday, 1985), chap. 5.
13. Peter Scalabrini, "History," International Migration Network, n.d., http://simn-global.org/history/; Peter Scalabrini, *For the Love of Immigrants: Migration Writings and Letters of*

Bishop John Baptist Scalabrini (1839–1905) (New York: Center for Migration Studies of New York, 2000).

14. Dolan, *The American Catholic Experience,* 277.

15. National Catholic Educational Association, "About Us," n.d., https://www.ncea.org /NCEA/About_Us/NCEA/About/About_Us.aspx?hkey=5470d2fe-6f67–4aae-8b5b -4385a9a39082.

16. Association of Catholic Colleges and Universities, "About Catholic Higher Ed.," n.d., https://www.accunet.org/About-Catholic-Higher-Education.

17. Dolan, *The American Catholic Experience,* 325.

18. Catholic Health Association of the United States, "A Passionate Voice for Compassionate Care," Catholic Health Association of the United States, n.d., https://www.chausa .org/docs/default-source/default-document-library/cha-corporate-brochure-2018.pdf ?sfvrsn=0.

19. Dolan, *The American Catholic Experience,* 257.

20. Genesis 1:27.

21. David Hollenbach, *Humanity in Crisis: Ethical and Religious Response to Refugees* (Washington, DC: Georgetown University Press, 2019); Hollenbach, chap. 10 herein; Hollenbach, "Religion and Forced Migration," in *The Oxford Handbook of Refugee and Forced Migration Studies,* ed. Elena Fiddian-Qasmiyeh, Gil Loescher, Katy Long, and Nando Sidona (Oxford: Oxford University Press, 2014), 447–59.

22. USCCB, "Economic Justice for All (Pastoral Letter on Catholic Social Teaching and the U.S. Economy)," in *Catholic Social Thought: The Documentary Heritage,* ed. David O'Brien and Shannon Thomas (Maryknoll, NY: Orbis, 1986), 715.

23. Pope Francis, *Evangelii Gaudium (The Joy of the Gospel)* (Vatican City: Libreria Editrice Vaticana, 2013).

24. USCCB, "Economic Justice for All," no. 79.

25. Pope Francis, "Homily of Holy Father Francis, Arena Sports Camp, Salina Quarter, Lampedusa," 2013, http://w2.vatican.va/content/francesco/en/homilies/2013/docu ments/papa-francesco_20130708_omelia-lampedusa.html.

26. Pope Francis, "Migrants and Refugees: Men and Women in Search of Peace." Message of His Holiness Pope Francis for the celebration of the 51st World Day of Peace, January 1, 2018, http://w2.vatican.va/content/francesco/en/messages/peace/documents/papa -francesco_20171113_messaggio-51giornatamondiale-pace2018.html.

27. Pope Francis, "Statutes of the Dicastery for Promoting Integral Human Development," 2016, http://w2.vatican.va/content/francesco/en/motu_proprio/documents/papa -francesco_20160817_statuto-dicastero-servizio-sviluppo-umano-integrale.html.

28. Matthew 7:12; Pope Francis, "Address to Joint Session of U.S. Congress," September 24, 2015, http://w2.vatican.va/content/francesco/en/speeches/2015/september /documents/papa-francesco_20150924_usa-us-congress.html.

29. Donald Kerwin and Kyle Barron, "Building Structures of Solidarity and Instruments of Justice: The Catholic Immigrant Integration Surveys," *CMS Report,* 2017, http://cmsny .org/publications/ciiisurveysreport/.

30. Catholic Charities USA, "Immigrant and Refugee Services," n.d., https://www.catholic charitiesusa.org/our-ministry/immigration-refugee-services/.

31. Donald Kerwin and Mike Nicholson, "The Effects of Immigration Enforcement on Faith-based Organizations: An Analysis of the FEER Survey," *Journal on Migration and Human Security* 7, no. 2 (2019): 46.

232 NOTES

32. Center for Applied Research in the Apostolate, "Frequently Requested Church Statistics," n.d., https://cara.georgetown.edu/frequently-requested-church-statistics/.
33. Silvano M. Tomasi, *Piety and Power: The Role of Italian Parishes in the New York Metropolitan Area (1889–1930)* (Staten Island, NY: Center for Migration Studies, 1975).
34. Center for Applied Research in the Apostolate, "Frequently Requested Church Statistics."
35. Hosffman Ospino, "National Study of Catholic Parishes with Hispanic Ministries" (Boston: Boston College School of Theology and Ministry, 2017), 17, https://www.bc.edu/content/dam/files/schools/stm/pdf/2014/BC-NatlStudyParishesHM-Rep1–201405.pdf.
36. Center for Applied Research in the Apostolate, "Frequently Requested Church Statistics."
37. Kevin Wallsten and Tatishe M. Nteta, "For You Were Strangers in the Land of Egypt: Clergy, Religiosity, and Public Opinion toward Immigration Reform in the United States," *Politics and Religion* 9, no. 3 (2016): 585.
38. PRRI, "Data Shows How Passionate and Partisan Americans Are about the Border Wall," 2019, https://www.prri.org/spotlight/data-shows-how-passionate-and-partisan-americans-are-about-the-border-wall/.
39. PRRI, "Data Shows."
40. Robert P. Jones et al., "How Immigration and Concerns about Cultural Changes Are Shaping the 2016 Election: Findings from the 2016 PRRI/Brookings Immigration Survey" (Washington, DC: PRRI and Brookings Institution, 2016), 38.
41. Jones et al., 42.
42. Kerwin and Barron, "Building Structures of Solidarity."
43. Daniel Cox, Rachel Lienesch, and Robert P. Jones, "Beyond Economics: Fears of Cultural Displacement Pushed the White Working Class to Trump," *Public Religion Research Institute/The Atlantic*, 2017, https://www.prri.org/research/white-working-class-attitudes-economy-trade-immigration-election-donald-trump/.
44. Pew Research Center, "Most Border Wall Opponents, Supporters Say Shutdown Concessions Are Unacceptable," 2019, https://www.people-press.org/2019/01/16/most-border-wall-opponents-supporters-say-shutdown-concessions-are-unacceptable/.
45. Wallsten and Nteta, "For You Were Strangers in the Land of Egypt, 585–86.
46. Michael Lipka and Gregory A. Smith, "Like Americans Overall, U.S. Catholics Are Sharply Divided by Party," *Facttank: News in the Numbers*, 2019, https://www.pewresearch.org/fact-tank/2019/01/24/like-americans-overall-u-s-catholics-are-sharply-divided-by-party/.
47. Kerwin and Barron, "Building Structures of Solidarity," 42.
48. PRRI statistics from 2013, cited by Kerwin and Barron.
49. Donald Kerwin and Briana George, *US Catholic Institutions and Immigrant Integration: Will the Church Rise to the Challenge?* (Vatican City: Lateran University Press, 2014), 10.
50. Kerwin, "The US Refugee Resettlement Program," 2018.

CHAPTER 12

1. See, for example, Margaret A. Farley, "Feminism and Universal Morality," in *Prospects for a Common Morality*, ed. Gene Outka and John P. Reeder Jr. (Princeton, NJ: Princeton University Press, 1993), 170–90.
2. Chris C. Mojekwu, "International Human Rights: The African Perspective," in *International Human Rights: Contemporary Issues*, Jack L. Nelson and Vera M. Green (Stanfordville, NY: Human Rights Publishing Group, 1980), 92–93.

NOTES 233

3. Preamble to African Charter on Human and People's Rights, arts. 19–22, in *The International Law of Human Rights in Africa: Basic Documents and Annotated Bibliography*, ed. M. Hamalengwa, C. Flinterman, and E. V. O. Dankwa (Dordrecht: Martinus Nijhoff, 1988).

4. African Charter on Human and People's Rights, art. 29.

5. For a survey of such abuses in Kenya, see Korwa G. Adar and Isaac M Munyae, "Human Rights Abuse in Kenya under Daniel Arap Moi, 1978–2001," *African Studies Quarterly* 5, no. 1 (2001). *African Studies Quarterly* is an online-only journal; this article is available at http://web.africa.ufl.edu/asq/v5/v5i1a1.htm (accessed July 21, 2003).

6. For a discussion of how Moi fomented ethnic conflict and then argued that his form of rule was the only way to hold the country together, see Human Rights Watch/Africa Watch, *Divide and Rule: State-Sponsored Ethnic Violence in Kenya* (New York: Human Rights Watch, 1993); and "Multipartyism Betrayed in Kenya," *Human Rights Watch/ Africa* 6, no. 5 (July 1994).

7. Gibson Kamau Kuria's response to my lecture is cited in Stephen Mburu, "Rights Dodge the Poor," *Daily Nation* (Nairobi), December 17, 1996, 4. My lecture was published as "Human Rights in Development," *Independent Review* 1, no. 2 (1997): 154–60; a revised version appeared as "Solidarity, Development and Human Rights: The African Challenge," *Journal of Religious Ethics* 26, no. 2 (1998): 305–17.

8. *Documents of the Thirty-Fourth General Congregation of the Society of Jesus* (St. Louis: Institute of Jesuit Sources, 1995); Decree Fourteen, "Jesuits and the Situation of Women in Church and Civil Society," no. 362, 172.

9. Jomo Kenyatta, *Facing Mount Kenya: The Traditional Life of the Gikuyu* (Nairobi: Heinemann, 1982 [1938]), chap. 6.

10. Sandra D. Lane and Robert A. Rubenstein, "Judging the Other: Responding to Traditional Female Genital Surgeries," *Hastings Center Report*, May–June 1996, 31–40.

11. Amnesty International USA, "Female Genital Mutilation: A Fact Sheet," available at http://www.amnestyusa.org/women/fact_sheets/female_genital_mutilation.html (accessed July 22, 2003).

12. Martha C. Nussbaum, "Judging Other Cultures: The Case of Genital Mutilation," in *Sex and Social Justice* (New York: Oxford University Press, 1999), 126.

13. Nussbaum, 129.

14. Fuambai Ahmadu, "Rites and Wrongs: An Insider/Outsider Reflects on Power and Excision," in *Female "Circumcision" in Africa: Culture, Controversy and Change*, ed. Bettina Shell-Duncan and Ylva Hernlund (Boulder, CO: Lynne Rienner, 2000), 305–7.

15. Richard A Shweder cites Ahmadu throughout his study, "'What about Female Genital Mutilation'? And Why Understanding Culture Matters," in *Why Do Men Barbeque? Recipes for Cultural Psychology* (Cambridge: Harvard University Press, 2003), 168–216. The medical study to which he refers is that of Carla M. Obermeyer, "Female Genital Surgeries: The Known, the Unknown, and the Unknowable," *Medical Anthropology Quarterly* 13 (1999): 79–106.

16. Shweder, "'What about Female Genital Mutilation'?" 180, 188.

17. Universal Declaration of Human Rights, art. 2.

18. Margaret Farley proposes a similar approach to the basis of moral obligation. See her *Personal Commitments: Beginning, Keeping, Changing* (San Francisco: Harper and Row, 1986), chap. 7, esp. 80–84.

19. See William Luijpen, *Phenomenology of Natural Law* (Pittsburgh, PA: Duquesne University Press, 1967), chap. 6, "Justice as an Anthropological Form of Co-Existence," esp. 180.

234 NOTES

For approaches that are both similar and interestingly different from this, see also Jean-François Lyotard, "The Other's Rights," in *On Human Rights: The Oxford Amnesty Lectures 1993*, ed. Stephen Shute and Susan Hurley (New York: Basic, 1993), 135–47; and Jacques Derrida, *Of Hospitality* (Stanford, CA: Stanford University Press, 2000).

20. Needless to say, Kant's moral and political thought is only touched on here. See Kant's different but related statements of the categorical imperative in *The Foundations of the Metaphysics of Morals*, trans. Lewis White Beck (Indianapolis, IN: Bobbs-Merrill, 1959), esp. 39, 47. For the statement of Kant's cosmopolitan political orientation see especially *Idea for a Universal History with a Cosmopolitan Intent*, in *Perpetual Peace and Other Essays*, trans. Ted Humphrey (Indianapolis, IN: Hackett, 1983), 29–40.

21. Here I am influenced by Margaret A. Farley's suggestion that a practically reasonable approach to moral obligation means that it should "make sense" in light of one's best reflection on what human experience reveals about the human condition. See Farley, "Moral Discourse in the Public Arena," in *Vatican Authority and American Catholic Dissent*, ed. William W. May (New York: Crossroad, 1987), 174–75; and "Response to James Hanigan and Charles Curran," in *Sexual Orientation and Human Rights in American Religious Discourse*, ed. Saul M. Olyan and Martha C. Nussbaum (New York: Oxford University Press, 1998), 105–6.

22. Here I agree with the conclusion of Amartya Sen's *Reason before Identity: The Romanes Lecture for 1998* (Oxford: Oxford University Press, 1999). I do not, however, agree fully with Sen's linkage of rationality with choice as opposed to discovery. Practical reason, I maintain, can discover aspects of the genuinely human that take priority over cultural traditions.

23. See esp. Aristotle, *Nicomachean Ethics*, book X, chap. 4–6. This point is developed succinctly by Rawls's discussion of what he calls the "Aristotelian principle" in *A Theory of Justice*, rev. ed. (Cambridge, MA: Harvard University Press, 1999), no. 65, 372–80.

24. That human beings are neither beasts nor gods and should be treated accordingly is a presupposition of ethical politics. See Aristotle, *Politics*, book I, chap. 3 (1253a). Martha Nussbaum takes this as a fundamental presupposition of her "capabilities approach" to ethics in social and economic life. See, for example, Nussbaum, "Human Capabilities, Female Human Beings," in *Women, Culture, and Development: A Study of Human Capabilities*, ed. Martha Nussbaum and Jonathan Glover (Oxford: Oxford University Press, 1995), 73.

25. "U.N. Millennium Goals," available at http://www.un.org/millenniumgoals/index.html (downloaded August 1, 2002). For a fuller developments of these goals and some ways to work toward achieving them, see "The United Nations Development Declaration," September 18, 2000, at http://www.un.org/millennium/declaration/ares552e.pdf; and "Road Map towards the Implementation of the United Nations Millennium Declaration Report of the Secretary-General," September 6, 2001, at http://www.un.org/documents /ga/docs/56/a56326.pdf.

26. Cahill, "Toward Global Ethics," *Theological Studies* 63, no. 2 (October 2012): 337. Probably the most ambitious attempt to outline the goods that all people should have access to and should be able to choose to realize in their lives is presented by Martha Nussbaum. See, for example, Nussbaum's *Women and Human Development: The Capabilities Approach* (Cambridge: Cambridge University Press, 2000), esp. chap. 1, "In Defense of Universal Values."

27. Personal communication cited in Catharine A. MacKinnon, "Crimes of War, Crimes of Peace," in *On Human Rights: The Oxford Amnesty Lectures 1993*, ed. Stephen Shute and

NOTES   235

Susan Hurley (New York: Basic, 1993), 86. MacKinnon also cites a number of reports by human rights NGOs that present similar accounts of the sexual violation of women in war and in peace as well.

28. See MacKinnon, "Crimes of War, Crimes of Peace," 88–89.

29. International Criminal Tribunal for Rwanda, Case No. ICTR-96–4-T, "The Prosecutor versus Jean-Paul Akayesu," Decision of September 2, 1998, no. 732. Available at http://www.ictr.org/default.htm.

30. The English-language verdict and sentence delivered by the tribunal in the Akayesu case are available at http://www.ictr.org/ENGLISH/cases/Akayesu/judgement/ak81002e.html.

31. Roméo Dallaire, "The End of Innocence: Rwanda 1994," in *Hard Choices: Moral Dilemmas in Humanitarian Intervention*, ed. Jonathan Moore (Lanham, MD: Rowman and Littlefield, 1998), 71–86.

32. See Dallaire's own account of the events during and after his role in Rwanda in his *Shake Hands with the Devil: The Failure of Humanity in Rwanda* (Toronto: Random House of Canada, 2003).

33. J. Bryan Hehir, "Military Intervention and National Sovereignty: Recasting the Relationship," in *Hard Choices: Moral Dilemmas in Humanitarian Intervention*, ed. Jonathan Moore (Lanham, MD: Rowman and Littlefield, 1998), 48.

34. See my *The Common Good and Christian Ethics* (Cambridge: Cambridge University Press, 2001), chap. 6.

35. Henry Shue, *Basic Rights: Subsistence, Affluence, and U.S. Foreign Policy* (Princeton, NJ: Princeton University Press, 1980), 18.

36. Shue, *Basic Rights*, 20.

37. John Rawls, *The Law of Peoples, with "The Idea of Public Reason Revisited"* (Cambridge, MA: Harvard University Press, 1999), nos. 8 and 9.

38. Rawls illustrates what he has in mind through the example of a hypothetical country, Kazanistan. See Rawls, *The Law of Peoples*, no. 9.3.

39. Rawls, 79. This distinction is similar to that drawn by Michael Walzer, between minimal or thin rights and fuller or thick ones. See Walzer, *Thick and Thin: Moral Argument at Home and Abroad* (Notre Dame, IN: University of Notre Dame Press, 1994).

40. Rawls, *The Law of Peoples*, 81.

INDEX

abortion, 71–75, 77, 80–81, 100–101, 110–13
Abraham, 152, 171
ACA. *See* Affordable Care Act (ACA)
Acts of the Apostles, 96
Affordable Care Act (ACA), 71–72, 75–76, 80, 100–101, 103
Africa, 17, 33, 39–40, 42, 47–50, 120, 184–85. *See also specific countries*
African Charter on Human and Peoples' Rights, 47–48, 185
African Development Bank, 142
African Union (AU), 41, 160, 162
Ahmadu, Fuambai, 188–89, 197
AIDS, 144
Akayesu, Jean-Paul, 195–96
Al Hussein, Zeid Ra'ad, 31
Alito, Samuel, 101
Allen, John, 106
American Grace: How Religion Divides and Unites Us (Putnam and Campbell), 73–75
American Revolution, 36, 93
Americans with Disabilities Act, 102
Annan, Kofi, 145, 161–62
apartheid, 60–61, 95–96, 158. *See also* South Africa
Aquinas, Thomas, 24–27, 38, 76–78, 111, 113, 123, 125, 154, 215n44
Aquino, Corazon, 5
Argentina, 6

Aristotle, 21–22, 27, 57–59, 125, 192
Armenian genocide, 91
Assad, Bashar al-, 41
asylum, 6–8, 18, 150, 160, 163–64, 174
AU. *See* African Union (AU)
Augustine, 78, 127, 154, 214n37
authoritarianism, 68
autonomy, 16, 21, 47, 55–57, 212n32

Bane, Mary Jo, 76, 83
Banjul Charter, 47–48
Barnett, Richard, 168
Barth, Karl, 65
Bellarmine, Robert, 65
Benedict XVI (pope), 28–29, 42–43, 68–70, 137–38, 140–42
Benhabib, Seyla, 153
Biden, Joe, 104
bin Laden, Osama, 90
bioethics, 16
Boko Haram, 107–8
Bosnia, 156, 168, 195
Bostock v. Clayton County, Georgia, 101, 103
Bracton, Henry de, 127
Brexit, 31
Buddhism, 91–93
Burwell v. Hobby-Lobby, 100

Cahill, Lisa, 194
Cambodia, 44
Cameron, David, 163

Campbell, David E., 73–76
capability, in duty to respond, 160
capitalism, 48, 139
Carens, Joseph, 150
Caribbean, 37
Caritas in veritate (Benedict XVI), 42, 137, 140
Case, Anne, 8, 122
Cassin, René, 52
Catechism of the Catholic Church, 70
Catholic social thought, 137–39, 225n14
Central African Republic, 162
Chad, 92
Chile, 5
China, 91, 93, 105–6, 112, 114
citizenship, 153, 176–77
Civil Rights Act of 1964, 101
civil wars, 92, 157
class, 122
Cold War, 27, 49
Collier, Paul, 144, 226n34
colonialism, 17, 37–38, 185–86
communalism, 47–48, 184
Compendium of the Social Doctrine of the Church, 10
Confucianism, 17, 47, 49–50
Connell, Francis, 67
conscience, 2–3, 18, 25, 87, 124
contraception, 78, 100–101, 110, 112–13, 218n15
COVID-19 pandemic, 134, 136
Croatia, 195
Cushing, Richard, 78

Dalai Lama, 92–93, 129
Dallaire, Roméo, 197
Deaton, Angus, 8, 121–22
De Controversiis (Bellarmine), 65
democracy, 5–6, 45, 93–94, 125; Catholic Church and, 34; equality and, 129–30, 200; globalization and, 139; justice and, 93; in Rawls, 200; religious freedom and, 66–68, 99
Democratic Party, 74–75
Deng, Francis Mading, 41–42, 160–61
development policy, 146

Dignitatis Humanae (Second Vatican Council), 2, 35, 69, 87, 217n35, 223n31
dignity, 4–5, 10, 15–30; demands of, 23–24; equality and, 124; female genital mutilation and, 198–99; freedom and, 22, 89; inductive understanding of, 20–23; interaction of practical and theological interpretations of, 24–30; Kant and, 19–20, 151–52; objections to, 16–17; religious freedom and, 63–64; as social norm, context of emergence of, 17–20; as solidarity, 46–64; universality and, 151; of women, 201
"Dignity is a Useless Concept" (Macklin), 16
Dirty War, 6
displaced persons, 7–8, 104–5, 149–65
Djibouti, 159
Dolan, Timothy, 71, 104
Dreher, Rod, 102
duties: negative, 156–58; positive, 158–65

Economic Community of West African States, 162
"Economic Justice for All" (US Catholic Bishops), 133–34, 137, 142–43
economic rights, 4–5, 9, 27–28, 51–52, 112, 117
education, 8, 81, 169, 176
EJA. *See* "Economic Justice for All"
employment discrimination, 101–2
Enlightenment, 47, 53
equality, 1, 10–11, 60, 117; basic, in Christian tradition, 123–25; democracy and, 129–30, 200; economic implications of, 130–32; faith and, 124; justice and, 125–26; poverty and, 131–32; racial, 10, 77, 79, 121; today, development of tradition on, 128–32. *See also* inequality
Eritrea, 159
Espinoza v. Montana Department of Revenue, 218n15
Essay on the Development of Christian Doctrine, An (Newman), 128
Ethiopia, 159

Evidence for Hope: Making Human Rights Work in the 21st Century (Sikkink), 44

exclusion, 10, 57, 61, 131, 137–38, 172

faith: dignity and, 29–30; equality and, 124; freedom and, 88, 104

Farley, Margaret, 20, 183, 233n18, 234n21

female genital mutilation (FGM), 187–89, 196–99

Finke, Roger, 6, 90–91, 104–5

Finnemore, Martha, 164

France, 91, 162, 164

Francis, Pope, 7, 10, 106, 137, 152, 207n8; exclusion and, 172; inequality and, 131; refugees and, 166, 173–74; Responsibility to Protect and, 43; Rwanda and, 33–34; as too liberal, 178

fraternal societies, 170

freedom: challenge of, 85–98; dignity and, 22, 89, 124; equality and, 124; faith and, 88, 104; in Marx, 48; personalism and, 87–88; as personal reality, 86–89; relationality and, 57, 86–89; religious, 1–4, 25–26, 63–84, 95, 97–103, 110–11, 114, 127–28; Second Vatican Council and, 77–84; of speech, 51–52; Universal Declaration of Human Rights and, 50

French Revolution, 2, 13, 34, 36, 93, 103–4

Gadaffi, Muammar, 40, 162

Gandhi, Mahatma, 18, 129

Gaudium et Spes (Second Vatican Council), 3, 35, 85

gender, 9–11, 122

Genesis, Book of, 24, 96, 123

genital mutilation, 187–89, 196–99

genocide, 18, 31–45, 91, 162, 181. *See also* Holocaust; Rwanda

Genovese, Kitty, 158

Gilbert, Lela, 106

Ginsburg, Ruth Bader, 109

globalization, 133–46, 173

Glover, Jonathan, 208n18

Golden Rule, 115, 174

Gomez, José, 102

Gorsuch, Neil, 101

Gregory XVI (pope), 2, 65, 127–28

Grim, Brian, 6, 90–91, 104–5

Guterres, António, 149

health care, 61, 71, 169–70

Hehir, J. Bryan, 197–98

Helsinki Accords, 49–50

Hinduism, 92, 94

HIV/AIDS, 144

Holocaust, 13, 15, 18–19, 32–36, 91, 194, 205n8, 207n12

homosexuality, 29–30, 63, 70–72, 75, 77, 79–84, 101–3, 109–13, 218n15

Hooper, J. Leon, 214n40

Hopgood, Stephen, 2

Hosanna-Tabor Evangelical Lutheran Church and School v. Equal Opportunity Commission, 101

hospitals, 169–70

Hountondji, Paulin, 50

Human Dignity and Bioethics (President's Council on Bioethics), 16

humanitarian revolution, 36–38

human rights: Catholicism's developing approach to, 2–5; future of, 6–11; as individualistic, 34, 47–50; memory and, 32–33; mixed history of commitment to, 33–35; participation and, 61–62; recent action for, 5–6

Human Rights as Politics and Idolatry (Ignatieff), 16

Human Rights Watch, 49

Huntington, Samuel, 5–6, 68, 93

ICRC. *See* International Committee of the Red Cross (ICRC)

idolatry, 16–17

IGAD. *See* Intergovernmental Authority on Development (IGAD)

IGAD Plus, 160

Ignatieff, Michael, 16

IMF. *See* International Monetary Fund (IMF)

immigration, 152, 166–80. *See also* displaced persons; refugees

impartiality, 150–51

imperialism, 17, 39, 161, 192. *See also* colonialism

inclusion, 131, 139–40, 166–80

India, 18, 92

Indigenous peoples, 37–38

individualism, 21, 26–27, 34, 46–50, 86, 185

inequality, 5, 119–23, 126–28, 138, 146, 188. *See also* equality

integration, of refugees and migrants, 168–71, 175–76

Inter-American Development Bank, 146

interdependence, 45, 134–35, 137–38, 140

Intergovernmental Authority on Development (IGAD), 159–60

International Committee of the Red Cross (ICRC), 150–51

International Criminal Court (ICC), 48, 157–58

International Monetary Fund (IMF), 136, 139, 142

Iraq War, 106–7, 164

Islam, 29, 68, 91–94, 105–8, 152, 171, 201

Islamic State, 107, 164

Jesus Christ, 171

Jews, 59–60, 152, 154, 171. *See also* Holocaust

John Paul II, Pope, 5, 68, 92–93, 127, 129, 136–38, 223n31

John XXIII, Pope, 1, 4, 7, 67, 112, 130, 140–42, 153

Jordan, 160

Judaism, 34, 152, 154, 171

June Medical Services LLC v. Russo, 218n15

justice, 93, 98, 112; basic, 131–32, 138; equality and, 125–26; globalization and, 133–46; same-sex unions and, 82; social divisions and, 83; state and, 111, 113

just war, 156–57, 197–98

Kant, Immanuel, 19–20, 24, 55–59, 190–91, 234n20

"Kantian moment," 19

Kaveny, Cathleen, 115, 217n6

Kennedy, John F., 66–67, 73

Kenrick, Francis, 127

Kenya, 41, 145, 159, 161–62, 186–87

Kenyatta, Uhuru, 157

Keohane, Robert, 135

Kerry, John, 73

Kew Gardens Principle, 158–59

Kim Dae-jung, 49–50

King, Martin Luther, 129

Kissinger, Henry, 39

Knights of Columbus, 170

Kono people, 188–89

Kuria, Gibson Kamau, 185–86

las Casas, Bartolomé de, 3, 37, 208n20

law, 69–72, 77–84, 100–102, 111–12

Laycock, Douglas, 103, 109

Lebanon, 160

Lee Kuan Yew, 17, 47

Leo XIII (pope), 4, 67

Le Pen, Marine, 91

Leviticus, Book of, 59

Libya, 40, 92, 161–63

Little Sisters of the Poor v. Pennsylvania, 100–101, 109

Lugo, Juan de, 127

Lustre of Our Country, The (Noonan), 100

MacKinnon, Catharine, 195

Macklin, Ruth, 16

Madison, James, 100

Mali, 41, 162

Mamdani, Mahmood, 17, 39–40, 42, 48

Mandela, Nelson, 92

Manhattan Declaration, 71, 213n22

Marcos, Ferdinand, 5

Marfleet, Philip, 150

marginalization, 5, 86, 108, 136, 172

Maritain, Jacques, 23, 26, 96

Mark, Gospel of, 59

marriage, same-sex, 29–30, 63, 70–72, 75–80, 82–84, 101–4, 109, 112

Marshall, Paul, 106, 108, 110–11

Marx, Karl, 48

Marxism, 4, 48, 53

Masterpiece Cakeshop v. Colorado Civil Rights Commission, 101, 103

McConnell, Michael W., 99–100

McKeon, Richard, 54

memory, 32–33, 38–43, 45

migration, 152, 166–80. *See also* displaced persons; refugees
Migration and Refugee Services (MRS), 174–75
ministerial exception, 101–2
Mirari Vos (Gregory XVI), 2, 65
Moi, Daniel arap, 186, 233n6
Mojekwu, Chris, 47, 184–85
Montesinos, Antonio de, 37–38, 208n20
Morsink, Johannes, 50
Mounk, Yascha, 2
Moyn, Samuel, 2, 32, 48–49, 205nn8–9, 205n11, 207n12
Moyo, Dambisa, 143–44
MRS. *See* Migration and Refugee Services (MRS)
Muhammad, 171
Murray, John Courtney, 25–26, 63–73, 77–82, 87–90, 95–98, 110–14, 206n24, 214n40, 217n35
Muslims. *See* Islam
Myanmar, 105, 112, 114

negative duties, 156–58
neoliberalism, 2, 32, 49
Newman, John Henry, 128
Niebuhr, Reinhold, 65
Nigeria, 68, 92, 107–8
Noah, 154
Noonan, John T., 100, 127–28, 204n16
Nteta, Tatishe, 178
Nussbaum, Martha, 91, 150, 153, 188, 196, 205n16, 234n24
Nye, Joseph, 135

Obama, Barack, 71, 100
Oneal, John, 44–45
Organization of African Unity, 185
O'Rourke, Beto, 103
Ottaviani, Alfredo, 87
Our Lady of Guadalupe School v. Morrissey-Berru, 101–2

Pacem in Terris (John XXIII), 1, 4, 7, 35, 130, 140, 153
participation, 60–62, 67, 76–77, 125, 131–32, 138–39, 172

Paul, 127, 131
Pelikan Jaroslav, 1–2
persecution, religious, 6–7, 68, 90–92, 104–8, 110
personalism, 87–89, 95
personhood, 20–22, 57–60, 150, 192–93, 200
Philippines, 5
Philpott, Daniel, 93, 106, 130
Pictet, Jean, 150
Pinker, Steven, 16, 36–37
Pinochet, Augusto, 5
Pius XI (pope), 67
Pius XII (pope), 3–4, 35
pluralism, 16–17, 54–57, 63, 109–10, 114, 172
Poland, 5, 93, 130, 159
polarization, 66, 72–77
Politics (Aristotle), 57–58
positive duties, 158–65
poverty, 4–5, 119–22, 131–36, 139, 141–47, 194
prostitution, 77–78, 214n37
Putnam, Robert D., 73–76, 83

R2P. *See* responsibility to protect (R2P)
racial equality, 10, 77, 79, 121
rape, 194–95
Rawls, John, 200, 220n52
Red Cross. *See* International Committee of the Red Cross (ICRC)
refugees, 7–9, 18, 31, 41, 92, 107, 147, 166–80. *See also* displaced persons
relationality: dignity and, 20–21, 26–27, 58; freedom and, 57; God and, 26; personhood and, 59–60; religious freedom and, 69; rights and, 46–64
relativism, 26, 67, 81, 189
Republican Party, 74–75, 102, 178
Respect for Marriage Act, 104
Responsibility to Protect (R2P), 38–43, 161
Rohingyas, 105, 114
Rosazza, Peter, 133
Rosen, Michael, 206n25
Russett, Bruce, 44–45
Ruston, Roger, 37
Rwanda, 6, 31–45, 156, 162, 181, 195–99

Sachs, Jeffrey, 143
Saudi Arabia, 91
Scalabrini, John Baptist, 169
schools, 169, 176
Second Vatican Council: democracy
  and, 5–6; freedom and, 77–84; human
  rights and, 3, 26, 34; law and, 77–84;
  morality and, 77–84; Murray and,
  65–69; religious freedom and, 1–4,
  65–84, 87, 95, 110, 114
secularism, 2, 13, 34, 69–70, 108
self-transcendence, 21, 58, 191–93, 198
Sen, Amartya, 50, 234n22
sex abuse scandals, 178, 180
sexuality, 77–78
sexual violence, 194–95
Shah, Timothy Samuel, 93, 130
Shea, Nina, 106
Shoah. See Holocaust
Shue, Henry, 52, 199
Shweder, Richard, 189, 197
Sierra Leone, 188
Sikkink, Kathryn, 2, 44–45, 164
Sixtus V (pope), 77–78
slavery, 10, 22, 36–37, 77, 119, 127, 129
social Catholicism, 5. See also Catholic
  social thought
socialism, 48–49
social rights, 4, 60, 112, 117
social thought, Catholic, 137–39, 225n14
solidarity: dignity and, 46–64; intellectual,
  198; interdependence and, 138, 140;
  social, 54–57; subsidiarity and, 154;
  Universal Declaration of Human Rights
  and, 50–53
Somalia, 159
South Africa, 60–61, 92, 95–97, 158, 201
South Sudan, 8, 38–39, 42, 157, 159–60
sovereignty, 42–43, 160–61
Soviet Union, 5, 13, 49, 53, 93, 130
Spain, 37–38
Sri Lanka, 91–92
Stamatov, Peter, 37
Structural Adjustment Program, 136
"Stupidity of Dignity, The" (Pinker), 16
Suárez, Francisco, 42–43

subsidiarity, 140–42, 154–55
Sudan, 107, 159. See also South Sudan
Sustainable Development Goals, 137
Syria, 7, 40–41, 107, 157, 159–60, 163–64

Taliban, 201
terrorism, 105, 107, 164
Tierney, Brian, 99
Toft, Monica Duffy, 6, 93–94, 130
totalitarianism, 27, 49–50, 97, 111
Tower of Babel, 96
transgender, 101–2, 218n15
Trump, Donald, 31, 175, 177
Turkey, 90–91, 160
Tutu, Desmond, 90, 92, 129

UDHR. See Universal Declaration of
  Human Rights (UDHR)
Uganda, 8, 159–60
Uighurs, 105–6, 112, 114
Ukraine, 31, 120, 134, 136, 156–57, 159
unemployment, 28, 51, 83, 133
United States, 99–115, 121. See also
  Affordable Care Act (ACA)
Universal Declaration of Human Rights
  (UDHR), 1, 3–4, 13, 15, 35, 44;
  colonialism and, 18–19; dignity and,
  19–20, 151; freedom and, 50; Holocaust
  and, 18, 32, 207n12; human experience
  and, 193; personhood and, 22; solidarity
  and, 50–53; universality of, 47, 151
universality, 3, 6, 9–10, 47, 151, 190–202

Vatican II. See Second Vatican Council
Vitoria, Francisco de, 3, 37–38, 42

wages, 4, 125–26
Wallsten, Kevin, 178
Walt, Stephen, 164
war, just, 156–57, 197–98
Washington consensus, 136
Weakland, Rembert, 133–34
wealth, 119–22
We Hold These Truths: Catholic Reflections
  on the American Proposition (Murray),
  66–67

INDEX 243

Weigand, William, 133
Wolfe, Alan, 56–57
women, 9–11, 122
women's rights, 183–202
World Bank, 136, 139, 142, 146
World Conference on Human Rights, 53
World Trade Organization (WTO), 139
World War I, 3
World War II, 3, 94. *See also* Holocaust

WTO. *See* World Trade Organization (WTO)

Xi Jinping, 105–6

Yemen, 92
Yugoslavia, 44

Zenz, Adrian, 105
Zubik v. Burwell, 109

ABOUT THE AUTHOR

DAVID HOLLENBACH, SJ, is Pedro Arrupe Distinguished Research Professor at Georgetown University in Washington, DC. His teaching and research deal with human rights, religious and ethical responses to humanitarian crises, and religion in political life from the standpoint of Catholic social thought, theology, and the social sciences. His most recent book is *Humanity in Crisis: Ethical and Religious Response to Refugees*. Earlier works include *The Common Good and Christian Ethics*. He has taught often at Hekima University College in Nairobi, Kenya.